The Text *in* Play

The Text in Play

Experiments in Reading Scripture

MIKE HIGTON
and
RACHEL MUERS

CASCADE *Books* • Eugene, Oregon

THE TEXT IN PLAY
Experiments in Reading Scripture

Cascade Books
An Imprint of Wipf and Stock Publishers
199 W. 8th Ave., Suite 3
Eugene, OR 97401

www.wipfandstock.com

ISBN 13: 978-1-61097-859-0

Cataloguing-in-Publication data:

Higton, Mike.

The text in play : experiments in reading scripture / Mike Higton and Rachel Muers.

xii + 240 pp. ; 23 cm. Includes bibliographical references and indexes.

ISBN 13: 978-1-61097-859-0

1. Bible—Hermeneutics. 2. Bible—Criticism, interpretation, etc. 3. Sacred books. 4. Hermeneutics. I. Muers, Rachel. II. Title.

BL71 T35 2012

Manufactured in the U.S.A.

For David F. Ford

Contents

Acknowledgments

VARIOUS OF THE EXPERIMENTS in this book were first tried out on our friends and colleagues—particularly in various Scriptural Reasoning meetings, or sessions at the Society for the Study of Theology or the American Academy of Religion. We're grateful to all those who gave us feedback at those meetings, and to the various publishers with whom earlier portions of some of the chapters were published.

FROM MIKE HIGTON

"Spiritual Reading and Play: Augustine and the Good Samaritan." An earlier version was published as "Boldness and Reserve: A Lesson from St. Augustine," *Anglican Theological Review* 85/3 (2003) 445–56. Material from that version is reproduced here with the kind permission of the publishers. An even earlier version was presented at the Society for the Study of Theology conference at the University of Nottingham in 2001.

"Keeping a Hard Text in Play II: Judging and Being Judged." A version was presented to the Scriptural Reasoning Group at the 2009 American Academy of Religion meeting in Montréal.

"Unsettling Play: Negotiating with the Moabite Liberation Front." An earlier version was presented as "What's a Christian Theologian to Do with Psalm 2" to the Truro Theological Society in February 2008.

"Whose Psalm Is It Anyway?: Why Christians Cannot Read Alone." Earlier versions were presented to the Department of Theology and Religious Studies at King's College, London, in 2006 (as "Is Psalm 1 About Jesus?"), and to the Lichfield Centre for Christian Studies in 2009. A much shorter version was published as "The Irrepressibility of Scripture: Psalm 1 between Jews and Christians," *Journal of Scriptural Reasoning* 7/1

(2008), and is available online at http://etext.lib.virginia.edu/journals/ssr/issues/volume7/number1/ssr07_01_e02.html.

"What Is Scriptural Reasoning?: How Christians, Jews, and Muslims Can Read Together." An earlier version appears as "A Session of Scriptural Reasoning" on the blog *Kai euthus*, June 23, 2008, online at http://goringe.net/theology/?p=179. The version here also includes, with the kind permission of the editors, some materials drawn from an editorial in *Conversations in Religion and Theology* 7/2 (2009) 129–33—an issue devoted to Scriptural Reasoning—and from a review in that issue (pp. 147–55) of Nicholas Adams, *Habermas and Theology* (Cambridge: Cambridge University Press, 2006).

"Patterns of Inter-faith Reading I: Scriptural Settlements." A much earlier version was presented as part of a response to a Scriptural Reasoning Group session at the 2008 American Academy of Religion meeting in Chicago, in honor of Dan Hardy. An interim version of some of the material was published in the editorial in *Conversations in Religion and Theology* mentioned under the previous item.

"Why Inter-faith Reading Makes Christian Sense I: Hard Sayings." An earlier version was presented to the Scriptural Reasoning Group at the 2010 American Academy of Religion in Atlanta.

"Reading Within and Between Traditions II: Tradition, Invention, Recognition." Earlier versions were presented at the Society for the Study of Theology conference in Durham, and to the Department of Theology at the University of Exeter, both in 2008.

FROM RACHEL MUERS

"Critical Reading and Play: Demand Feeding and the Desire for God." An earlier version was published as "Demand Feeding and the Desire for God: A Brief Play at Exegesis" in the *Journal of Scriptural Reasoning* 7/1 (2008), and is available online at http://etext.lib.virginia.edu/journals/ssr/issues/volume7/number1/ssr07_01_e04.html.

"Keeping a Hard Text in Play III: Fearful Bodies." An earlier version was published as part of Ayesha Siddiqua Chaudhry, Rachel Muers, and Randi Rashkover, "Women Reading Texts on Marriage," *Feminist Theology* 17/2 (2009) 192–209.

"Reading Within and Between Traditions I: It Takes At Least Two to Reproduce." An earlier version was published as "It Takes Two to Reproduce" in *Cross Currents* 55/2 (Summer 2005) 162–71.

"Reading the Rainbow: Playing with the Text and Living in the World." An earlier version was published as "Reading the Rainbow" in the *Journal of Scriptural Reasoning* 3/1 (2003), and is available online at http://etext.virginia.edu/journals/ssr/issues/volume3/number1/ssr03-01-e04.html. Material from that version is published here with the kind permission of the editors.

"Literal Reading and Other Animals I: Setting Free the Mother Bird." An earlier version was published as "Setting Free the Mother Bird: On Reading a Strange Text" in *Modern Theology* 22/4 (2006) 555–76.

"Literal Reading and Other Animals II: The Animals We Write On." An earlier version was published as "The Animals We Write On: Encountering Animals in Texts" in *Creaturely Theology: On God, Humans and Other Animals*, edited by Celia Deane-Drummond and David Clough, 138–50 (London: SCM, 2009).

FROM BOTH OF US

Much of the writing in this book arose out of our participation in various small groups engaged in scriptural study—especially Scriptural Reasoning groups. There were many such groups, and it would be impossible now to generate a list of all those who helped shaped our approaches to these texts. We are especially grateful, however, to David Ford, Basit Koshul, Peter Ochs, and the late Dan Hardy for pioneering the practice of Scriptural Reasoning, and to all the many people with whom we have enjoyed discussing scriptural texts over several years, among them Ahmad Achtar, Nick Adams, Adam Afterman, Rumee Ahmed, Redha Ameur, Jeff Bailey, Jason Byassee, Michael Cartwright, Ayesha Chaudhry, Aryeh Cohen, Jon K. Cooley, Valerie Cooper, Maria Dakake, Oliver Davies, Lejla Demiri, Anver Emon, Emily Filler, Menachem Fisch, Gavin Flood, Jim Fodor, Jason Fout, Ben Fulford, Bob Gibbs, Shari Goldberg, Jacob Goodson, Tom Greggs, Hannah Hashkes, Martin Kavka, Annabel Keeler, Steven Kepnes, Catriona Laing, Diana Lipton, Miriam Lorie, Shaul Magid, Yamine Mermer, Matthias Müller, Aref Nayed, Feodor Nikolay, Chad Pecknold, Ben Quash, Randi Rashkover, Esther Reed, Eugene Rogers, Sarah Snyder, William Taylor, Susannah Ticciati, Muhammed Umar, Daniel Weiss, Tim Winter, Isra Yazicioglu, Willie Young, Simeon Zahl, and Laurie Zoloth. We are also deeply grateful to Jake Andrews for the indexes, and to Patrick Harrison for his careful typographical work.

1 Introduction

This book does not attempt to offer either a systematic doctrine of scripture or a complete biblical hermeneutics. It is, rather, the description of a series of experiments undertaken by two Christian readers of scripture over the past several years (roughly speaking, interconnected experiments in spiritual exegesis and in inter-faith reading) and their attempts to see how those experiments made sense within, and made a difference to, their existing practices of reading.

The book is, therefore, neither a systematic whole nor a collection of disconnected essays. It is something like an explorer's map, created and revised in the course of a series of exploratory journeys, which has now reached the point where it seems to be worth inking in the pencil lines, rubbing out some of the early mistakes, and sending the whole thing off to the printers. It has become, we hope, a coherent enough sketch of the terrain to be of use to others wandering across the same steppes.

The explorations that underlie this book have been of two main kinds. In the first place, the two of us have been involved for several years in a practice called Scriptural Reasoning, which involves meeting regularly and intensively with Jewish and Muslim friends to study our respective scriptures together. The central section of this book contains our explicit reflections on those exploratory conversations: our emerging sense of why we do it, what it is good for, what assumptions about similarities and differences between the participants are necessary, and so on.

In the second place, however, we have both found that one of the effects of our participation in Scriptural Reasoning has been a reinvigoration of our reading of the Bible as Christian theologians, for the sake of our Christian theological work. The first and third sections of this book try to display that reinvigoration: they show us engaged in such theological reading, and recount our experimental discovery of new ways in which our theological conversations can be driven, interrupted, redirected, and empowered by detailed attention to biblical texts.

PLAYING WITH THE TEXT

By means of a series of related experiments in biblical reading, Part I sets out the kind of hermeneutical approach that we have found ourselves adopting in these experiments. We make no claim that this is, or should be, the whole of Christian theological reading of scripture—as we have already said, this book is neither a systematic doctrine of scripture nor a complete biblical hermeneutics. We do claim, however, that a coherent account of one aspect of Christian reading, which we call "playing with the text," emerges. Roughly speaking, that phrase names a renewed practice of *spiritual* reading that is not divorced from, but is rather animated by, *literal* reading and *critical* reading. This part of the book, taken as a whole, provides a roughly coherent examination of what it means to read the Bible with serious playfulness, in the midst of communities already formed and being formed by scripture and already in possession of some kind of rule of faith to guide reading.

We begin with fairly unproblematic and benign forms of play, looking at ways in which scripture can be read so as to drive readers deeper into their existing faith. But we then move on to more difficult texts, asking what it means to play with texts with a worrying potential to be read in oppressive and terrorizing ways, without seeking simply to neutralize those texts. Finally, we move on to forms of play that can unlock similar difficulties in apparently benign texts. All the time, we ask how serious playfulness might allow Christian communities to live fruitfully with difficult texts, in serious and constant engagement with them, without denying or forgetting their abiding difficulty.

So we begin, in chapter 2, with one of Augustine's expositions of the parable of the Good Samaritan. The chapter introduces the idea of "play" and shows that the kind of play in which Augustine indulges (in which the Samaritan suddenly becomes Christ), extravagant though it appears, is simply what happens when the various texts that Christians read are thrown into promiscuous collusion with one another, and allowed by means of the connections that are established to take the reader on unexpected journeys deeper into their faith. The tone is primarily celebratory, an attempt to understand and share Augustine's *delight* in these connections, but we also note the ways in which that delight sometimes threatens to wash over the detailed contours of the text. We suggest that a renewed practice of scriptural play will combine Augustinian play with repeated acknowledgement of the abiding awkwardness of its texts.

In chapter 3, we play with another example: a text from 1 Peter that uses the image of breastfeeding to talk about the nourishment of the church. It is a text that, as its history of interpretation shows, lends itself well to being played with. In one sense the chapter simply illustrates again the process of playing that we have already explored—but it is not now a matter of watching someone else (i.e., Augustine) play, but of playing seriously for ourselves. In the process, the chapter demonstrates two things. First, it shows how the discourses, narratives, and systems that we inhabit and that constitute our world get caught up, unavoidably and problematically, in this process of playful reading; play is not an activity marked off and separated from the serious business of living (that's a theme that we return to in Part Three). Second, we begin to see that the kind of play we are advocating is not at all a way of avoiding *critical* reading. That remains our theme for the next three chapters, and the whole central section of Part One could be thought of as an exploration of what play looks like when we are reading challenging texts.

Chapter 4 tackles a "hard text" head on, and asks how playing works when the material is so explosive. We explore different strategies of play that can be drawn on to make it possible to live with a hard text from 1 Timothy about the silence of women—and end up calling into question the apparent opposition between these playful strategies and strategies that supposedly face the text with more sobriety. But this chapter also calls into question the idea that the end of such play can or should be a comfortable settlement with such a difficult text—the removal of its sting. Our play does not *end* anywhere satisfactory, but sets up and leaves open a process of disputation, wrestling with problems that do not go away. Play is not a form of exegesis primarily concerned with finding *answers*.

Chapter 5 highlights one element of the practice described in the fourth: the place in play of continued interaction between interpreters who differ. The kind of play we advocate tries to combine the making of real judgments about the relative adequacy of differing interpretations with an insistence on keeping conflicting voices *together* in the reading process. This chapter gives a brief exploration of debates about the proper interpretation of the controversial verses in Romans 1 that speak of sexual relations. We note that the text itself calls for reasoned judgment, poising it between God's once and future revelation in the first and second advents, but calls into question forms of that judgment that would too easily *divide* right interpreters from wrong. The chapter therefore lays some important groundwork for Part Two.

Chapter 6 is a partner to the fourth, and explores another hard text about women—this one from Ephesians. It once again shows what it means to play seriously with the text: to find possibilities of blessing, by weaving it into the pattern of the good news that is the reading community's rule of faith, without losing sight of the text's difficulty, and of the real patterns of broken relationship in the communities of its readers to which the text connects—and for which it is, to some extent, responsible.

The final chapter in Part One is rather different. Rather than showing what happens when we play with hard texts, finding ways of living with them without betraying either the text or the reading community, we now turn to a text that has proved easy to live with—a relatively unproblematic text that Christian readers have found easy to weave into the good news and their communal lives. Here our playing does not involve overcoming or responding to difficulties but deliberately uncovering them—making things *more* difficult. We look at Psalm 2, and play with it until the easy ways in which it yields to christological reading start to look a whole lot more problematic. Play is not a way of avoiding or overcoming difficulty: it is not intended to make the Bible easier to live with; sometimes the opposite may be what we most need.

SCRIPTURAL REASONING

Part Two of the book is devoted to Scriptural Reasoning, a practice in which Jewish, Christian, and Muslim readers meet to read their scriptures together, without assuming that such reading together is made possible by any consensus about the authority, place, or proper interpretation of the respective scriptures within each of the three traditions (and without even assuming that "scripture" or "tradition" means the same thing in each case). The whole section can be read as an attempt to *describe* Scriptural Reasoning, starting with fairly straightforward practical descriptions of what it involves, and moving on to more complex attempts to describe the kind of interaction between religious traditions that it involves (although by the end of the section it will prove quite difficult to use this "religious traditions" terminology in this easy way). As well as *describing* Scriptural Reasoning, however, we also *advocate* it—in the sense that we explain why it makes sense to engage in this as Christian theologians committed to Christian theological, christological reading of the Bible.

Chapter 8 forms a bridge between Part One and Part Two. It matches chapter 7's exploration of Psalm 2 with an exploration of Psalm 1, examining the kind of christological play in which Christians have engaged for centuries when reading this text. The chapter asks how this Christian reading relates to Jewish readings of the same text, and argues that the kind of play we have been advocating calls for readings that are not *supersessionist* (claiming a right as Christians to interpret this text and denying that right to Jews) but *con-sessionist* (claiming that Christians are called to read side by side with Jews, serious about reading the text within the terms set by their rule of faith, but equally serious about listening to the other's readings).

Chapter 9 introduces Scriptural Reasoning, a broader and more complex practice of *con-sessionist* reading than that described in the previous chapter, because it includes Muslims as well. Scriptural Reasoning is an established practice, and this chapter simply aims to provide a description of what happens in some Scriptural Reasoning meetings. We provide a fictionalized transcription of a single meeting, and then a commentary that points to some of the dynamics of this kind of inter-faith conversation.

Chapter 10 attempts a different kind of description of Scriptural Reasoning, building up a conceptual vocabulary capable of describing fairly formally how a common practice is possible without consensus. We present a description of the activity of settling by which religious individuals and communities seek a roughly coherent settlement between their lives, their contexts and their scriptures—and then describe the ways in which differing settling activities can mesh to produce a sustainable practice. This is the only chapter in the book that is not driven by a particular piece of exegesis, and that should rightly make readers suspicious of it. The concepts it provides are no more than useful placeholders—and the next six chapters are devoted to making the simple description of Scriptural Reasoning that they allow richer and more complicated.

Chapter 11 remains at a fairly simplistic level of description, and simply tries to put some flesh on the conceptual bones provided in chapter 10. It provides a simple model of Scriptural Reasoning by examining three texts, one from each tradition. Each text suggests a different logic of interpretation—logics of digression, kenosis, and hospitality—and for the purposes of this simple model we take each of these logics as if it were a characteristic of the respective tradition. It is possible to see how participants following each of these three differing logics might work together in a common practice of Scriptural Reasoning, without the differences between them being erased.

Chapter 12 starts in earnest to make things more complicated. Rather than operating, as the last three chapters have done, with simplistic descriptions of the three traditions from which participants come, this chapter asks whether and how Scriptural Reasoning works from the point of view of one very specific Christian tradition: charismatic evangelical Anglicanism—in fact, British charismatic evangelical Anglicanism of a very particular vintage. We look at how a Scriptural Reasoning conversation about one of Jesus' "hard sayings" (his instruction to let the dead bury their own dead) connects with, and in some senses continues, the kinds of reading of that passage found within that particular Christian tradition.

Chapter 13 parallels chapter 12 (this book does, after all, have two authors) and asks how the "tent" of Scriptural Reasoning looks when one enters it from a Quaker meeting house: a religious tradition or "house" defined in part by its absence from, and marginality to, established religious houses, and one that classically described its homelessness in terms of imagery drawn from Hebrew Bible descriptions of Israel. In this context, Scriptural Reasoning appears as a practice of "waiting upon God"—a practice that makes deep Quaker sense.

Much of the description of Scriptural Reasoning offered to this point in this book has focused on what happens when a participant from a particular tradition reads texts from her own tradition with the help of her fellow Scriptural Reasoners. Yet participants actually spend quite a bit of their time reading texts from the traditions of others. Chapter 14 provides the results of just such a reading: a Christian theologian reading a Qur'anic text, asking what "prophecy" means in that text and how he as a Christian reader stands towards it.

Chapters 15 and 16 form a pair. Even with the complications added by the previous three chapters, we have still been powering our descriptions of Scriptural Reasoning with a relatively unexamined notion of tradition. Chapter 15 explores the metaphors of reproduction, generation, and fidelity that crop up in almost any discussion of the continuity of a tradition. Chapter 16 asks what our account of tradition will look like if the disciples, John the Baptist, and Jesus himself, as depicted in Mark 1, can be said to stand in one. Both chapters tend in the same direction: a denial that tradition can simply mean a reproduction of the same; a denial that Scriptural Reasoning participants can be considered to be straightforward representatives of a tradition, telling the group the one thing that their tradition says; and an insistence that the differing members of a "single" tradition who take part in Scriptural Reasoning are not so much representatives of as *agents in* their traditions, seeking for the innovations that will allow more faithful continuation.

READING THE BOOK OF NATURE

Part Three picks up on the point insisted on back in chapter 3: that the discourses, narratives, and systems that constitute our world are unavoidably caught up in the processes by which we play with the text. In particular, it focuses on the way in which attitudes to and claims about the natural world—particularly about animals—are caught up in our playing. Playful reading of the kind we have been exploring is not meant to provide a retreat from the responsibilities of ordinary life: it is a practice by which those responsibilities can be explored, deepened, challenged, and reordered—in which the settlements we have entered into with text and world can be unsettled again, and we can be thrown again into the hunt for coherence. These chapters do not resolve the issues they raise; they clarify what is at stake, they set a process of conversation and reflection going, and they make some suggestions for new ways forward in those conversations—while pointing out some of the dangers that might attend following these ways too glibly.

Chapter 17 provides a brief overture to the section, exploring connections between the stories of Jonah and Noah. It asks what it means for playful readers of these texts to find themselves in the natural world: the world of rainbows, bushes, and fish—the world of "all flesh" (and more)—and to know that world as the world of God's mercy.

Chapters 18 and 19 go closely together. They are both driven by a disturbing parallelism in the history of Christian reading: claims about animals, claims about the literal sense, and claims about Jews have often gone together. Chapter 18 examines the Deuteronomic command to set free the mother bird when one comes upon its nest; chapter 19 examines a string of texts about animals, but also the fact that scriptural texts have often been written *on* animals, and have had animals drawn in the margins. Each of these explorations provides an opportunity to exemplify the kind of play described in Part One, and to do so in implicit and explicit conversation with Jewish interpreters of a kind that coheres with the practice described in Part Two, but pushing the boundaries of concern still further. The kind of play we have been advocating is shown to be at once a matter of *hermeneutical* concerns, *inter-faith* concerns, and *ethical* concerns.

part one

Playing with the Text

2 Spiritual Reading and Play

Augustine and the Good Samaritan

[25]Just then a lawyer stood up to test Jesus. "Teacher," he said, "what must I do to inherit eternal life?" [26]He said to him, "What is written in the law? What do you read there?" [27]He answered, "You shall love the Lord your God with all your heart, and with all your soul, and with all your strength, and with all your mind; and your neighbour as yourself." [28]And he said to him, "You have given the right answer; do this, and you will live."

[29]But wanting to justify himself, he asked Jesus, "And who is my neighbour?"

[30]Jesus replied, "A certain man went down from Jerusalem to Jericho, and fell into the hands of thieves, who stripped him, and beat him, and went away, and left him half dead. [31]Now by chance a priest was going down that road; and when he saw him, he passed by on the other side. [32]So likewise a Levite, when he came to the place and saw him, passed by on the other side. [33]But a Samaritan while travelling came near him; and when he saw him, he was moved with pity. [34]He went to him and bound his wounds, having poured oil and wine on them. Then he put him on his own beast, brought him to an inn, and took care of him. [35]The next day he took out two pence, gave them to the innkeeper, and said, 'Take care of him; and when I come back, I will repay you whatever more you spend.' [36]Which of these three, do you think, was a neighbour to the man who fell into the hands of the robbers?" [37]He said, "The one who showed him mercy." Jesus said to him, "Go and do likewise."

—Luke 10[1]

1. NRSV, but modified in order to match the quotations from the KJV in Dodd's translation of Augustine's commentary, below.

IN 1658 A POSTHUMOUS work by the Anglican clergyman Samuel Crook was edited and published by his colleagues Christopher Barker and William Garrett: *Ta Diapheronta, or, Divine Characters*. Turning in his nineteenth chapter to "the preaching hypocrite" who "preacheth Christ, but not *for* Christ," Crook wrote:

> As the godly minister extracts honey out of weeds, and makes an holy use of secular and profane literature, so this hypocrite, with a carnal spirit and profane heart, pollutes the holy things of God, and staines all that Word of God which he laies his hand upon, dallying with words, mincing of Texts, playing with Scripture, and darkening it with Allegorical, or other senses, refusing to rest in the plaine meaning which the words naturally afford, and the context amply gives witnesse to.[2]

Interpreting scripture is a serious business for Crook; it is the business of winning souls, of binding and loosing the conscience. It is not a matter for *play*.

Our topic in the first part of this book is precisely such play. We ask what it means to play with scripture, what reasons one might have for doing so, and what integrity such play might have in the face of suspicions like those of Crook. We begin, therefore, with a text that has become a stock example of allegory's unnatural restlessness—an example of playful exegesis that led C. H. Dodd, with something of Crook's repulsion, to say: "To the ordinary person of intelligence who approaches the Gospels with some sense for literature this mystification must appear quite perverse." The passage in question is an interpretation of the parable of the Good Samaritan in Augustine's *Quaestiones evangeliorum*, and if we can see the sense in this "famous example" of play[3] then we will have travelled a long way towards an understanding the nature of play more generally.

Augustine writes:

> *A certain man went down from Jerusalem to Jericho*: Adam himself is meant; Jerusalem is the heavenly city of peace, from whose

2. Crook, *Ta Diapheronta*, 212; emphasis added in the first, brief quotation. The full title of Crook's work is TA ΔΙΑΦERONTA [*sic*], *or, Divine Characters: in Two Parts: Acutely Distinguishing the More Secret and Undiscerned Differences between* 1. *the Hypocrite in His Best Dresse of Seeming Virtues and Formal Duties. And the True Christian in His Real Graces and Sincere Obedience. As also between* 2. *The Blackest Weeds of Dayly Infirmities of the Truly Godly, Eclipsing Saving Grace, and the Reigning Sinnes of the Unregenerate that Pretend unto that Godlinesse They Never Had.*

3. Dodd, *Parables of the Kingdom*, 13.

> blessedness Adam fell; Jericho means "the moon," and signifies our mortality, because it is born, waxes, wanes, and dies. *Thieves* are the devil and his angels. *Who stripped him*, namely, of his immortality; *and beat him*, by persuading him to sin; *and left him half dead*, because in so far as man can understand and know God, he lives, but in so far as he is wasted and oppressed by sin, he is dead—he is therefore called half dead. The *Priest and Levite* who saw him and passed by signify the priesthood and ministry of the Old Testament, which could profit nothing for salvation. *Samaritan* means "guardian," and therefore the Lord himself is signified by this name. The *binding of the wounds* is the restraint of sin. *Oil* is the comfort of good hope; *wine* the exhortation to work with fervent spirit. The *beast* is the flesh in which he deigned to come to us. The *being set upon the beast* is belief in the incarnation of Christ. The *inn* is the Church, where travellers are refreshed on their return from pilgrimage to their heavenly country. The *morrow* is after the resurrection of the Lord. The *two pence* are either the two precepts of love, or the promise of this life and of that which is to come. The *innkeeper* is the Apostle. The supererogatory payment is either his counsel of celibacy, or the fact that he worked with his own hands lest he should be a burden to any of the weaker brethren when the Gospel was new, though it was lawful for him "to live by the Gospel."[4]

It is not hard to understand the consternation that this exegesis provoked in Dodd. Augustine has, it would seem, played with the text so roughly that the joints holding together its various parts have been broken, and each piece has had its surface rubbed off, to reveal a mirror in which he sees reflected the bright light of some ecclesiastical doctrine. Dodd's "ordinary person of intelligence" can no longer see the original parable through the fragmented dazzle. How are we to make sense of what Augustine has done?

Our clue is provided by Augustine himself. He provides several other very different interpretations of the same parable, including two in the first book of *De doctrina christiana*, and if we look at these two interpretations first we will be able to approach Augustine's questionable playfulness by degrees.

4. *Quaestiones evangeliorum* 2.19, in Dodd's slightly abridged translation in *Parables*, 11–12. The original can be found in PL 35:1340.

The first interpretation he offers is one which we might call moral:[5] Augustine takes his cue from the commentary found on Jesus' lips, "Go and do thou likewise," and takes the parable as a moral lesson in neighbour-love.

> The man to whom our Lord delivered the two love commandments, and to whom he said that on these hang all the law and the prophets, asked him, "And who is my neighbour?" He told him of a certain man who, going down from Jerusalem to Jericho, fell among thieves, and was severely wounded by them, and left naked and half dead. And he showed him that nobody was neighbour to this man except him who took pity upon him and came forward to relieve and care for him. And the man who had asked the question admitted the truth of this when he was himself interrogated in turn. To whom our Lord says, "Go and do thou likewise;" teaching us that he is our neighbour whom it is our duty to help in his need, or whom it would be our duty to help if he were in need. Whence it follows that he whose duty it would be in turn to help us is our neighbour. For the name "neighbour" is a relative one, and no one can be neighbour except to a neighbour.[6]

Though this reading is more complex than first meets the eye, *allegory* has not yet raised its head, and one might imagine Crook reading on, unperturbed.[7] A little later in the same book, however, Augustine says: "Even God himself, our Lord, desired to be called our neighbour. For our Lord Jesus Christ points to himself under the figure of the man who brought aid to him who was lying half dead on the road, wounded and abandoned

5. Augustine might be thought already to have taken a step in the wrong direction: from the parable as solvent for our existential horizons to parable as vehicle for moral teaching. Yet the opposition between existential and moral interpretation is perhaps not so great as has sometimes been supposed, and the inclusion of the "go and do thou likewise" command after the parable—whether we ascribe it to Jesus, to the oral tradition, to proto-Luke, to the Lucan redactor, or to anyone else who takes our fancy—shows how deeply some kind of move to a moral interpretation is embedded in the reception history of this parable.

6. *De doctrina christiana* 1.31; the Latin text can be found in PL 34:15–22. The *Quaestiones evangeliorum* passage is probably to be dated to 399 or 400; the first book of *De doctrina christiana* to 397.

7. Augustine has paid attention to the strange logic of the exchange between Jesus and the lawyer. The lawyer asked who the neighbor is to whom he should show love; Jesus replies that the neighbor is the one who shows mercy—but then commands the lawyer not to love this neighbor but to emulate him. Augustine's somewhat laborious last three sentences untie this little knot.

by the robbers."[8] Here Augustine moves from a moral interpretation to a figural interpretation: Jesus was referring to himself "under the figure" of the Samaritan. This is, I suspect, the crucial move in the journey from "rest[ing] in the plaine meaning" to "playing with scripture." This is where the subject matter ceases to be a moral lesson, let alone a horizon-shifting existential speech-act, and instead becomes Christian doctrine; any further allegorization of individual details in service of a more precise correspondence to Christian doctrine is simply an elaboration of this move.

Yet Augustine might ask how a theological reader could possibly do anything different. How could one take this lesson about love and isolate it from the broader evangelical context? Love, for a Christian reader, cannot be taken simply as one existential possibility amongst others; nor can it simply be one piece of moral advice amongst others—even a piece of moral advice that comes with the backing of dominical authority. This parable speaks of love more seriously than that. In speaking of love, this parable speaks (as its context suggests) of the one true content of the law, and so the one true subject matter of theology. It speaks of the self-same subject matter that is spoken of, as Augustine might insist, in every other theological locus, every other scriptural text. To deny this is to refuse to treat the subject matter of this parable seriously; it is to diminish the parable. It not only severs it from the dual love command that immediately precedes it in the Gospels; it removes it from the gospel. A Christian interpreter cannot interpret this parable without realizing that, even if she is talking about the revelation of an existential possibility or about a moral lesson, she is at the very same time talking about things that are grounded in the deepest ways of God with the world, things that are established, revealed, and confirmed in the incarnation, on the cross, and in the resurrection. Once that fundamental unity of the subject matter of the gospel is admitted, it must be an act of extraordinary and artificial restraint *not* to see Christ in the figure of the Good Samaritan, as if a literate person were to strain for a moment to see letters and words simply as oddly shaped marks on a page. This is not to say that the historical critics are wrong to claim that Jesus did not have all this in mind when he told the parable (and to that extent, we might place a demurral against the *form* of Augustine's comments) but they are wrong if they think that Augustine's move to a figural exegesis is essentially a betrayal of the parable. It is the refusal to take this step that betrays the parable.

8. *De doctrina christiana* 1.33.

In one sense, this does mean that Augustine knows in advance what the parable must mean. As he famously says later on in *De doctrina christiana*, the subject matter of the whole Bible is love of God and love of neighbor. We should not, however, assume from this that for Augustine this parable is therefore dispensable, a redundant repetition of a message already known from elsewhere. If that were the case, then the object of Augustinian exegesis would indeed be to annihilate particular texts. No, this interpretation has its context in a book in which Augustine is struggling with the realization *prompted by his exegesis* that the one self-identical subject matter of theology is not quite as he had thought. He is struggling to find the proper way to place the "love thy neighbour" command alongside the "love the Lord thy God" command. His famous discussion of *usus* and *fruitio* (which Oliver O'Donovan's detailed discussion has shown us *is* a struggle)[9] is a temporary stage in an evolving process by which he tries to come to terms with the intractable shape of the dominical commands, which resist the terms in which he had previously identified and described the one subject matter of theology. What is found here is the same truth that is found elsewhere, but here it is found differently, and Augustine discovers more of the one, identical subject matter of scripture by discovering it again here.

So, this figural interpretation is not eisegesis in the sense of an arbitrary squashing of the gospel *into* a parable that is *really* about something else. It is rather the discovery that, whatever this parable is really about, it is for the Christian reader properly understood *within* the context of the whole gospel, and that the gospel is properly understood *through* this parable.

Even if this sketch of an argument is accepted, however, what are we to say of the more elaborate allegorical interpretation with which I started? Nothing I have said so far appears to justify taking Jericho as signifying mortality, for instance, or the supererogatory payment as indicating Paul's teaching on celibacy. One might well worry that, although Augustine was right to work on this parable until it became transparent onto the gospel, he might finally have worked it so hard that all its contingency and particularity, all the grit it picked up from the time and place where it was told, has been smoothed away. That is, Augustine's tour de force of exegetical cleverness might well appear to prevent readers from seeing the details of the parable itself, prevent the parable's peculiarities from shaping or

9. O'Donovan "*Usus* and *Fruitio*."

disturbing the view Christian readers have of the one theological mystery which is its subject matter.

This worry becomes more serious when we hear Augustine, later in the first book of *De doctrina christiana*, saying that

> we may learn how essential it is that nothing should detain us on the way, when not even our Lord Himself, so far as He has condescended to be our way, is willing to detain us, but wishes us rather to press on; and, instead of weakly clinging to temporal things, even though these have been put on and worn by Him for our salvation, to pass over them quickly, and to struggle to attain unto Himself, who has freed our nature from the bondage of temporal things, and has set it down at the right hand of His Father.[10]

Augustine here speaks of Christ's humanity almost as if it were a ladder that could be kicked away once it had been climbed, as if the spiritually mature person will have no more need of that humanity once he has gained the lessons it has to teach and can contemplate divinity without it. Drawing on Paul's language of "knowing Christ no more after the flesh" from 2 Corinthians 5, Augustine speaks as if the process of theological education might be one in which the humanity of Christ becomes ever more transparent until the divinity which is bodied forth in it is grasped, and the humanity ceases to appear. This disappearance of the grit of temporal things is precisely the process one might think has taken place in Augustine's dealings with Christ's parable: the move from figural interpretation to full-blown, detailed allegorization hints at a similar sensibility, one which allows no real room for creaturely participation *as creaturely* in the life of God.

A reader who, wrestling with Augustine's interpretation of this parable, did think that such a denial of creatureliness had taken place might thereby come to a point where she had to part company with him: where, despite accepting his move to figural interpretation, she would hold back from following him all the way, and insist on doing more justice to what I have called the abiding grit of Jesus' humanity (his bodiliness, his particularity) *and* to the grit of Jesus' parable.

Is this parting of the ways fair, however? On the one hand, there are plenty of resources in Augustine for repairing the christological lacuna I have gestured towards, and plenty of resources even in the first book of *De doctrina christiana* to help us take the conversation about particularity and bodiliness further: Augustine has important things to say here about

10. *De doctrina christiana* 1.38.

love of one's body, for instance, and about what it means to love in particularity, as one contingently thrown into a particular set of relationships. On the other hand, we can take a hint from the fact that Augustine was steeped in the culture of late antique North Africa, and had inherited the endemic love of riddles and wordplay and conjurer's erudition that mark that place and time. Augustine here is surely being deliberately excessive: this is in-your-face, outrageous playfulness, wearing its questionability on its sleeve. It plays, and at the same time it *shows* you that it is playing—and it is perhaps that very fact, the playfulness of the play, that allows the opacity of the parable to be glimpsed again.

Such a balance between playfulness and acknowledgment makes deep theological sense. The full unity between opacity and transparency is a unity that will only be manifested eschatologically, for it is only at the eschaton that it can become clear how each particular, without diminution of its particularity, stands, in the Spirit, in relation to God in Christ, and speaks of and to that God. Here, before the eschaton, Christian interpretation can only be a partial anticipation of that eschatological unity, an anticipation that must witness *both* to that anticipated unity *and* to its own eschatologically provisional nature. Christian interpretations, in order to do justice to these constraints, will therefore have to have a certain rhythm to them. They will have to oscillate between, on the one hand, moments when they take up Augustine's gauntlet and press the parable until the reader can see reflected in it its deepest subject matter, and on the other hand, moments when the playfulness of the play and the abiding particular grittiness of the parable are both registered, as a witness against any claim to total clarity.

On the one hand, then, Christian readers need something of Augustine's ambition: his desire to find the way in which any and every scriptural text speaks of the self-same love—love of God and love of neighbor. It might just be that they should join Augustine even in full-blown allegorization, if such playful bravado can witness to the claim that any story in the Bible of love, of God, or of neighbor is in the end identical with the story of God's ways in Christ. The story of the Good Samaritan *is* the story of God's way to the cross in Christ and God's turning of the world to himself on Calvary; and if, in order to push that essential point seriously, Christians say playfully that "The *beast* is the flesh in which he deigned to come to us. The *being set upon the beast* is belief in the incarnation of Christ," so be it.

On the other hand, Christian readers also need to handle this bravado in such a way as to *display* their playfulness. Their playful exegesis needs to tip its hat and acknowledge to the crowd the extent to which it is running ahead of the game, compelled by the subject matter to outrun its secure hermeneutical capability. Alongside their boldness, Christian readers therefore need reserve—they need what has been called the "ploddingly exegetical."[11] The Crooks and the Dodds, the critics and commentators who deride Augustine's allegorical interpretation, provide a constant reminder of the intractable historical messiness of the parable that readers might too easily magic away, and to which they must constantly return. If in one breath they can say that "the *beast* is the flesh in which he deigned to come to us," in the next breath Christian readers must be ready to say, "That isn't quite right, of course; let's read that again."

What, then, do we mean by "play"? On the one hand, it involves the Christian reader proposing readings of biblical texts that weave them into the broader context of the Christian good news—willing, in the process, to step beyond the plain sense of those texts for the sake of the good news. On the other hand, it involves that reader taking seriously the challenges that such readings face: acknowledging the grit of the texts, their particularity, awkwardness, and difficulty—the call of the literal. We do not, in this book, offer a resolution. We have no formula for integration of boldness and reserve. Rather, we advocate a rhythm of reading practice, a certain style of ongoing interpretative argument.

As it stands, that two-sided description of play is only a gesture in the direction of the kind of reading that interests us in this book. We have seen roughly what it might mean in relation to Augustine's multiple readings of the Good Samaritan parable, but not enough to know what it might look like in relation to other texts—not enough, that is, to make it any kind of followable rule. We do not intend, however, to make up for that lack by a detailed theoretical explanation of the hermeneutic exemplified by such play. Rather, we intend to specify the nature of play more closely, and (we hope) render our play followable, simply by engaging in it—repeatedly. In the remainder of this book, therefore, we offer, not a systematic doctrine of scripture, not a complete biblical hermeneutics, but a series of experiments in scriptural reading, exploring further in relation to specific texts the interplay between spirited play and the awkward plain sense.

11. Milbank, Ward, and Pickstock, "Suspending the Material," 2, describing "Barthianism."

3 Critical Reading and Play

Demand Feeding and the Desire for God[1]

[2]Like newborn infants, long for the pure, spiritual milk, so that by it you may grow into salvation—[3]if indeed you have tasted that the Lord is good.

—1 PETER 2

IN THE LAST CHAPTER, we watched Augustine playing with scripture. In this chapter, we start the process for ourselves, beginning with a text that lends itself to play. This passage from 1 Peter has its fair share of debatable points of translation and interpretation, few of which constitute or relate to troubling problems for doctrine or ethics, and at least some of which are not about to be settled.[2] It has the (for Western Christian scholars) exotic appeal of possible connections to Syriac texts;[3] it has an interpretation history that allows a succession of serious thinkers to show

1. I am grateful to David Horrell for his help with this chapter. An earlier version of it appeared in a celebration of the work of David Ford, who, while he has never been prepared to compromise on the seriousness of the theological task and its significance for what he describes as "the world's great challenges," has also taken seriously the *playfulness* of theology, a consequence of its orientation towards God for God's own sake and "for naught" else. See especially David Ford, *Christian Wisdom*, 14–18, a discussion of Luke 7:18–35.

2. As Karen Jobes notes, in certain Christian communities the text is a focus for reflection on the inerrancy and sufficiency of scripture, and there are issues in translation and interpretation that would affect those debates. Jobes, "Got Milk?," 1.

3. *Odes of Solomon*, esp. 8 and 35.

their gentler sides[4]—a history that can be followed through the developments of metaphors, images, and symbols rather than chiefly through doctrinal debates. It is, you might say, cute—even if it does, on longer acquaintance, become messier and even threaten to keep one awake at night.

My playing with this text, like many games with children, begins by noticing something that grown-ups normally presume to be incidental (such as the detail of an illustration), and for a moment taking it to be the main point. I focus, for the sake of the game, on the image of the newborn baby that "longs for" milk—and, presumably, lets the world know about it—and on the various possible responses to that baby, the various approaches to (as Winston Churchill put it, in his inimitable style) "putting milk into babies."[5] I can imagine a range of readings of this text corresponding to a range of approaches to infant feeding, all variously supported within the rest of 1 Peter and the scholarly literature.

Thus: my grandparents' generation, following an approach that is now returning to fashion, were encouraged from a very early stage to regulate their children's desire for milk according to a predetermined timetable—a timetable that would, according to the experts, ensure that the children grew up both adequately nourished and properly disciplined. First Peter, we note, addresses its readers frequently as "obedient" children (1:14, 22), necessarily subjected to discipline to ensure that their life remains appropriate to their new birth (1:13; 4:7; 5:8), existing (for their own good) within somebody else's timetable (e.g., 5:6), suppressing or eliminating wrong desires (1:14; 2:11).

Again: one generation of parents after another has been warned of the dangers of deceptive, or contaminated, milk for their children—whether that is the dangerous milk of lower-class wet-nurses, the formula milk that was presented in a recent set of U.S. television advertisements as placing children at unacceptable risk, or breast milk contaminated through environmental pollution. The authors of 1 Peter want to ensure that their readers receive only the right kind of sustenance, unadulterated or undeceitful (taking a range of possible translations of *adolon* in 2:2); they want to separate this community out (as a holy nation, 2:9, a people

4. See for example the discussion of the imagery of the "milk of the word" in Puritan rhetoric in Marylynn Salmon, "Cultural Significance of Breastfeeding."

5. Radio broadcast on March 21, 1943, in Churchill, *Onwards to Victory*, 43. He was not actually talking about breastfeeding; he was talking about the distribution of cows'-milk-based products during wartime, and its contribution to national security. See Carter, *Feminism, Breasts, and Breast-Feeding*, 55.

in "exile," 1:1) from the contaminants of the surrounding environment. There is good and bad milk out there, and it is crucial for their healthy "growth," their growth into salvation, that the believers obtain a steady supply of the *best* sort of milk.

But then again: my parents, and I, learned about child-led or "demand" breastfeeding. We were told, moreover, that this is how things have worked in most times and places. The child's desire for milk, on this understanding, is part of what ensures that there *is* milk for her to drink; in a breastfeeding relationship, demand regulates supply. It makes sense to tell newborn children not only to keep drinking (the right kind of) milk, but to keep crying out for the milk. The all-encompassing need of the infant, felt and expressed with her entire being—a need that makes her, as David Ford writes, "all cry"[6]—enables her to be nourished and to grow. And the infant will only go on crying if she meets with a response—so the injunction to "long for the milk," to go on crying, implies on this reading the promise of a response.

The commentators on this verse who note, rightly, that newborn children do not need to be told to want milk, do not note that children can be (and all eventually are, regardless of childrearing philosophy) taught not to want it at the "wrong" times or from the "wrong" people.[7] At this point in 1 Peter, however, as it seems to me, the readers are not being encouraged to moderate their desires or become "good children" ("contented little babies," to quote Gina Ford[8])—demanding only when it suits their parents, demanding only at the approved times, demanding only the right things. Nor, as commentators note, are they being gently encouraged to wean themselves off their current food and onto something more solid—this by contrast with other New Testament texts in which the imagery of milk is used (such as 1 Cor 3:2 and Heb 5:12–14). Their desire—*for* something or other (and we must come to that)—is being encouraged as essential to their growth—*into* something or other. Before they can be obedient children, or disciplined children, or patient children,

6. Ford, *Christian Wisdom*, 23.

7. In fact, the commentaries tend to assume, as they explain the metaphorical "vehicle," that the longing of a baby to be fed—if we can even articulate the desire so clearly—is straightforwardly identifiable as a longing for breastmilk, taken as the obvious literal referent of "unadulterated milk." Babies, a recent advertising campaign in the U.S. claimed, are born to breastfeed. I am not so sure; my experience and anecdotal evidence suggests that suckling, as much as feeding from a bottle, is something babies learn to do, and learn to want to do.

8. G. Ford, *Contented Little Baby Book*.

or a holy nation, they have to be the newborn children who cry out with their whole being.

However, this is all to ignore the issue that has most preoccupied commentators on this verse: what is actually being referred to here, given that the addressees are *not* newborn children? Crucial here is the interpretation of *logikon*, which the NRSV renders as "spiritual." A first glance at the literature makes depressing reading for an interpreter (like me) who would like to use this passage to help her reassert the materiality of Christian hope and the inadequacy of dualistic presentations of Christianity. *Logikos*, which appears only twice in the New Testament, denotes, in philosophical texts of the period, that which distinguishes humanity from the animals, or spirit from matter. At the very least, *logikos* in this text alerts the reader (as if it were necessary, as if there were some particular risk to be averted here) to the presence of a metaphor.[9] *Logikos* milk is, apparently, anything but the runny white stuff—which still leaves open the question about what it is, and about how the milk metaphor functions. I shall play a little more with two options that appear in the history of interpretation.

The King James Version, emphasizing the *logos* in *logikos*, translated the passage as "the sincere milk of the word." Many recent commentaries take up, if not the letter of this translation, at least its spirit (or its logic).[10] Milk is, after all, used elsewhere in the New Testament and in early Christian writings as a metaphor for proclamation or instruction. On such a reading, the addressees of 1 Peter are called to desire words, preaching, proclamation, perhaps the prophecies and the good news to which reference is made earlier in the letter (1:10–13)—as babies want milk.

This reading appears at first sight to keep the "newborn baby" metaphor within strict limits. People who want words, who feed on words, *cannot* be very like newborn babies; *logikos* reaffirms the paradox of addressing the people who hear or read this text as babies. Becoming *logikos* or able to appreciate the *logikos* means moving beyond the stage where desires are nameless, immediate, and all-encompassing, to the point where they can be described, examined, judged, learned or unlearned—where they can appear in words. At this point the possibility of a (gendered) dualism arises again in the mind of a suspicious interpreter. The text acknowledges materiality, acknowledges that which exceeds representation, and then hastens to bring it under the control of the *logos/logikos*. Children have

9. On all this see Michaels, 1 *Peter*, 87.

10. See on this Jobes, "Got Milk?"

to grow up quickly, get beyond attachments to material things, and prove that they are *logikos* by submitting to the proper (paternal/patriarchal) authorities (see 2:13—3:7).

Some other recent readings of *logikon gala* regard the link to "word" as largely irrelevant, and seek instead a more expansive meaning. Thus for Karen Jobes the milk in question is the sustaining grace of God, which the believers show themselves to have "ingested" insofar as their lives are transformed, and which they continue to desire as a precondition of their continuing transformation. Again, this interpretation may threaten to spiritualize the processes of Christian identity formation and to separate the longing for spiritual milk even further from anything material (or maternal). What is desired is perhaps not even something as "tangible" as words or preaching.

I wonder, however, whether *logikos* here admits of another reading, one that would not silence the suspicious voices but might do more justice to the scope of concern evidenced in this letter. The passage we are considering is not explicitly christological, but the words of verse 3—in their materiality, in the sounds they make—contain an echo: *chrestos ho kurios*, "the Lord is good"; *Christos ho kurios*, "Christ is Lord." This echo in turn serves as a reminder that the addressees of 1 Peter are being asked to relearn their desire in relationship to Jesus Christ. The indispensable condition of their need being met, of their being able to "grow up to salvation," is a particular human body. They do not long for just "any old milk," nor the milk that could be determined, through a detached assessment of their situation and needs, to be the best for them.

As various feminist critiques have pointed out, certain medical discussions of infant feeding do their best to ignore the fact that the breast milk consumed by a baby comes in each case from somebody's breasts. A range of alternative approaches attempt to read breastfeeding as a relationship, and the "production" and "consumption" of milk as intelligible only within the context of that relationship. It is probably not implausible to find in a text written before the modern science of infant nutrition connotations of profound intimacy in a reference to a baby's desire for milk. What is received in response to the cry is not just something that meets the immediate need of which the cry is a symptom (the need for adequate nutrition); it is personal presence. All the other New Testament uses of *epipotheō*, "long for," apart from the much-debated James 4:5, refer to the desire of one person for the presence of another or some others.

So the baby-like longing described in 1 Peter 2:2 may be linked not only to a greater propensity to cry out but to "indescribable and glorious joy" (1:8), said to be experienced *now* by the addressees of the letter. The longing to see somebody face to face, and the joy of the face-to-face meeting, is not "describable" as a list of desired items. Perhaps the word-as-milk might, also, be received through, and inseparable from, the love of particular others. The joy it gives might be "indescribable" not only because it transcends the fulfilment of specific needs, but because it is found in these particular relationships of love.

The recipients of this letter are, I suggest, being reminded about the multiple embodied relationships through which they receive what they need for their "growth" and learn to cry out for it. Christ is one from whom their food comes, who meets and calls out their needs, and whose presence they desire—and he is not spiritual *as opposed to* material. But then Christ is also the milk itself, *logikon gala*, because he is the gift they receive—the one they "taste and see" within the community of which they are part, as they tell his story and eat together, and as they experience each other's presence.

The readers of 1 Peter are, after all—hence the emphasis at other points on discipline and holiness—engaged in an intense process of communal transformation. Just as the words of this text do not allow the reader to forget their "materiality" (working through their sounds, *chrestos/Christos*), the letter as a whole does not allow its readers to forget the particular historical means through which "life-sustaining" gifts are mediated to those who read it. The letter comes from somebody in particular (Peter, 1:1, but then also Silvanus, 5:12, and the "sister church in Babylon," and Mark, 5:13) to somebody in particular ("the exiles of the Dispersion in Pontus, Galatia, Cappadocia, Asia and Bithynia," 1:1). More problematically, it speaks to and presupposes various specific institutions (including not only ecclesial institutions, but slavery, the Roman Empire, and the patriarchal family), which are offering some means of supplying material needs and forming embodied life—something a bit like milk—to the readers of the letter.

Even if, however, it is right to read *logikon gala* as "wordy milk"—scripture or proclamation—perhaps this text says something about the approaches to scripture that are appropriate to those who "taste and see that the Lord is good." Perhaps the text is not talking about a word that comes "unadulterated" by anything material—purely logical, or simply spiritual—but about a word that is historical and embodied, that is only *itself* as historical and embodied, that does not transcend materiality by escaping it. In which case, the word-as-received, scripture read in communities, might turn out to be a little more like milk. It might have something to do with the meeting of real needs in the present, as well as something to do with helping people to grow beyond those needs (in ways they cannot identify in advance and may not be concerned with in advance). The word-as-received in communities might respond to cries—including the most "basic" cries, the cries of children to be fed—and call forth more cries from those who read and hear it. It might also bring about "indescribable joy," joy in being in the presence of others (within the texts and within the communities) through the encounter with whom the presence of Christ is made real.

As I read this text, I find that the milk metaphor is hard to contain. It refuses to keep its distance from the realities it is being used to describe—because its primary reference is to something universal and unavoidable. All the readers of this letter really were once crying children who needed milk and a cuddle, and all of them really still are people who exist in some particular set of relationships of dependence and love, and who have crying needs and profound longings that arise within those relationships. They are now, as 1 Peter repeatedly recalls, in a position to recognize that they might have learned to "long for" things that are not good for them, and that the process of unlearning this longing—coming off the junk food—could be difficult.

Playing with this text, however, suggests to me that the result of such unlearning is an equally, or more, profound longing that is equally, or even more, concerned with the whole person (the *logikos* and the infant)—and the "growth" to which that longing is essential might have an equally wide reference. Playing with this text is not simply a game: it has the capacity to unsettle and reorder the practices and discourses, the relationships and the longings, the bodies to which its words connect, and which are "in play" as we read. There might be genuine Christian wisdom about the feeding of infants; it might even be worth crying out for, or losing sleep over. But the pursuit of this or any other urgent concern would not—as 1 Peter suggests—be incompatible with rejoicing in God for God's own sake.

4 Keeping a Hard Text in Play I

Will the Real Women Please Stand Up?[1]

[8]I desire, then, that in every place the men should pray, lifting up holy hands without anger or argument; [9]also that the women should dress themselves modestly and decently in suitable clothing, not with their hair braided, or with gold, pearls, or expensive clothes, [10]but with good works, as is proper for women who profess reverence for God. [11]Let a woman learn in silence with full submission. [12]I permit no woman to teach or to have authority over a man; she is to keep silent. [13]For Adam was formed first, then Eve; [14]and Adam was not deceived, but the woman was deceived and became a transgressor. [15]Yet she will be saved through childbearing, provided they continue in faith and love and holiness, with modesty.

—1 Timothy 2

As the previous chapter has already begun to suggest, play is a serious matter because the texts with which we play do not exist in isolation but in communities of people with bodies, relationships, needs, and histories. The next step in our exploration of play takes that suggestion further, by turning directly to one of the Bible's "hard texts": a text

1. This chapter emerged from the discussions of a small group at the Scriptural Reasoning in the University meeting in Cambridge, June 2008. The group included David Ford, Steven Kepnes, Shari Goldberg, and others. Jacob Goodson's contributions to that group were particularly important in shaping the paper, and many of the most interesting ideas in this chapter are his.

from 1 Timothy with all-too-visible connections to neuralgic divisions in the communities in which it has been read.

FIRST READING

We can begin with a first reading, which seems to read verses 11–15 quite straightforwardly. For this first reading, this is clearly a text that teaches that women are not to take up roles in church that involve teaching men or that involve exercising authority over men. In communities that are used to reading these New Testament epistolary texts as clear authoritative addresses to all Christians (whenever it is possible to do so), this is the plain sense of the text.

However, it is worth noting that there are in contemporary Christian interpretations of this passage various neutralizing strategies that, though they assume this first plain reading, then seek rather directly to cut the lines between this reading and a direct contemporary obedience to the teaching. For instance, one may point out the contextual specificity of this ruling—it belongs to a specific culture, a specific moment in time, now past. Or one may seek, somehow, for the *spirit* of this ruling beyond the letter, saying (for instance) that it is *really* about the need for the church where possible to so order its life as not to cause unnecessary offense to the surrounding culture—and that we need to find the appropriate application of that deeper principle in our own time.

It is worth noting that such escape routes from the text are not simply tricks thought up in modernity and imposed upon the text; both, after all, can find some support within the wider text of which this is a part. On the one hand, this is a letter which is explicitly addressed to a specific individual in a particular context, and in general Christian readings of the Epistles have *always* been able to make some distinction between matters that belong, as it were, purely to the lives of the original sender and recipients and matters that are of wider import. On the other hand, it is not difficult to find in the wider corpus of Pauline literature a spirit/letter distinction, and some explicit training in theological-ethical reasoning that might already support a search for the "real," "deeper" meaning of the text.

SECOND READING

Instead of finding a way in which women might be set free from the strictures imposed by this text, however, we might look at what happened if men joined them under those strictures—taking a more playful route out of our difficulty. What if, even though this is a text that originally addressed women and called them to silence, the appropriate Christian response to it is to recognize that Christian readers are *all* called to learn in silence with full submission? What if, in the terms of this text, we are *all* women now?

What forms of reasoning might support such a reading—which initially seems rather obviously "made up," rather obviously arbitrary (and which will continue to seem so for as long as one holds to modern assumptions about the relationship between the proper meaning of this text and the intentions of the original human author or the likely understanding of the original audience)? Several such patterns of biblical reasoning are possible.

First, there is the route that takes us via Mary. In a broader Christian theological context, the paradigm of the woman who is saved through childbirth, and who learns in submissive silence (speaking only to say, "Be it unto me according to thy word"), is Mary.[2] Mary is, at least for some Christians, the paradigmatic instantiation of the "woman" of this passage—and yet, in much Christian theology, Mary is also a type of the whole church: Christians are *all* Mary. To travel down this route is not (necessarily) to claim that the original author of this text was deliberately referring to Mary; it simply involves noting that existing patterns of Christian scriptural reasoning focused on Mary (specifically, typological patterns) enable one to reread this text differently.

Two further points are worth making about the rereading that emerges along this Marian route. First, the decision to travel in this interpretive direction finds support elsewhere in the New Testament, where submission is explicitly enjoined on all in the church. Second, if Christians are *all* to be silent, it follows that this silence is not an absolute silence, since they are all also called to prophesy (as Paul says in 1 Cor 14:5, albeit in a passage which contains its own injunctions to women to be silent, 14:33–36). Travelling down this route is going to involve some deeper thinking about what "silence" actually involves.

Alongside this Marian route, there is a second path that takes us via the unstable way in which the Genesis story is used in this passage—a matter of some import, since the whole of 1 Timothy 2:11–15 is rooted in Genesis 3. One could argue, against 1 Timothy's own reading, that *both*

2. Those Marian resonances are deeply entangled with the depiction of Eve in Genesis 3, on which this passage draws so heavily. I am grateful to Jacob Goodson for teaching me to see these connections.

Adam and Eve were deceived, albeit by somewhat different routes, and that *both* transgressed, so that, if having been deceived and having thereby become a transgressor is the ground on which silent submission is enjoined, men should be no less silent than women.

Once one recognizes the oddness of the claims that this 1 Timothy text makes about Genesis 3, one's confidence in the "obviousness" of the first, plain sense reading begins to crumble. That first reading itself leads us over questionable ground, and our second reading could plausibly claim to be on "plainer" ground when it came to reading the Genesis passage. After all, 1 Timothy's reading of Genesis appears to rely upon the fact that whilst the narrative of Eve's deception is given in full the text is very laconic when it comes to Adam: it simply says that Eve, having eaten the fruit, "also gave some to her husband, who was with her, and he ate." Adam's motivations, the process by which he moved from obedience to disobedience, are (unlike Eve's) not narrated. Indeed, until the verb "ate," it is only the serpent and the women who perform any action, or speak or deliberate in any way. First Timothy's reading of this seems to rely upon the reader *not* filling in the gaps in the Genesis narrative in the way that "plain" reading might seem to demand.

A third route takes us via the fact that women elsewhere in the Christian scriptural canon do speak; indeed, they teach men. One should first note that, if one asks what kind of teaching is being talked about in this passage, the early part of the passage answers: the author calls himself a teacher insofar as he is a herald of the gospel, a proclaimer of Christ. The women in the resurrection stories, the woman of Samaria, and others, apparently including Timothy's own mother and grandmother (see 2 Tim 3:14–15 and 1:5)—there are plenty of women who are given precisely this teaching role elsewhere in the Christian canon.[3] So, reading canonically, one has to choose. Either one cannot take the plain sense of this passage, or one cannot take the plain sense of those other passages. There is no unified plain sense; *something* has to give. For proponents of our second reading to allegorize "woman" in this passage in order to create a canonically consistent reading is to do no more than proponents of the first reading already have to do. Examining the logic of the second reading exposes the logic of the first reading too; the patterns of reasoning upholding the two readings are not so very different.

3. Think what would happen if one applied the Genesis 3 Eve paradigm, as read by 1 Timothy, to the Samaritan woman at the well from John 4. One would end up with the woman as Eve, the townspeople (who this Eve goes to after her encounter, persuading them to eat the fruit she has just tasted) as Adam—and Jesus as the serpent.

FIRST AND SECOND READING

The neat opposition between a first, plain reading and a second, playful reading begins, therefore, to crumble. The relationship between the two readings is more complex than that. The existence of the second reading does not deny the continued existence of the first; second readers can still acknowledge that it is possible to read the first way faithfully. A second reader will, however, argue that to claim *finality* for the first reading involves a misrecognition of the reasoning processes involved; the examination we have just undertaken of the reasoning involved in the first and the second reading does not allow us to present the debate between the two as one between, say, plain and allegorical reading, or authorized and arbitrary reading. The second reader can see the debate between first and second as a conversation between different faithful readings, rather than a debate between faithful and unfaithful. Both sides are faced with not with asking simply what this text meant for its original author and audience (as if they were simply historical critics), but with asking what it means for *us*, where "us" means Christians who are readers of the whole canon.

Of course, the second reader may well argue that his or her reading is a *still more faithful reading* than the first—but the kind of argument that will support such a claim will not be the kind of argument designed to secure the single meaning of an unambiguous text: they have more to do with the capaciousness and resilience of a whole pattern of reading that takes in this and many other texts—and the process of making judgments between two such capacious and resilient patterns of reading is never a simple matter. In chapter 6 we will look at another text which leaves open two mutually opposed patterns of reading, and ask further about what it means to read alongside those whose reading opposes one's own—especially in a context where simply agreeing to differ seems to be an abdication of responsibility.

The continued presence of the first reading matters in another way, however: it is a reminder to second readers that real people get caught in the gender divides erected or sustained by texts like this. And the presence of the first reading as a warning may make us realize that the second reading itself is in real danger of reinforcing destructive gender binaries. You don't need to read far in feminist critiques of Christian Marian discourse, for instance, to spot some quite large potential problems with the "We are *all* women" route, to the extent that it both leaves the definition of "woman" heavily loaded with passivity and submission, and evacuates it of materiality and bodiliness. Chapter 7 will take an equally difficult text and try a different kind of play: one that works precisely by refusing an erasure of difference that might seem at first to be the most obvious escape root from the terror of the text.

Taking this charge seriously will mean that second readers can't rest content with the settlement their reading has reached. Their playfulness has not reached a stopping point, an interpretation that will suffice—but in destabilising a first reading that was understood as a stopping point, it has initiated an ongoing process of rereading and reflection. The play must go on, and what drives it on is not simply an abstract curiosity interested in seeing what more can be made of this text, but the needs and pains of the communities in which the text is read: the play goes on as long as they hold on for a blessing.

5 Keeping a Hard Text in Play II

Judging and Being Judged

[18]For the wrath of God is revealed from heaven against all ungodliness and wickedness of those who by their wickedness suppress the truth ... [21]for though they knew God, they did not honour him as God or give thanks to him, but they became futile in their thinking, and their senseless minds were darkened ...

[24]Therefore God gave them up in the lusts of their hearts to impurity, to the degrading of their bodies among themselves, [25]because they exchanged the truth about God for a lie and worshipped and served the creature rather than the Creator, who is blessed for ever! Amen.

[26]For this reason God gave them up to degrading passions. Their women exchanged natural intercourse for unnatural, [27]and in the same way also the men, giving up natural intercourse with women, were consumed with passion for one another. Men committed shameless acts with men and received in their own persons the due penalty for their error.

[28]And since they did not see fit to acknowledge God, God gave them up to a debased mind and to things that should not be done. [29]They were filled with every kind of wickedness, evil, covetousness, malice. Full of envy, murder, strife, deceit, craftiness, they are gossips, [30]slanderers, God-haters, insolent, haughty, boastful, inventors of evil, rebellious towards parents, [31]foolish, faithless, heartless, ruthless. [32]They know God's decree, that those who practise such things deserve to die—yet they not only do them but even applaud others who practise them.

> 2:1 Therefore you have no excuse, whoever you are, when you judge others; for in passing judgement on another you condemn yourself, because you, the judge, are doing the very same things. [2]You say, "We know that God's judgement on those who do such things is in accordance with truth." [3]Do you imagine, whoever you are, that when you judge those who do such things and yet do them yourself, you will escape the judgement of God? . . . [5]But by your hard and impenitent heart you are storing up wrath for yourself on the day of wrath, when God's righteous judgement will be revealed.
>
> —ROMANS 1–2

As in the last chapter, this chapter explores a text that has proved susceptible to opposed readings, and to consequent divisions in the communities of its readers. The existence of that debate calls readers to make judgments—but this text is also a text *about* judgment. This chapter therefore asks where judgment appears in this passage, and whose judgment it is. It provides five different answers: *God's* judgment; then our *concurring* judgment, our *suspicious* judgment, and our *reasoned* judgment; and finally a strange switch that the text performs, whereby the judgers become the judged.

1

The most obvious way in which "judgment" appears in this passage is as God's revealed judgment—indeed God's wrath. It begins with God's wrath revealed from heaven: God acts as lawgiver and as judge, and condemns all manner of ungodliness, wickedness, and deceit. God sentences the evildoers to suffer the appropriate consequences for their acts. The act of divine judgment divides right from wrong, lifting up the former and casting down the latter.

The Christian reader—one who stands under the judgment of scripture—is, first of all, one who simply watches this judgment fall. You can imagine her standing and waiting, seeing the shadow of God's falling judgment growing larger and darker on the ground—and then breathing a sigh of relief as the judgment smashes into the earth some distance away, squashing the idolaters.

2

The second way in which "judgment" appears in this text is implicit. It is found in that sigh of relief of the Christian reader. For a reader who regards himself as called to stand under the judgment of this text, this description of divine judgment will form *his* judgment. He will learn to condemn what God condemns, and to leave standing what God leaves standing.

That might take many forms: cheering along as God's judgment falls, perhaps, or, for the suddenly convicted sinner, rushing out from under the shadow of God's wrath to stand in the light, pausing only to grab his fallen hat from the ground an instant before that judgment lands with a thump.

3

So, if the first kind of judgment in the text is the divine judgment dividing right from wrong, and the second is the reader's judgment affirming and repeating the divine, the third place that judgment might appear in or around this text is suggested by my rather tendentious wording so far. The picture of the Christian reader cheering along as judgment falls inevitably raises the suspicion that the supposedly divine judgment depicted by this text is in fact a *projection* of what was in the first place a human judgment—a suspicion that the condemnation that slammed into the earth squashing the idolaters over *there* was in fact lobbed into the air by the jubilant believers over *here*—and was nothing more than that.

The possibility of judging this text—judging it as simply prejudiced perhaps, as wrongly judgmental—is certainly there. Yet it is also a difficult one for those Christian readers who regard themselves as standing in some sense under the judgment of their scriptures. Is *dismissal* of a judging text a sentence that they as judges are authorized to pass—and, if so, on what grounds? To put the question another way, can the suspicion of the text find any grounds within the text itself, or is it a judgment *on* but not *in* the text?

4

In depicting God's judgment, this text does not simply pronounce a verdict—it is not simply a syllabus of errors. Rather it tells a story, and provides a kind of explanation, and so invites the reader to *understand* where its condemnations come from, and why they fall as they do.

Alongside the divine judgment, the consenting believer's judgment, and the suspicious judgment of the critic, we therefore have a fourth kind of judgment. The fourth place in which we find judgment in this text is in the formation of understanding to which the reader is called: the formation of her ability to make *reasoned* judgments.

Let me spend just a little longer on this. The text contains a pattern of reasoning, and the reader is implicitly invited to reason along with it in order to become a judge. And that means that the reader is enabled to ask questions about the precise nature of the divine judgment depicted here. She is, for instance, enabled, even invited, to ask what precisely the wicked sexual relationships are that are judged in verses 26–27, if culpable idolatry is the root form of wickedness, and if ruthless rapacity is the end to which wickedness tends. And asking what is meant by "degrading passions" or "shameless acts" is not simply an *etymological* question—as it were, a simple exercise of lower criticism, preparatory to the real business of learning from the text. There is a higher-level question about the meanings of those terms that make sense within the broader sweep of the reasoning presented. Rather than simply *acquiescing* to having her judgment shaped according to the divine judgment displayed here, the Christian reader and would-be judge is invited—by the very fact that this is a text that reasons—into an active process of reasoning.

That means, I think, that a Christian reader faithfully standing under the judgment of scripture can expect quite properly to get involved in the kinds of exegetical arguments that infamously surround this specific text. Arguing about it is *not* an indication that its judgment is not being taken seriously.

So, one can imagine an argument between a more conservative and a more liberal exegete. The two might agree that verses 19–25 describe the loss of a right ordering of life—a life centered upon true worship of God. They might agree that verses 26–27 suggest that this right ordering is also, perhaps fundamentally, a right ordering of desire, an ordering centered upon desire of God, but within which there is a place for proper sexual desire ("natural" sexual relationships in some sense). They might agree that sin is presented as a breakdown of this proper ordering so that, although it will have many symptoms, the disordering of specifically sexual desire will loom large amongst them—such that it will, from at least one angle of vision, be (along with explicit idolatry) the characteristic sin. That, however, is where their agreement will end.

The more conservative exegete might see here a window into the connection between two fundamental natural orderings in which human beings stand: the primary ordering of Creator and creature, and the subordinate ordering of male and female that is a divinely ordained figure of the Creator/creature ordering. The disordering of the Creator/creature ordering—a matter of the creature's desire slipping its moorings from its most proper divine object, and attaching itself to creatures—is then dramatized or figured by a similar disordering of the desire properly associated with the male/female ordering, before showing its true colors in all the other forms of disordered desire represented by the vice list in verses 29–31.[1] The exegete who treads *this* path ends up not simply with an affirmation of a straightforward literal reading of the particular condemnations voiced by the text, but with a whole pattern of reasoning that makes sense of those condemnations. And her exegesis leaves her with the task of reasoning this out: exploring the right ordering of male to female, and creature to Creator, and the way in which those orderings are linked and are to be honored—a much more open and complex task than simply acquiescing in a condemnation. There's work to do to justify such a reading—serious argumentative work.

On the other hand, the more liberal exegete might focus precisely on the way in which the vice list in verses 29–31 describes the general character of disordered life: it is malicious, covetous, envious; it is haughty, boastful, proud. Recalling another famous Pauline passage, this exegete might say that disordered life is fundamentally life devoid of that Christ-like love that is patient, kind, and not envious or boastful or arrogant or rude; disordered life is characterized by a turning away from selflessness to self-gratification. He might argue that it only makes sense for Paul to put a description of certain patterns of sexual desire in the center of this passage if, for Paul, those desires are inherently desires in which the individual's gratification is the central, the all-consuming element—if, that is, same-sex desire automatically means for him a form of sexual desire which by its very nature is incapable of truly loving mutuality. The liberal exegete might note that in the specific context in which Paul wrote it is not *too* difficult to see how the forms of homosexual relationship visible to him might well have led him precisely to such a supposition.

1. This account is loosely based on Piper, "Other Dark Exchange."

It is then open to the exegete to argue that, nevertheless, there are other forms of same-sex sexual relationship, forms unimagined by Paul, that are fully capable—no less capable than heterosexual relationships—of displaying a godly love and faithfulness. And this reading will involve the more liberal exegete in a rereading of discourses about what is natural and unnatural—detaching them from claims about natural complementarity between the sexes, say, and making them more thoroughly christological, so that what is natural is, for us, understood as what is capable of conformity to Christlike love. This exegete is not, then, engaged in dismissal of the text—he is driven by its judgment to the task of exploring the contours of selflessness and self-gratification, and to taking seriously the ways in which selflessness and gratification play themselves out in a whole variety of sexual relationships, regardless of the sex of the participants.[2] This exegete too has the task of reasoning his judgment out, seriously and attentively.

I'm only sketching these arguments, of course, and it is not my purpose here to pursue either of them any further. My point is simply this: that each of these exegetical arguments might be seen as an attempt at *reasoned faithfulness*—indeed as faithful *only if* reasoned. Each is, or should be if it wants to be taken seriously, an attempt to pursue the reasoning of the passage, to join in with it and work with it, and in *that* way to let the reader's judgment be formed by a divine judgment that comes with reasons attached. Having this kind of serious exegetical argument, and pursuing the wider reasoning that it prompts, is the form that standing under the judgment of this text takes.

5

So, we have seen four forms of judgment in and around this text: first, divine judgment; second, human judgment concurring with that divine judgment; third, suspicious judgment worrying that there is nothing more than human judgment here; and then, fourth, the *reasoning* judgment that is made possible—made necessary—by a reasoning text.

The text makes clear, however, that the stakes in this reasoning are very high: after all, the idolaters that the text condemns have also reasoned for themselves—and they ended up exchanging the truth of God

2. This account is very loosely based on an argument in Williams, "Knowing Myself in Christ"; see also Higton, *Deciding Differently*.

for a lie. Facing us as it does with that kind of threat, can we really say that this text calls for the process of reasoned judgment that I have described? Does it really leave the reader with that kind of freedom?

I think we have to say that it does. Look what happens at the start of chapter 2. The Christian reader has seen the shadow of God's judgment falling, and has run into the light. She has thereby aligned herself with the divine judgment, and confidently imagined that she will escape condemnation . . . when—wham!—it falls on her anyway, squashing her flat. "Therefore you have no excuse, whoever you are, when you condemn others. . . ." This is the fifth kind of judgment I have found in or around this text.

Now, the reader at the start of chapter 2 is not simply judged for judging others. This is not a text that condemns judgment per se. The problem is not that the reader has been unduly ready to see others standing under divine judgment, but that she has been unduly *un*ready to see that she too still stands condemned.

But notice what this means. It means that some kind of reasoned judgment is unavoidable. The reader who gets condemned here is one who has not taken the process of reasoning about divine judgment seriously enough. He has not dug down to the patterns of deep reasoning that are expressed in the surface condemnations that he knows and echoes, and he has not risen back up to see what other patterns of his own life and thought might unexpectedly, unobviously, stand under the judgment of those deep reasonings. His reasoning with the text has stopped short—and these verses in chapter 2 condemn him not because he has reasoned for himself instead of simply taking the text at face value, but because he has *failed* to reason seriously for himself.

This is, then, a very uncomfortable text—and not simply for the obvious reason that it touches on controversial issues of sexuality. It is uncomfortable in that it both calls for processes of reasoned judgment *and* makes the outcome of that reasoning a matter of life and death: failing to reason leaves one condemned, but so does reasoning that leads one in the wrong direction.

The very verses at the start of chapter 2 that sharpen the dilemma, however, give a hint of one kind of resolution to it. They suggest that the process of learning to judge *well*—learning to reason in a way that does not deliver one to condemnation—must mean first and foremost learning to judge *oneself and one's own people*.

The mark of a community or an individual learning to judge well, this passage suggests, is first of all self-judgment, and only second of all judgment turned outward towards others. The mark of a community or an individual learning to judge well is that their outward-turned judgment is simply an echo of one that their lives show they have themselves already taken as seriously, as deeply as possible, in ways that go beyond simple literalism.

Perhaps we might say that the form of judgment called for is not one that first of all places a dividing line between me and those whom I judge to be in the wrong, but one in which I begin by recognizing my community with them.

So: five kinds of judgment. Recognizing the complexity of the relationship between divine and human judgment in this passage does nothing to make the passage an easy one. It will not stop conservatives judging it to include a condemnation of homosexuality as we know it today, nor will it stop people like me judging it to include no such thing. And recognizing the complexity of the passage does nothing to ameliorate the text's insistence that these are matters of real seriousness—matters of right and wrong, life and death. There's no comfort here for a *laissez-faire* pluralism, one that lets multiple readings flourish without concerning itself about the ways in which they differ, the patterns of reasoning that sustain them, and the ways in which they might be shown to be wrong. Christian readers can and should and must argue about it, and can and should and must make judgments—and, yes, that means taking responsibility for the task of arguing that a given reading is wrong.

Nevertheless, this text, for all its frightening deployment of judgments that divide—truth from falsehood, natural from unnatural, idolatry from proper worship—does, with the twist in its tail, suggest that there's something disordered about a pattern of reading that would *either* allow me too easily to say that those people over there, with their lifestyles and sexual practices and desires, are in the wrong while I am in the right; *or* allow me too easily to say that those *readers* over there, with their condemnations and exclusions and failures of mercy, are in the wrong while I am in the right, without digging into the underlying patterns of reasoning and asking whether I too am caught in their nets. So I find in this text a call to dig into the reasonings that structure my own readings of this text *and* those that structure the readings I oppose—to take seriously the job of arguing it out, and to refuse the simplistic vision that would suggest that tussles over this text can be solved simply by name calling or labeling.

There is, this text suggests, no obedient judgment without that kind of play we know as reasoning.

6 Keeping a Hard Text in Play III

Fearful Bodies

[21]Be subject to one another out of reverence [Gk phobos, fear] for Christ. [22]Wives, be subject to [Gk lacks verb here] your husbands as you are to the Lord. [23]For the husband is the head of the wife just as Christ is the head of the church, the body of which he is the saviour [Gk *himself the savior of the body*]. [24]Just as the church is subject to Christ, so also wives ought to be, in everything, to their husbands.

[25]Husbands, love your wives, just as Christ loved the church and gave himself up for her, [26]in order to make her holy by cleansing her with the washing of water by the word, [27]so as to present the church to himself in splendor, without a spot or wrinkle or anything of the kind—yes, so that she may be holy and without blemish. [28]In the same way, husbands should love their wives as they do their own bodies. He who loves his wife loves himself. [29]For no one ever hates his own body, but he nourishes and tenderly cares for it, just as Christ does for the church, [30]because we are members of his body. [31]"For this reason a man will leave his father and mother and be joined to his wife, and the two will become one flesh." [32]This is a great mystery, and I am applying it to Christ and the church.

[33]Each of you, however, should love his wife as himself, and a wife should respect [phobetai] her husband.

—Ephesians 5

JUST LIKE THE PASSAGES we have explored from 1 Timothy 2 and Romans 1, Ephesians 5:21–33 is a hard text. In fact, it is a contentious text all the way down—the translation, the sources, the argumentation, the theology, the ethics—and I would not like to speculate about how many pages of scholarly argument have been written for every word of it. It's a text about love and fear that is both beloved and (I think) fearful. My aim is to provide a gender-critical reading that moves beyond the binary question, "Is this text all right or not?" but I want, in doing that, to acknowledge that there are some genuine and not particularly complex binaries associated with the reading of this text and others like it (men really batter women, and that's really *not* all right, however difficult it may be to stop it happening).

I initially wrote this chapter for a panel discussion entitled "Women Reading Texts on Marriage." But when I start looking at this text, I was not sure I wanted to call it a "text on marriage," because I was concerned about how that detaches me as a reader from the particular, embodied, asymmetrical relationships into which the text speaks. If I start by saying, "What is this text saying about marriage?" I am assuming I can step back from the address to "wives" and the address to "husbands," assess them both from a single perspective, and see what they add up to.

To cut a long argument short: I think that such a single perspective—"What does this say about marriage?"—is implicitly a male perspective, because, in the historical context this text addresses and in most of the contexts in which it has been read, men control the institution of marriage, symbolically and practically. They are the heads, or the providers and maintainers, because of their greater economic power; they are the ones for whom children are born. That's reflected in the structure of the text before us. Husbands receive far more instructions here than do wives, and this can be linked to their greater power—among the original hearers of the text at least—to affect how marriage works. Women do not do much in this text. It's less obvious in the English translation, but the Greek in verses 22–24 is at least ambivalent about whether wives are spoken of in the second person or in the third. This is the first of the many grammatical strains in the text, and one of the very many obvious asymmetries—an asymmetry of address, such that we're not even sure whether women are fully included among the readers, hearers, and doers.

The asymmetry of address is particularly disturbing in Ephesians, because of the pervasiveness in the rest of the letter of the language of fullness, unity, inclusion, and abundance. The text I'm looking at is fearful because it makes one wonder who is really, in practice, in body, included in the "all of you" and "each of you" of this letter—and how, and on what terms. (And there's that neat rhetorical inclusio, a pair of references to "fear" in verses 21 and 33, which most translations soften but most commentaries on the Greek insist really do mean "fear.") What's the cost of the unity the letter talks about? Given that we are different and are in relationships that make our differences, what is this singleness of vision, this drawing together of all things, going to do to us; can it be done without violence? Has marriage in this text become the way divine order is liturgically formed and secured, and if so does that happen through the suppression or erasure of women?

Focusing on sexual difference within a text immediately means that nobody has a neutral perspective and that nobody can avoid the question of his or her relation to what is different. I would like to find a way of reading our texts that performs this relational non-neutrality. So what I want to look at here is, rather than a single "text on marriage," some sort of address to "wives" and some sort of address to "husbands," which in each case directs attention primarily at an embodied relation to the other. It seems to me that the text both says and performs that we live our bodies through and as relationships to others. That's not proclaimed as news here—it's really a presupposition of the text. And it is both one of the most promising and one of the riskiest dimensions of the text as regards women. In this text, marriage changes embodied identities, even (to quote Luce Irigaray) "prior to the child." And this means that women-becoming-wives don't seem to be offered any assurance of rights or adjudication, nor a sphere of activity that remains theirs (bearing and naming children).

So what do women-as-wives get that mitigates the terror of the text? I have one suggestion. It is very striking that the expression "savior of the body," used of Christ, occurs only here (verse 23) in the entire New Testament. Discussion in commentaries tends to focus on the links to the later image of the church as body, and on what this "interruption" of a point of unlikeness in the middle of a discussion of likeness does to the Christ-husband, church-wife comparison. But on a first reading of the text, I was inclined to take it simply as what it sounded like—an avowal, addressed at least indirectly to women, that, in Christ, bodies are saved.

This I find to be disruptive of more than the Christ-husband comparison, and of more than a particular model of "being in subjection." It is disruptive of whatever and whoever does violence to women's bodies, takes control of them, claims objectifying possession of them. And it allows women to hope for the salvation of their bodies from the condition of being blank pages onto which other people's fantasies, or analogies, or even theologies, can be inscribed. And it places this talk about "saving the body" within talk about marriage, thereby holding out the possibility that marriage, the giving over of one's body to be another's, is not in and of itself what you need to be saved from. This I find to be quite radical stuff. It sharpens my anger against the real abuse that this text continues to sanction. It makes it even harder to take the end of verse 33 ("the wife should fear her husband") as anything other than part of the problem.

But talking about Christ as "himself savior of the body" also serves, I find, as a challenge to "disembodying" readings of this text. It stops me running away to "one true meaning" that would apply in all times and places or that would enable the text to be rejected once and for all.

If with this in mind we look to the address to husbands, we find the statement that "nobody hates his own body" (in the Greek that's *sarx*, "flesh"). This is more puzzling. Obviously many people do hate their own flesh, and the form and manifestation of that hatred is strongly gendered; the idea of the body as saved and healed and taken up in transformation is disturbing partly because of this widespread body hatred. What is going on?

The main point here in this sentence seems to be about the nurture that flesh needs—using terms that are strongly evocative, as commentators note, of the care of infants. We may see here, in the middle of an address to husbands, an acknowledgement of a kind of demand most obviously and easily attributed to nursing mothers. There's a demand for care that comes from someone who is your own flesh and blood, and is addressed, as it were, to and through your flesh and blood, so you could no more deny it than you could cut off your arm. It's not the giving away of a previously self-possessed self; it's the realization that you are always already a body in relation. And talk of demand and need doesn't do full justice to the text here; the surrounding imagery is about marriage and sex, and hence about how the pleasure of the body is also found in recognising another as "flesh of my flesh." (Notice also how the use of this quotation seems to make the husband his wife's child; his relationship to her is compared to his relationship to his parents. He's somehow dependent on her in order to become himself).

So it seems to me that even if there's one dynamic in this text that is trying to keep all the asymmetrical relations where they always were, and project them forward into eternity—to assume that husbands have all the choices and all the agency, and then to give them some advice about what to do with it—there's another dynamic that's disturbing the order or threatening to reorder it. Commentators have noted that the metaphors in this text are unstable—so, for example, that the "one flesh" image invites thoughts of reciprocity and mutuality, of applying every injunction to both husbands and wives, even though it's embedded firmly in the instructions to husbands and followed quickly by the call for the wife to fear her husband. What they haven't always noted is that the instability of the metaphors has to do with the fact that they aren't "just" metaphors; they're pointers to real connections in embodied historical existence. The Christian community isn't the same sort of body as the body of an individual, but it's some sort of body and it has something to do with the bodies of individuals. And life within marriages and communities does change people.

I'm not sure as I read this text—and I'm not alone in this—where one person starts and another ends, what belongs to whom. It's not clear with regard to Christ and the church (hence at least some of the extensive spilling of ink), and it's not clear with regard to husbands and wives. To whom does that language about nursing and nurturing really belong? The acknowledgement of a "savior of the body" (who isn't any one person's husband) puts a stop to the appropriation of one person's body to another's control, but it doesn't render bodies impermeable or ungiveable. It promises, I think, something like a genuine erotic mutuality, liberated from false ideals either of total self-denial or of total self-possession—and other parts of the Letter to the Ephesians suggest that this kind of mutual rejoicing is already real, is the most real thing there is, is the reality of "all things" in relation to God. But that promise is only part of what's going on, and I find that in order to voice such a hopeful reading of the text I already have to de-gender and depoliticize my reading a little, and to distance myself from the perspective of the wives who are still under instruction to be in subjection and to be afraid, and who only get the promised "salvation of the body" with fear attached. I retain the suspicion that this is also a text of terror, and I want an escape route.

This raises questions about the distribution and allocation of risk in the reading of scriptural texts. It is all very well to say that when we read we must risk complexity, we must risk being disturbed, we must risk having our assumptions overturned—but how do we handle the fact that the reading of these texts as scripture imposes on some women the risk of multiple forms of abuse? How appropriate is "play" in that kind of context?

7 Unsettling Play

Negotiating with the Moabite Liberation Front

[1]Why do the nations conspire,
and the peoples plot in vain?
[2]The kings of the earth set themselves,
and the rulers take counsel together,
against the Lord and his anointed, saying,
[3]"Let us burst their bonds asunder,
and cast their cords from us."
[4]He who sits in the heavens laughs;
the Lord has them in derision.
[5]Then he will speak to them in his wrath,
and terrify them in his fury, saying,
[6]"I have set my king on Zion, my holy hill."
[7]I will tell of the decree of the Lord:
He said to me, "You are my son;
today I have begotten you.
[8]Ask of me, and I will make the nations your heritage,
and the ends of the earth your possession.
[9]You shall break them with a rod of iron,
and dash them in pieces like a potter's vessel."
[10]Now therefore, O kings, be wise;
be warned, O rulers of the earth.
[11]Serve the Lord with fear,

with trembling [12]kiss his feet,
or he will be angry, and you will perish in the way;
for his wrath is quickly kindled.
Happy are all who take refuge in him.

—PSALM 2

WE FINISH PART I of this book with a very different kind of text. It is a text where a certain kind of playful reading—a christological reading—quickly became the Christian plain sense. Playing with *this* kind of text is not so much a matter of learning how to weave it in to a wider pattern of Christian reading and living, but discovering what happens when the loose threads in that weave are yanked hard enough to start pulling the cloth apart. First, however, we need to see just how deeply ingrained the christological reading of this text has been.

At the Second Council of Constantinople in the year 553, Theodore of Mopsuestia was vilified as a heretic, and his writings were condemned. "If anyone," the council fathers said, "offers a defence for this . . . heretical Theodore, and his heretical books in which he throws up . . . many . . . blasphemies against our great God and savior Jesus Christ . . . let him be anathema."[1] There were some doubts at the time about the propriety of this condemnation, because Theodore had already been dead for 125 years, but he was condemned for his christological teaching, and the christological controversy in which he had participated had by no means died with him.[2]

In the symphony of criticism that sounded around his decaying head during the council, an interesting hermeneutical note sounds. Among the works of his that subsequently disappeared from library shelves was his commentary on the Psalms, yet it disappeared not because it said particularly objectionable things about Christ, but because it said practically *nothing* about Christ. Theodore was criticized for having rejected the traditional reading of many psalms, the traditional reading that took

1. Second Council of Constantinople, "Anathemas against the Twelve Chapters," Anathema 12.

2. I wrote the paper on which this chapter is based in 2008, exactly 125 years after the death of Karl Marx in 1883. Were a council in 2008 to anathematize Marx and those who still propagated his ideas, its sense of timing would be rather like that of the Second Council of Constantinople with its combination of Theodore.

them to refer clearly to Christ.[3] Instead, he preferred to read nearly all of them "historically"—as, in effect, glosses on the Old Testament's historical narratives of David and the Davidic kingdom. For Theodore, the Davidic historical context from which the Psalms came provided the only horizon within which they could meaningfully be thought to speak.[4]

Even Theodore, though, probably the patristic commentator least likely to find references to Christ in any Old Testament text, made one of his rare exceptions for Psalm 2.[5] In this psalm, Theodore says, "David in his inspired composition narrates everything carried out by the Jews at the time of the Lord's passion; he recalls their sacrilegious plotting against the Lord, vain and futile as they were, and recounts their vicious and futile efforts. He suggests also [the Lord's] right to command, and hints at the power of control that, after the resurrection as a human being taken up by God, he received for exercise over all." As if that were not clear enough, Theodore—the very theologian who was to be accuse of a Judaizing interpretation of the Bible—continued: "issue is to be taken with the Jews, who endeavor to deflect the reference in this prophecy away from the person of the Lord, some wanting to take the words of the present psalm in reference to Zerubbabel, some to David."[6]

It is worth noting that for Theodore the reference to Christ in this psalm is *not* a matter of an allegorical or spiritual sense. Christ is spoken of by the plain, literal sense. Theodore reads the text as if it were spoken by its historical author (David, he thinks), and claims that what David said in his historical context was explicitly and deliberately, thanks to the inspiration of God's Spirit, a prophecy foretelling the passion and triumph of Christ. There is but one meaning to this psalm, for Theodore, and that meaning concerns Christ.

Theodore may have stood outside the mainstream in his reluctance to find Christ in many other places in the Psalms, but even he had no doubt that Christ was firmly and clearly spoken of here. And if even poor anathematized Theodore, notorious eraser of Christ from the Psalms, insists on such a Christ-focused reading in this case, you can be confident

3. See Greidanus, *Preaching Christ*, 93, and Tyng, "Theodore of Mopsuestia," 303.

4. See O'Keefe, "'Letter That Killeth,'" and Hill, "His Master's Voice"; see also Greer, *Theodore of Mopsuestia*, ch. 5.

5. Along with Pss 7, 14, and 110.

6. Hill, *Theodore of Mopsuestia*, 15. Very little of the original Greek remains, but Latin and Syriac translations have survived. The relationship between christological interpretation of the Psalms and relationships between Christians and Jews will be the subject of chapter 8.

that the early church is going to give no quarter to any who wish to read the Psalm another way.

A DEEP TRADITION

The kind of Christ-focused reading of this psalm that Theodore performed was, of course, deeply rooted in the Christian tradition, and one of the reasons that Theodore clung to it was that it was already evident in several places in the New Testament: in Acts, Hebrews, and Revelation.[7] In Acts 4, for instance, when Peter and John are released from captivity and return to their friends, they respond by proclaiming:

[24]Sovereign Lord, who made the heaven and the earth, the sea, and everything in them, [25]it is you who said by the Holy Spirit through our ancestor David, your servant:

> "Why did the Gentiles rage,
> and the peoples imagine vain things?
> [26]The kings of the earth took their stand,
> and the rulers have gathered together
> against the Lord and against his Messiah."

[27]For in this city, in fact, both Herod and Pontius Pilate, with the Gentiles and the peoples of Israel, gathered together against your holy servant Jesus, whom you anointed, [28]to do whatever your hand and your plan had predestined to take place. [29]And now, Lord, look at their threats, and grant to your servants to speak your word with all boldness, [30]while you stretch out your hand to heal, and signs and wonders are performed through the name of your holy servant Jesus."

At least by the time of the composition of Acts, then, the psalm was being used to make sense of the passion of Christ—to insist that Christ's suffering was predestined by God's hand, and to provide a way of making sense of the sufferings of Christ's followers.

It was this New Testament quotation, with its explanation that in the psalm God was speaking by the Spirit through David, that provided the bedrock for later Christian exegesis. When a theologian like Theodore asked what he was to do with this psalm, the book of Acts told him:

7. For discussions, see Weren, "Psalm 2 in Luke–Acts"; Steyn, "Psalm 2 in Hebrews."

marvel that the passion was no accident but the outworking of God's plan, laid out already in the Psalms for those who have eyes to read it.

In Hebrews 5:5–6 we find a quotation from Psalm 2 joined to one from Psalm 110: "Christ did not glorify himself in becoming a high priest, but was appointed by the one who said to him, 'You are my Son, today I have begotten you'; as he says also in another place, 'You are a priest for ever, according to the order of Melchizedek.'" Sonship, kingship, priestly office, anointing—these psalms provided the author of Hebrews with a set of concepts to conjure with, a palette of colors that enable him to paint his Christology. When a theologian like Theodore asked what to do with this psalm, the book of Hebrews told him: use it to begin understanding the meaning of Christ's anointing and appointing; use it to explore the meaning of his divine nature.

It is not just Theodore, of course, who found his answers here. The ball that the authors of Acts, Hebrews, and Revelation set rolling continued to spin all the way down Christian history, and until very recently the direction of its spin went unquestioned. *Of course* the psalm was about Jesus. *Of course* Christians should understand it as a prophecy or prefiguration of Jesus' passion.[8] Even those who, like Theodore, were most sceptical, most likely to be suspicious of extravagant typological and allegorical readings, would agree: there is nothing else for Christian readers to do with this psalm than read what it tells them about Christ.

REJECTING THE CONSENSUS

If you look hard, there is *one* slight tension amongst traditional Christian interpreters of the psalm—a tension between those who see it more as a "prophecy" and those who see it more as a "prefiguration" of Christ. This tension barely creates a ripple in the pool of Christian consensus about this psalm, but it is worth mentioning because of what happens next.

The prophetic end of the spectrum is that occupied by Theodore: the text is a prophecy spoken by David; that prophecy—and therefore the psalm in which it is recorded—has a single meaning: Christ. For other readers, however, the psalm has a double meaning: it is not just *by* David, it is *about* David, but David in turn is a figure of Christ, and so by being

8. See, for example, the commentary of Aquinas cited below. See also Byassee, *Praise Seeking Understanding*, 68; Parsons, *Martin Luther's Interpretation*, ch. 4; Jenkins, "Erasmus' Commentary on Psalm 2."

about David the psalm is also about Christ. For instance, Aquinas in his commentary says, "[T]his Psalm is David's, because it was composed by him, and it treats of his kingdom in the figure of the kingdom of Christ [*et de regno eius in figura regni Christus agit*]. For by David Christ is suitably signified."[9] The prophet, in Aquinas' view, is God himself, and David is his prophecy: God has given us David as a pointer to Christ. To the extent that David is also a prophet he is so in a secondary, derivative sense—as one allowed by God's inspiration to see the prophecy that he himself is.

Now, as I said, for the most part, and except in rather extreme cases like that of Theodore, this distinction between prefiguration and prophecy is not a matter for controversy or even notice. But if we scroll down to more recent writings, we find it becoming more visible—as, for instance in Robert Lowth's 1753 *Lectures on the Sacred Poetry of the Hebrews*, a landmark in the development of modern critical studies of the Hebrew Bible.

Lowth was writing in an era where a Theodorian sensibility was becoming the norm, in that the whole un-Theodorian idea of multiple meanings was becoming suspect, and needed explicitly to be *argued* for. Lowth says:

> The subject of the second Psalm is the establishment of David upon the throne, agreeably to the Almighty decree, notwithstanding the fruitless opposition of his enemies. The character which David sustains in this poem is twofold, literal and allegorical. If on the first reading of the psalm we consider the character of David in the literal sense, the composition appears sufficiently perspicuous, and abundantly illustrated by facts from the sacred history.

9. Thomas Aquinas, *Commentary on the Psalms*, Ps 2. Aquinas keeps both referents in view for some time. For example: he says, "In the first [part] is related the trickery of those struggling against the kingdom of David and of Christ"; he explains that kings are called "christs," anointed ones; he explains that the "yoke" that the rebels would throw off is David's royal power, but that "Spiritually, in Christ, the yoke is the law of charity—Matthew 11: *My yoke is easy* etc." When he gets to v. 7, however, he says that it was "not always [*usquequaque*] fulfilled concerning David, and thus is understood concerning Christ"; he does not attempt to explain in what sense David was God's son, but instead launches into a christological discussion of the nature of Jesus' divine sonship. From that point on, though the Davidic reference is not wholly absent, Aquinas loses interest in it.

That is, if read as coming *from* its Davidic historical context, and speaking *about* that context, the psalm makes perfect sense. There is more, however. Lowth continues:

> Through the whole, indeed, there is an unusual fervour of language, a brilliancy of metaphor; and sometimes the diction is uncommonly elevated, as if to intimate, that something of a more sublime and important nature lay concealed within; and as if the poet had some intention of admitting us to the secret recesses of his subject. If, in consequence of this indication, we turn our minds to contemplate the *internal* sense, and apply the same passages to the *allegorical* David, a nobler series of events is presented to us, and a meaning not only more sublime, but even more perspicuous, rises to the view.[10]

Lowth's lectures were originally given in Latin. When they were published in an English translation they came complete with notes from a German biblical scholar, Johann David Michaelis, who had been present at the original lectures in the 1740s. Michaelis, with all the uneasiness of a modern Theodore with the very idea of multiple meanings, wrote: "If, as we learn from the apostle Paul, this Psalm relates chiefly to Christ, his resurrection and kingdom; why should we at all apply it to David? . . . If Christ, therefore, be the subject of this poem, let us set aside David altogether."[11] Theodore would have been proud.

Later, in the nineteenth and twentieth centuries, historical-critical scholarship comprehensively and convincingly demonstrated that the psalm itself gives no hints that it is a prophetic description of a distant future; it demonstrated that the psalm talks not about universal kingship but about the domination of particular rebellious vassal kingdoms, near and far; it demonstrated that there is nothing in the psalm to suggest that the sonship ascribed to the anointed is any kind of mysterious ontological state, rather than another example of a familiar Hebraic and ancient Near Eastern metaphor for sacrally instituted kings. In short, historical-critical

10. Lowth, *Lectures on the Sacred Poetry*, 151–52, my emphasis. Lowth continues, "Should any thing at first appear bolder and more elevated than the obvious sense would bear, it will now at once appear clear, expressive, and admirably adapted to the dignity of the principle subject. If, after having considered attentively the subjects apart, we examine them at length in a united view, the beauty and sublimity of this most elegant poem will be improved. We may then perceive the vast disparity of the two images, and yet the continual harmony and agreement that subsists between them, the amazing resemblance, as between near relations, in every feature and lineament."

11. Lowth, *Sacred Poetry*, 152, footnote.

scholarship has amply and in detail demonstrated that there is no difficulty at all in taking the psalm, in its historical context, as a statement that belongs wholly within the political and ideological history of Judah.

It may be part of a coronation ceremony for the kings in Jerusalem, or from some ritualized annual reminder of coronation; it may have originated from a specific historical context in which the reassertion of the king's authority was needed. But nothing about it (no "unusual fervour of language," no "brilliancy of metaphor," no uncommon elevation of diction) hints at anything beyond the ancient Israelite horizon. Modern historical critics stand with Theodore in focusing on the literal-historical meaning of the text; they stand with Theodore in believing that the psalm should be interpreted within the horizon of the kings of Israel of Judah; they stand with Theodore in their deep suspicion of spiritual or allegorical readings—but they utterly reject Theodore's insistence that the psalm is clearly and literally a prophecy. If I might parody Michaelis for a moment, the modern historical critic says: "If, as we learn from the historical critics, this Psalm relates chiefly to the king in Jerusalem, his authority and his vassal states; why should we at all apply it to Christ? . . . If the Jerusalem king, therefore, be the subject of this poem, *let us set aside Christ altogether*."

RETURNING TO CHRIST

On the one hand, then, as a Christian reader of Psalm 2, I am heir to a long and rich tradition of reading that takes this psalm to be about Jesus—a tradition that has its roots firmly established in New Testament soil. I think that, as a Christian theologian interested in these things, I am bound to ask whether it is any longer possible to stand within that tradition of reading. On the other hand, I am faced with the general finding of historical criticism: that this psalm makes perfectly good sense within its own original historical context. And I have to say that I find the historical critics wholly convincing on this point. I don't think that David was, consciously or unconsciously, prophesying. I don't think the psalm was written by David at all. I do think the psalm emerged perfectly naturally within the context of the monarchy in Jerusalem, even if I'm yet to be convinced that any of the proposals of a more detailed historical setting has got beyond the level of plausible speculation.

In order to understand what freedom I think the Christian reader of this psalm might nevertheless still have, I will make a provisional distinction between the *literal* and *spiritual* senses of the psalm.[12] I do so with some trepidation, because I'm very aware that this distinction can be made in several different ways, and in particular that "literal" can mean all sorts of different, sometimes mutually incompatible things. But for present purposes I will distinguish spiritual reading (which I'll come to in a moment) from literal-historical reading, where by "literal-historical" I mean the form of reading that sees the text as an artefact produced in a particular historical context, amongst particular people, and that looks for the sense it would have had *in* that context, *for* those people. Mainstream forms of historical-critical reading are one form of literal-historical reading, but the precritical approach of Theodore of Mopsuestia would be another.

We may provisionally distinguish this literal reading from *spiritual* reading—aware, once again, that "spiritual reading" can mean several rather different things. For my purposes, though, and as a first approximation, I mean that kind of reading that finds other senses alongside or beyond the literal: the kind of reading that explores the ways in which the text as it stands contains the possibility of being read *differently*—of being read as *also* about Christ, or as about Christian life, or as about the future God has for the world. In the terms of our presentation so far, you might say that it is the kind of reading willing to play with the text.

My initial claim is that Christian theologians can talk about such spiritual reading, and about the spiritual senses of the psalm, without upsetting the historical critics by making the wrong sort of claims about the original historical context in which the text was produced, or about its original author or recipients. That is, I think that Christian theologians can talk about spiritual reading, about the spiritual sense of the psalm, without making the kind of claims about its original setting and production that cry out to be measured by canons of historical-critical plausibility.

The kind of distinction I am operating with might be clearer if I give an unrelated example. The author of 1 Peter says this (3:19–21): "[Jesus] went and made a proclamation to the spirits in prison, who in former times did not obey, when God waited patiently in the days of Noah, during the building of the ark, in which a few . . . were saved through water.

12. This distinction is one we will be returning to several times in the remainder of this book.

And baptism, which this prefigured, now saves you— not as a removal of dirt from the body, but as an appeal to God . . ." Look at how the author uses the Noah story. In the first place, he uses it in some kind of literal-historical way—which means, in his case, taking it as a factual story whose (rather mysterious) implications (the fate of the spirits of those who did not obey in the time of Noah) concern him. In the second place, however, he uses it spiritually: that story of salvation through water prefigures another salvation through water—baptism. That second, spiritual reading became the dominant way of reading the flood story in Christianity, until very recently.

Now, the literal-historical reading of that story might look rather different for a modern reader. It will probably not involve the assumption that the flood really happened. It might, on the one hand, involve a clarification of the nature of the story itself, as it would have been understood in the contexts where it originally circulated—what the action of the story is, who the characters are and what they are doing. It might, on the other hand, involve asking what role this story played in those original contexts: what it said to, and what it says about, the people amongst whom it was told and retold. But that revised literal-historical reading could still be accompanied by a continuation of the spiritual reading—the reading for which the floating ark of the narrative prefigures the ecclesial font of baptism.

To persist with that spiritual reading need not imply any claim that the original authors or audiences of this story had this kind of theological use of their story in mind, nor that they regarded these words as pointing, however vaguely or incipiently, beyond the story that they told to some future fulfilment; it need involve no claim that they were in some way manipulated or nudged into writing something that would have that extra referent built in, despite their best intentions. To set out this spiritual reading is not necessarily to make *any* kind of claim about the events of the text's production in its original historical contexts—at least not any kind of claim that needs to vie with alternative, historical-critical explanations.

Rather, it is to make a claim about what Christians can do with the text, or more properly what the text can do with them, now. Put it this way: if you join the ranks of those who don't believe that the flood stories are literally true, that wouldn't imply any duty to remove the carving of Noah's ark from the side of your church's baptismal font.

Now, to turn to such spiritual reading involves a turn away from the text as information-providing, or more generally, away from the text as a container in which authors or editors have wittingly or unwittingly deposited something that it is the readers' task to extract. To put it in more traditional language, it is to turn from those uses of the text designed to tell you what the faith is, or to "prove doctrine." It is to turn instead to those uses designed to drive you deeper into the faith already known.[13] The text becomes a serious playground, a vehicle for re-presenting familiar truths in unfamiliar clothing, so as to rewrite the patterns of Christian thinking about them. The flood story does not convey *information* about baptism; one could not (or should not) use it to settle controversies about baptismal theology or practice. Nevertheless, it *does* something to one's grasp of baptism if one sees it in the light of the flood stories, if those stories become a lens through which to look again at what one already knows.

With that distinction between in mind, I can say that the only thing imposed upon me by the findings of historical criticism that so impress me with regard to Psalm 2 is that, in this case, I have to abandon the claim that there is a *literal* reference to Christ in this psalm. I accept what historical criticism has taught me, and agree that there is no hint of anything in this text that does not belong in its original historical context. There is no hint that, for its original author and for its original recipients, there was any earthly referent beyond their own political situation. They did not understand themselves as prophesying, their original audiences would not have understood these words as a prophecy, and there is no fact (or gap in the facts) about the production and reception of this psalm that either those authors or those audiences were missing.

But what about spiritual reading? What about the reader who says, "I know this is not the literal sense—I know it's not what the author originally meant, or what his audiences heard—but *look what happens* when I read it, with the kind of serious playfulness that we saw in Augustine's interpretation of the Good Samaritan, as being about Christ"? In that direction, I think, we find some interesting room for manoeuvering.

The first thing to say about such a suggestion is, "Well, why not?" After all, any historical critic who indignantly says, "But it's not *about*

13. Thomas Aquinas, *Summa Theologiae* 1a.1.10: "all meanings are based on one, namely the literal sense. From this alone can arguments be drawn, and not . . . from the things said by allegory. . . . [N]othing necessary for faith is contained under the spiritual sense that is not openly conveyed through the literal sense elsewhere."

that!" will have missed the point of the literal-spiritual distinction. From the point of view of the historical critic, however insistent he or she may be upon the necessity and integrity of a purely historical-critical reading, there is nothing untoward here: from his or her point of view, to attend to the strange emergence and persistence of this spiritual reading is not to listen to some challenge or contribution to the reconstruction of the text's origins; it is simply to attend to the strange history of reception that this text has had. It is to attend to the rather banal fact that, whatever it may have meant in their original contexts, it went on to mean other, different things as it was successively recontextualized over a long history. The historical critic will probably want to police quite carefully the border between literal and spiritual, of course, and make sure that the spiritual reader does not turn an edifying thought into an implausible historical claim—but that bit of intellectual hygiene is not itself destructive to the spiritual reading project. To think otherwise would be like thinking that a manufacturer of ladies' stockings has some right or duty to object when they are filled not with women's legs but with hastily wrapped Christmas presents. The reception history of the stocking is not wholly determined by the contexts and meanings of its original production. So, the first thing to say about a spiritual reading in which Christians takes the psalm to be, for them, about Christ is that it is a *possibility*.

The second thing to say again that such a reading may well be productive—not of new information about Christ, but of new thinking about what the Christian reader otherwise knows. That is, it is not just something that a Christian reader might be able to do, but something she might profit from doing. And one need only look with a generous eye at what precritical interpreters did with the text to see some of what such spiritual reading might lead to. It might be, for instance, one of the ways in which a Christian reader explores the nature of Christ's kingship, looking at it through the lens of the text so as to see it from a new angle. That is, reading this psalm might be part of the process whereby the Christian reader takes the existing idea of Christ's kingship (a doctrine established by the literal reading of other texts) and rolls it around on her tongue, tasting it, testing its limits, letting it percolate more deeply down to the roots of her imagination. The power of such reading is the power of metaphor: the unpredictable power unlocked by the juxtaposition of two distinct worlds of meaning. The implied story of a king on Zion, vying with rebellious vassal kings, is sandwiched against the story of an itinerant preacher, executed on Zion at the behest of its legitimate political rulers. What happens to one's imaginative grasp when those two stories are read in each other's terms? What happens to the reader's grasp of herself as a follower of the Lord's anointed? What happens to her grasp of her world as lying under this Lord's sway? These are not the kinds of questions that have any new facts as an answer. They are answered by the percolation of forms of imagination, by tectonic shifts in self-perception. The reader does not leave the text with new information, but dwells with it for ongoing edification.

If the first thing to say about such spiritual reading is that it is possible, and the second is that it might be beneficial, the third is that, for a Christian reader, such spiritual reading is, in fact, unavoidable. After all, the Jesus who is the focus of Christian attention emerged against the background of the Hebrew Bible, and only makes sense when read against that background. The Hebrew scriptures provide the primary terms of reference in which he makes sense, and so inevitably provide the primary terms in which the sense he makes is judged. He is, if you like, a commentary upon the Hebrew Bible—his whole life was a kind of embodied reading of those scriptures in a specific context—and so Christians can't help but read the Hebrew Bible as a commentary upon him.

Lest that sound implausible, think what it means in the case of Psalm 2. Christians ended up early on thinking of Jesus as a king. What they meant by that was shaped in significant part by the meanings of kingship that they found in the Hebrew Bible—even if that was not their only source. A text like Psalm 2 is part of the backdrop to Jesus' life and ministry, and the meaning of Jesus' life and ministry is in part constituted by the sense his life made of Psalm 2. To understand Jesus (or, at very least, to understand the Jesus of early Christian proclamation) you have to understand how early Christians took up themes, motifs, texts from the Hebrew Bible and applied them to Jesus, and had their reading of those scriptures and their understanding of him reshaped in the process. But this is more than simply a fact about the interpretive processes at work during Jesus' life and ministry, and the years immediately following. It is an ongoing task. Christians receive Christ as an embodied *proposal* for the reading of the Hebrew Bible; and so in receiving him, they receive the reading of that Hebrew Bible as their ongoing task. Christians are given, in Christ, the texts of the Hebrew Bible as *also* Christian texts—as texts that they need to read to make sense of their faith. Hebrew Bible becomes Old Testament—and to read it as Old Testament is to read it as it is caught up in this role of making sense of Christ. Reading the Old Testament in the light of the Christ who is a commentary upon it, and reading Christ in the light of the Old Testament scriptures that make sense of him, become practices that are constitutive for Christianity.

Faced with a text like Psalm 2, Christians cannot—or should not—resist the temptation to read it around Christ. Spiritual reading is not simply possible, not simply potentially beneficial: it is a core Christian practice. What is a Christian theologian to do with Psalm 2? Whatever literal-historical sense he or she makes of it, the Christian reader is *also* to read it around Christ: he or she is *also* to use it as a lens through which to consider Christ's kingship; he or she is *also* to see Christ's kingship as a response to, a *reading* of, the kingship depicted in the psalm.

RECONNECTING THE SENSES

So all is well. There is a neat and unproblematic resolution to find between the historical critic and the theological reader who stands firmly within the Christian tradition of Christ-centered reading. That resolution largely involves the two parties walking off in separate directions, yes, but that has to be better than a pitched battle.

Except, of course, that all is not well: the solution I have just offered is simply too easy. Are things in the hermeneutical garden really that *nice*? I glossed over rather rapidly, for instance, the fact that the Christian tradition I'm working with does not actually accept the severance of the literal and spiritual in quite the way I have described. I've made it sound like the christological reading is simply something that playful and creative Christian readers manage to do with the free-floating text once it has been cast free from its litera-historical moorings. But that is certainly not how spiritual reading was understood in the earlier Christian tradition. Take Aquinas, for example. He says:

> That God is the author of Holy Scripture should be acknowledged, and he has the power, not only of adapting words to convey meanings (which men also can do), but of adapting things themselves. In every branch of knowledge words have meaning, but what is special here is that the things that the words point to also themselves mean something. The first meaning, whereby words signify things, belongs to the . . . historical or literal [sense]. That meaning, however, whereby the things that the words point to in their turn also signify other things,

> is called the spiritual sense; it is based on and presupposes the literal sense.[14]

In other words, it is not, for Aquinas, that Psalm 2 talks about David and that the words it uses can, once cut loose from that historical referent, also fortuitously be used by Christians to speak about Jesus. Rather, for Aquinas, as I explained earlier, the words of Psalm 2 signify David, but *David* himself signifies Jesus: God has given David himself to the world as a prophecy of Jesus. The spiritual reading of the text, for Aquinas, is a reading of the historical referent of the text—a reading of David as *he* illuminates Christ. Spiritual reading, for Aquinas, is based on and presupposes the literal sense.

To take this tradition of reading more seriously than I have done so far involves two challenges to the solution I have offered. In the first place, Aquinas claims that the spiritual sense that this text possesses, it possesses not because the Christian reader invents it, but because God placed it there. In the second place, it claims that the spiritual sense is inextricably bound up with the literal-historical.

The first of these, the question of divine authorship, is not the focus of my attention at this point, but a couple of pointers are in order. In the first place, we might note that a claim to divine authorship is not necessarily a *causal* claim; that is, it is not necessarily a claim that God intervened in or otherwise arranged the pattern of efficient causes in the world at the time of the text's production in order to ensure that the text, or the events about which the text speaks, took a form that would prove to be edifying or transformative for Christian readers today. After all, *all* good things come from God (and, we might add, all good things are on their way to God): all good things are to be understood not simply as accidents whose significance stops with themselves, but are to be seen as part of a broader narrative sweep in which the world comes from God and is being drawn back to God. So when Christians find a genuinely edifying reading of this text, beyond the literal sense, then they *must* receive that edification as a gift from God, rather than as their own achievement: Christians can't but say that God is its author—and that claim to authorship is not a claim that competes with explanations of the creaturely contexts and processes involved in the production of the text. In the second place, we might note that if we can make sense of the life of Jesus of Nazareth as a fully creaturely life and yet as wholly a gift from God to the world of God's

14. Thomas Aquinas, *Summa Theologiae* 1a.1.10.

own life, we have to be able to say that the history that is as it were given in Christ, and that gives us Christ, is itself a gift. And that includes the textual history that gives us Christ, and that Christ gives us.

The second question, concerning the relation between spiritual and literal sense, is my main focus in this chapter. We have seen that traditional figural interpretation says that this psalm can be read spiritually because David himself is God's prophecy; it is *as read historically-literally* that the psalm goes on to have a spiritual sense. *David himself* is a figure of Christ, by God's design. Is that an aspect of traditional reading that my Christian reader will simply have to abandon? After all, we don't actually know when this psalm was written, we don't know whether it has anything to do with the historical David (though almost no critic I've read thinks for a moment that it does), and we don't even know for certain—as one of my colleagues regularly reminds me—whether David himself ever existed.

However, I don't think we *can* simply sever the literal-spiritual connection. Christians are, as I said, given the Hebrew Bible as Old Testament by Christ: these are *their* scriptures because they are *his* scriptures: they are the backdrop against which he makes sense, and on which he is a commentary. But what Christians are given in Christ is not simply a free-floating text, wrested from the people who wrote it and passed it on and revised it and read it: they are given a *history*. Christians understand themselves to be grafted into a people, a people with a history, with all the complexity and ambiguity and difficulty that comes with such a highly charged inheritance.

And that means, I think, that instead of thinking that this psalm could be, for Christians, simply a pattern of free-floating words that comment on Jesus and on which Jesus comments, and that the exploration of this mutual interpretation is an entirely ahistorical task bequeathed to Jesus' followers, it is *the text as it comes from and speaks of its history* (what we can tell of it, fitful, murky and complex though that might be) that Christians are given. Or at least saying something like that seems to me to be in firmer continuity with the Christian traditional of figural reading. The literal sense simply will not go away; the people by whom and for whom it was written will not go away. Christians do not operate in an enclave of spiritual reading cut off from that history—or, if they try to do so, they will find their reverie is interrupted by strange faces at the window.

READING WITH THE MOABITES

Let me put this more concretely by turning to perhaps the most striking of historical-critical readings of Psalm 2, provided by David Clines in a wonderful article, "Psalm 2 and the MLF (Moabite Liberation Front)."[15]

Since the psalm portrays a conflict between two parties, Clines says, it is worth noting that it can be looked at from the perspective of *either* party. If one party is the king of Judah, backed up by Judah's God, and by the psalmist, the other party looks like a real or imaginary coalition of vassal kingdoms: kings and peoples subject to the rule of Jerusalem. Clines, simply in order to give this second party a name, chooses to call them "Moabites," without claiming that this is any kind of secure historical identification. These Moabites as they appear in the psalm represent themselves as slaves (as bound in chains, burdened by a yoke), and their slavery is presented as primarily *political*—that is, it is simply the fact that they are clients or subjects of a foreign king that is at issue, not the nature of that king's laws, nor the nature of that king's God: their struggle is presented as a struggle for political emancipation. But their struggle for freedom is resisted by Jerusalem, and not simply resisted but scorned, with all the marks of "insensitive imperial despotism."[16] They are brought back into subjection not by being shown the benefits of their subordinate position, nor by having the justice of Jerusalem's laws or the love of Jerusalem's God displayed to them, but by crude threats of violence, and the promise that unless they kowtow they will find that violence flaring out against them. The psalmist portrays Jerusalem's rule quite explicitly and deliberately as a reign of terror: the vassal kings must live in perpetual fear, bowing to the king in fear for their lives. They should not think that they have any right to independence or self-determination: they are vassals, and Jerusalem has the right to destroy them if need be. For the king in Jerusalem, there is no question but that he exercises this dominion by divine right, and that he has divine right to support it by sudden violence; he has (he thinks) God on his side, and all resistance is useless. That the Moabites might not themselves believe that right is on the side of might, that they might not agree that the true God sanctions Jerusalem's violent maintenance of its imperial power, does not cross the psalmist's mind.

Much of Clines's paper is spent on a trawl through endless commentaries on the Psalms, looking for any hint that the commentators have

15. Clines, "Psalm 2 and the MLF (Moabite Liberation Front)."

16. Ibid., 161.

seen the possibility that this psalm looks rather brutal when viewed from the position of those the psalm reads as enemies. But every flicker that he finds in the commentaries of such a recognition is instantly doused by convoluted arguments that right really is on the side on which the psalm places it, and that the despotic, violent power that it so clearly portrays is really compatible with—indeed, another name for—compassion.

Clines acknowledges that the passion with which he pursues his rereading of the psalm is grounded in his own political views (how could it be otherwise?). He writes, after all, as someone who instinctively values political self-determination, freedom from political slavery or vassalage, and the right to independence, and as someone who deplores the use of violence or threats of violence to secure political advantage. But his accusation of this text goes deeper than that: it is, he says, even in its own historical context a demonstration of bad faith. In a nation that defined itself in terms of political liberation from Egypt—for whom stories of liberation from a state of vassalage and slavery were identity-defining, and for whom continued political independence was ideologically crucial—a psalm emerges that denies those things to others. Only Israel can experience liberation: for everyone else, oppression is the order of the day.

Faced with Clines's critique of the disastrous politics and ethics of Psalm 2, what is a Christian theologian to do with the psalm? He or she might, of course, be tempted simply to say, "That was then; this is now. Who cares what the text *meant* in whatever Judean context it emerged from; let's concentrate on the very different things it now *means*, when we read it as referring to Christ." If I am right that the literal and spiritual cannot be so neatly separated, because the spiritual is based on and presupposes the literal, then we are simply not going to get away with that kind of evasion. The "Moabite" faces at the window will not let us.

Christians are, in some sense, heirs to the history that produced this text, and that is still visible in it. And that means trouble. As Clines himself says, "the quotation of Psalm 2 in the New Testament by no means legitimates the ethics of the Psalm, but rather *problematizes the New Testament*."[17] The connections between literal and spiritual are, we might say, strong enough for Clines's critique of the literal to travel along to the spiritual. If Christians persist—as I have said that they should—in reading *this* psalm around Jesus, they should be very clear about the implications of what they are doing.

17. Ibid., 183, my emphasis.

CHRIST AS KING?

If Christians are to read Psalm 2 as part of the way they make sense of Christ—and I think they quite properly can't avoid doing so—then Clines's interrogation of the psalm inevitably becomes an interrogation of ways in which Christians make sense of Christ. What *kind* of kingship have Christians attributed to Christ, if it is a kind that is aptly described by this troubling psalm?

Clines quotes one example of a Christian reading of the psalm from the nineteenth century: "When [Christ] burst the bands of the grave . . . He purchased for Himself an universal dominion. Henceforth His kingdom has been established in Zion, and all people of the earth will be subdued either to His love or to His wrath. What remains for us but to yield ourselves reverently to His sway . . . ?"[18] When reading this psalm, Theodore, with whom we started, says of Christ, "With a rod he struck, dislodged, and threatened the condition of both Gentiles and Jews . . . to . . . force the to lay aside the old self and advance to the new"; he speaks of the "wrath of the avenging Lord," of God instilling fear by threat.[19] Aquinas says that "the gentiles were idolaters: and thus they had to be broken into pieces, so that they might accept another form."[20] Charles Spurgeon, in his *Treasury of David*, comments: "Yes! Jehovah hath given to his Anointed a rod of iron with which he shall break rebellious nations in pieces, and, despite their imperial strength, they shall be but as potters' vessels, easily dashed into shivers, when the rod of iron is in the hand of the omnipotent Son of God. Those who will not bend must break. Potters' vessels are not to be restored if dashed in pieces, and the ruin of sinners will be hopeless if Jesus shall smite them."[21] Joseph Seiss wrote a commentary on Revelation in the late nineteenth century, and when writing about the two witnesses in Revelation 11 had this to say that drew on Revelation's citations of Psalm 2: "They [the two witnesses] witness for Christ, not as the bleeding and pleading Lamb of God, but as the avenger of his elect, who is about to break his enemies with a rod of iron, and dash them to pieces like a potter's vessel. They are Judgment prophets sent to

18. Young, "Book of Psalms."

19. Theodore of Mopsuestia, *Commentary on Psalms 1–81*, 33.

20. Thomas Aquinas, *Commentary on the Psalms*, Ps 2.

21. Spurgeon, *Treasury of David*, 1:12.

. . . give the infatuated world its last awful warning, [and] assure of the coming avalanche of destruction."[22]

A quick search on the Internet quickly turns up scores of contemporary examples. Listen, for instance, to what a preacher called William Einwechter does with the psalm

> The authority of Christ in the political sphere is absolute. He is the Prince. All magistrates are under His command, and are responsible to conduct their office in conscious submission to His law as it has been revealed to them in the Word of God. Civil rulers are in office first and foremost to serve Christ by carrying out His will. Christ rules over the kings of the earth as surely as He rules over the elders of the church. Rulers who do not recognize this are rebels, fit only to be smashed by Christ's rod of iron (Ps. 2:9-12; Rev. 12:5) for their impertinence to their prince.[23]

However they coat it (and they have all sorts of ways of softening the harshness of their language), there is no getting away from the fact that these Christian commentators are drawing a central support for their ideas about Christ's rule from a depiction of despotic kingship, of violent and oppressive domination. And that is rightly troubling.

But that, I suggest, is the point. If Christians want an edifying, spiritual reading of Psalm 2, *here* is at least one part of the real edification that it has to offer. Precisely as it is illuminated by historical criticism—and historical criticism at its most urgently critical—this psalm has the capacity to send Christians back again to examine their faith, to examine the sense they have made of Jesus, and to see that sense with new eyes. How much of Christian description of Jesus—particularly Christian *eschatological* claims about Jesus—involves some kind of revenge fantasy, some kind of barely suppressed violence? How much of it yells that Christ will *get* his enemies in the end? How much of it revels in the idea that Christ may have come first time round with words and acts of love, but he'll be coming back with a rod of iron, and *then you'll see*, you nations? To what extent have Christians adopted the same bad faith that Clines finds in Psalm 2: as those who have been liberated, refusing liberation to others; as those who have been loved into freedom, fantasizing about the imperious, irresistible overthrow of those who have not joined them?

22. Seiss, *The Apocalypse*, 219, emphasis mine.

23. Einwechter, "Christ's Political Authority."

Those are questions worth asking; they are, in the deeper sense of the word, "edifying": not nice, pious, and heart-warming, but interrogative, disturbing, and potentially transformative.

It is not *despite* Clines's exposure of the psalm that I am advocating a continued Christian spiritual reading of it. I do not think that such spiritual reading can only get to work once Clines's argument has been brushed under the carpet. I think it is important that Christian readers let the difficulties of the text stand, and pay attention to them—that they avoid trying to find answers and resolutions that would mean they didn't have to face them, but instead placed the difficulties squarely in front of them, with the help of critics like Clines. I think Christian spiritual reading of the Psalm 2 can and should be *impelled* by what Clines has elucidated. And I think that, if and when it is, Christians will find not that spiritual reading is made impossible but that it takes on itself a more critical and interrogative edge—that it exposes some of the violence buried (not too deeply) in some Christian thinking and believing, and calls Christians to repentance.

Christian spiritual reading needs historical criticism—particularly criticism that concerns itself with ideological and ethical criticism—in order to be more fully itself. If Christians are called to see not just Christ, not just the scriptures that enable them to make sense of Christ, but also the history from which Christ and those scriptures come, as God's gift to the world—as the product of God's authorship, if you like—then I think they're also called to see this kind of historical criticism, restlessly probing the darker side of biblical texts, as no less a gift of God, no less a product of God's authorship.

What are Christian readers to do with Psalm 2? Read it literally and spiritually; read it for all it is worth; read it with eyes wide open. And, perhaps, read it in such a way as to expose in their faith all kinds of despotic violence, including the violence that is comfortable with the condemnation and vilification of biblical interpreters—however mistaken might have been their readings—125 years after they were dead and buried. Such reading might be playful, but it is a very serious kind of play indeed.

part two

Scriptural Reasoning

8 Whose Psalm Is It Anyway?

Why Christians Cannot Read Alone

[1]Blessed is the man
who walks not in the counsel of the wicked,
nor stands in the way of sinners,
nor sits in the seat of scoffers;
[2]but his delight is in the law of the Lord,
and on his law he meditates day and night.
[3]He is like a tree
planted by streams of water,
that yields its fruit in its season,
and its leaf does not wither.
In all that he does, he prospers.
[4]The wicked are not so,
but are like chaff which the wind drives away.
[5]Therefore the wicked will not stand in the judgement,
nor sinners in the congregation of the righteous;
[6]for the Lord knows the way of the righteous,
but the way of the wicked will perish.

—Psalm 1[1]

1. I have chosen the RSV translation over the NRSV, my normal first choice for an English translation, for two reasons: first, it does not have the inclusive-language "blessed are those" but the older "blessed is the man," which highlights a controversial point to which we will be returning; and second, it preserves the apparent progression of "walk," "stand," "sit" in v. 1, even though commentators are divided on whether it was originally intended as a progression—see, e.g., Kraus, *Psalms 1–59*, 115: "The

THE PLAIN SENSE

What is the plain sense of this psalm? It sets out a contrast between two ways of life—or rather, it sets out a contrast between a way of life and a way of death, the way of righteousness and the so-called "way" of wickedness.

The wicked at first sight seem to be substantial, to amount to something: they have a position, a path, a way of thinking, such that one might be tempted to walk with them, stand with them, sit with them. But there is in fact nothing substantial about them: they will blow away on the breeze to nothingness. They will find themselves on the wrong side of God's judgment, and find they have no place amongst God's people.

The righteous, on the other hand, may at first sight seem less substantial than the wicked: they are initially defined only negatively as those who do not take part in the ideas, conduct or speech of the wicked. Yet the righteous know where true stability lies: they hold fast to God's word, the *Torah*. They are the ones who have true stability, like well-rooted trees; their way does not lead to nothing, but to substance, to location, to identity, to prosperity. God knows them, and they will stand firm in the face of God's judgment.

What does it mean to call this reading a "plain-sense" reading, though? I might be tempted to say that I have simply paraphrased the "surface meaning" of the text, that I have stuck "close" to the text, but if I stopped there I would be obscuring the ways in which those metaphors—*plain* reading, *surface* reading, *close* reading—gain their content because of the company I keep.

In the first place, this "plain-sense" reading is shaped by the *human* company that I keep: my claim that I was giving a plain sense rests upon my guess that my readers will recognize what I have done as a fairly obvious, fairly banal thing to do with this text: the "plain sense" is a reading formally unremarkable in some specific company.[2]

In the second place, my "plain-sense" reading is shaped by the *textual* company that I keep. My ability to paraphrase, to identify meanings and

climax is worth noting"; but see Craigie, *Psalms 1–50*, 60: "it would be stretching the text beyond its natural meaning to see in these lines three distinct phases in the deterioration of a person's conduct and character"; and for a detailed discussion see Anderson, "Note on Psalm 1:1," 231–33—though his discussion does not actually touch on the progression of the verbs, but simply demonstrates that there is no progression in the descriptions of the wicked or their ways.

2. This is one of the meanings of *sensus literalis* discussed by Hans Frei in *Types of Christian Theology*, 16.

put them into my own words, was conditioned by my familiarity with texts *like* this one. It was dependent upon my having learnt how to speak the kind of language in which this psalm and other texts with which it keeps textual company are written.

In both senses, what counts as "plain sense" depends upon the company that one keeps. When meditating on the law of the Lord day and night, everything depends on the company with whom you walk, stand, and sit.

HISTORICAL-CRITICAL READINGS

One of the proper tasks of historical criticism is to uncover *different* plain senses of texts. After all, in different human and textual company, the "obvious" meaning of this text might have been rather different—and specifically in the contexts of the text's initial production, reception, redaction, and preservation it may have sounded very differently from the way it will sound when read in the RSV translation by the readers of a twenty-first-century theology book.

Some forms of historical criticism concentrate upon the *textual* company that the text in question keeps. For example, some historical-critical interpretations of Psalm 1 are driven by the close company it has kept with Psalm 2. There are indications both in the rabbinic tradition and in early Christian writings[3] that the two psalms may at some point have been joined together (despite their differences in style and subject matter), and this is exploited in a 1971 article by William Brownlee, who argues that Psalms 1 and 2 together formed a coronation liturgy at some point in their history. Common verbal and thematic threads help him stitch the two psalms together, and then a crowd of other texts are brought into the company to establish the propriety of reading various words in Psalm 1 in a royal or political sense. For Brownlee, in the ancient coronation context the plain sense of the psalm would have been a declaration of the happiness of a king who does not give himself over to wicked counselors or surround himself with scoffers, but who lets his rule be guided by the recitation of the *Torah*; that king will be a strong tree whose policies

3. Some early manuscripts of Acts 13:3 cite Ps 2:7 as from "the first psalm"; Justin Martyr, in *First Apology* 40, gives the two psalms together as if they were one text, and in the Babylonian Talmud (*Berakoth* 9b) there is a discussion of the first psalm beginning with blessing (1:1) and ending with it (2:12). See also the articles cited in the following note.

will succeed, and who will throw the wicked and feckless from his court.[4] That's what the plain sense of the text would have been, in the textual and human company into which it was born.

A broader and perhaps more typical historical-critical attempt to construct an appropriate textual company for Psalm 1 is provided by Jerome Creach, writing in the *Catholic Biblical Quarterly* in 1999. He focuses on verse 3a, "He shall be like a tree planted beside streams of water," and finds appropriate biblical and extra-biblical parallels to the tree image, and more detailed parallels to the particular choice of Hebrew word for "stream." His argument is, roughly speaking, that were this the textual company you kept, the thing that would strike you about Psalm 1 is the way in which it takes a familiar image from the wisdom tradition, splices in vocabulary that would have made you think of a tree planted and tended in the temple precincts, and then uses this now temple-flavored image to speak about the security provided by *Torah*. "Thus," Creach says, "*tôrâ* is implicitly compared to the temple, and is perhaps seen as the temple's replacement" and "Psalm 1:3 seems to indicate a shift in the perceived source of safety, from temple to *tôrâ*."[5] In its original textual company, this is what he thinks Psalm 1 would have plainly meant.

In other historical-critical readings, the emphasis falls more clearly on establishing the *human* company for the text. Hermann Gunkel suggested that the context was the post-exilic attempt to repudiate foreign wives as described in Nehemiah—which certainly gives the psalm a whole new spin (as you will see if you go back and read it now with that context in mind).[6] Others have suggested that the psalm emerged from a Deuteronomic party in pre-exilic Judah—perhaps the kind of circle responsible for the "Law of the King" in Deuteronomy 17:14–21—a circle that, it has been argued, was pursuing the double task of enjoining obedience to *Torah* as a limit upon the king's power, and arguing that such restraint would help the king remain a loyal vassal of Assyria.[7]

4. Brownlee, "Psalms 1–2 as a Coronation Liturgy." The details of his approach have not been much favored by later commentators. A less speculative attempt to make sense of Psalms 1 and 2 together is provided by Høgenhaven, "Opening of the Psalter."

5. Creach, "Like a Tree," 46.

6. Cited in Kraus, *Psalms* 1–59, 114–15.

7. The connection to the Deuteronomists is made by, amongst others, von Rad, *Old Testament Theology*, 1:200, Creach, "Like a Tree," 332, and Brueggemann, "Trusted Creature," 487. The analysis of the nature of the Deuteronomistic party is provided by Patricia Dutcher-Walls in "Circumscription of the King."

In every one of these cases, placing the psalm in different human or textual company makes its words resonate in different ways, reshaping what meaning will seem "obvious": the plain sense.

We can analyse the nature of such historical critical readings under four familiar headings: *literal*, *allegorical*, *tropological* (or moral), and *anagogical* (or eschatological)—though I'm going to be using these terms rather loosely. Under the heading "literal," I'm going to ask an ontological question: what *is* the text, for this kind of reading? Under the heading "allegory" I'll ask how it can say more than is obvious—what new thing does the text make *possible*? Under the heading "tropology" I'll ask what this kind of reading is *for*—how does this kind of reading shape the reader's life? And under the heading "anagogy," I'll ask what vision of true reading, full reading, guides this approach—what is this reading's eschatology?

So, *literally*, the text for these kinds of historical critics is a historical artefact, or family of historical artefacts: the text most properly *is what it was* in the contexts of its original production and reception; everything that comes after is not so much the text as the text's repercussions, or the telltale trails of evidence that can lead us back to the text.

Allegorically, the text can speak to the historical critic not just of its apparent subject matter (the subject matter of the plain sense for its original audience) but of its historical context—of the patterns of thought, the changes in culture, and the historical events that formed the womb from which it was born. It is a text that can speak between its lines: the text is what it was in its original contexts, and those original contexts speak to us through the text.

Tropologically, historical criticism is supposed to lead towards truer knowledge—but the real *moral* thrust of this is perhaps better seen when this is put negatively: this kind of reading is meant to produce what can be a painful tearing of the veils of delusion and misapprehension that have prevented the text from being its historical self for us. We are our history, and to the extent that we misread and misappropriate our history we misread ourselves. Historical criticism is a necessary purgative; it kicks down the artificial props with which we have supported the current pattern of our lives, and opens our eyes to the true strangeness, the not-for-us-ness, of the text.

Anagogically, this is a reading carried out with a certain kind of yearning to it; it has a certain kind of eschatology to it. Ultimately, the historical-critical reading is oriented towards an ideal, longed-for drawing together of all the diverse strands of evidence, and the making clear of all the connections between strands that would make it possible to see the texts in terms of their proper original contexts, and the contexts in terms of all available texts—and so, ultimately, to see ourselves in proper relation to our history. This is an unattainable vision, of course, which does not so much tell the critic when to stop as tell her *not* to stop: it is a vision that unsettles all the partial answers that it calls forth, and keeps the critic on the quest for deeper, wider, more comprehensive vision.

Is Psalm 1 a Christian text for this kind of historical criticism? Well—why on earth would anyone think so?

AUGUSTINE'S READING

Of course, Psalm 1 did not stay in its original textual or human company, whatever that company was. It was transplanted from company to company, and eventually ended up, amongst other places, in the company of New Testament texts and Christian readers. In that company, what happened next was probably inevitable—and is best illustrated by the opening of the exposition provided by Augustine:

> *Blessed is the man who has not gone off* [*abiit*] *in the counsel of the ungodly*. This should be understood to be about our Lord Jesus Christ, the man of the Lord [*homine Dominico*]. *Blessed is the man who has not gone off in the counsel of the ungodly*, as did the earthly man [i.e., Adam—see 1 Cor 15:47] who gave in to his serpent-deceived wife, and transgressed the commandment of God. *Nor stood in the way of sinners*. For although he entered the way of sinners by being born as sinners are, he did not "stand" in it because the enticements of the world did not hold him.[8]

The broad structure of Augustine's interpretation of the psalm is provided by this contrast between Christ and Adam, and he sees the psalm as a description of the roots and nature of sin and righteousness, the legacies of Adam and Christ.[9] He uses his exegesis of the psalm as an opportunity to lead his readers deeper into understanding of their own plight, and of their salvation; the whole tenor of his reading is pastoral and educative.

8. Augustine, *Enarrationes in Psalmos*, on Ps 1.1; my translation, loosely based on that in Coxe and Schaff's *Select Library of Nicene and Post-Nicene Fathers*.

9. It is worth noting in passing, by the way, that Christians were not the only ones up to this sort of thing. Rabbinic comments identify the righteous man variously as Adam, Abraham, and Levi. See *Midrash on the Psalms*, 2.13, 18, 19; noted in Creach, "Like a Tree," 44.

However different his purpose, much of his *method* is formally identical to (if substantively wildly divergent from) that of some historical critics. Augustine offers three interpretations of the streams of water, for instance, but whereas Jerome Creach discerned meanings related to Eden, Zion, and the temple, Augustine builds up a different company of texts to suggest that the streams might mean Christ's divinity, the Holy Spirit, or the sins of the people.[10] Of course, Augustine's justification for the tracing of these verbal connections is no picture of the chains of this-worldly cause and effect that surrounded the production of this text: he is not tracing influences or origins. He is chasing *canonical* connections, connections between the texts that God has given to God's people for their edification. The textual company that Augustine explores in order to make sense of this text is the company that it has been given by God.

However tenuous some of these connections might be, though, and however hard some of the more extravagant hypotheses might be to work into a coherent reading of the text, it is hard to see how Augustine could have avoided the basic move that takes this to be about Adam and Christ—just as I have argued that he could not avoid the christological reading of the parable of the Good Samaritan or of Psalm 2. How could this psalm be about the true nature of sin and the true nature of righteousness, and *not* be about Adam and Christ? It is just obvious, or "plain," for Augustine.

This basic hermeneutical move—taking the psalm to be about Adam and Christ—is one that enables Augustine to do substantive theological work through his reading the text, as when he discusses "delight in the law" and distinguishes between those for whom the law is a heteronomous burden, and those for whom the law is "discerned by the mind" (*mente conspicitur*), who, strictly speaking, do not *need* the letter of the law (because they are "in it," not "under it"). Precisely because he assumes that the psalm keeps company with the other biblical texts that ground his theology, the text's arrangements of words becomes a potential *re*arrangement of his theology: by bringing "delight" and "law" together and by (as Augustine could not but see it) applying the combination to Jesus, the psalm represents a challenge to his understanding of Christ's relationship to the law, and one that requires him to expend *effort* in order to make sense of it. That effort might not be the source of dazzling new insight, but it does

10. He draws respectively on "the river of God is full of water" (Ps 65:9), "he shall baptize you in the Holy Ghost" (Mt 3:11), and "The waters that you saw, where the whore is seated, are peoples and multitudes and nations and languages" (Rev 17:15), amongst other texts.

at least require him to phrase his old insights differently, to experiment until he can see how to say of Jesus that he *delights* in the law of the Lord.[11]

That reading the text this way does pose a difficulty, and does require interpretive work, is shown by Hilary of Poitiers's *Homilies on the Psalms*. Hilary states that

> the contents of the first Psalm *forbid* us to understand it either of the person of the Father or of the Son: *But his will has been in the law of the Lord, and in his law will he meditate day and night. . . .* [O]bviously it is not the Person of the Lord speaking concerning Himself, but the person of another, extolling the happiness of that man whose will is in the law of the Lord. Here, then, we are to recognize the person of the prophet by whose lips the Holy Spirit speaks, raising us by the instrumentality of his lips to the knowledge of a spiritual mystery.[12]

For Hilary, this psalm *could* in principle have been a psalm about Christ;[13] it is just that the attempt to work through such an interpretation coherently in this case proves it to be a mistake. It is only because Augustine has, as it were, dwelt with this difficulty for longer, and found a way to make sense of it, that he too is not forced to abandon christological reading.

Of course, there are others in the patristic tradition who don't consider a christological reading of the psalm—including such substantial figures as Basil of Caesarea in the East and Ambrose in the West. There are some who reject the whole idea more forcefully, such as Diodore of Tarsus and (as readers of the previous chapter will not be surprised to hear) Theodore of Mopsuestia. But the christological way of reading this psalm seems to have become dominant in the West before long, and was embedded not just in standard commentaries, but found its place in Western liturgy. A christological reading became the "plain-sense" reading of the text for generations of Christian readers.[14]

11. "'The law is not made for a righteous man,' says the Apostle (1 Tim 1:9). But it is one thing to be *in* the law, another to be *under* the law. If someone is *in* the law, she acts in accordance with it; if someone is *under* the law, she is acted upon by the law—the former is free, the latter a slave. The law that is written and imposed upon a servant is one thing, the law discerned by the mind by someone who does not need its letter, is quite another." *Enarrationes* on 1.2; translation adapted from the *NPNF* edition.

12. Hilary of Poitiers, *Homilies on the Psalms* 1.1.

13. He recognizes that a christological reading of this psalm is "inspired by a pious tendency of thought." Ibid., 1.2.

14. The patristic (and medieval) data has been usefully discussed by Waddell,

Let me turn again to my four questions: literal, allegorical, tropological, and anagogical. Literally, for this patristic and medieval tradition, the text is what it is in the context of the canon—which does not just mean in the context of the other books that made it into the accepted lists, but in the context of the rule of faith, the basic Christian narrative of salvation. The text simply *is* one voice in a choir singing the praises of the Christian God.

Strangely enough, in this particular case, there is not much to say about allegory. The christological reading is, for Augustine and the tradition, the *literal* reading of this prophetic text. This is a text that speaks pretty straightforwardly about Jesus, and there are few trips or traps to suggest to the alert reader that time needs to be spent unearthing a deeper, still more edifying meaning: allegory appears only as playfulness around the edges.

Tropology and anagogy, on the other hand, are all-important here, and go together: the text is given by God for *edification*, for the building up of life in Christ; reading it, understanding its meaning, is an aspect of the journey deeper into the life of God: "The fulfilment and the end of the law, and of all holy Scripture, is the love of one who is to be enjoyed, and the love of those who can enjoy that other in fellowship with ourselves."[15] Is Psalm 1 a Christian text? Of course it is, Augustine might say—what else does scripture teach?

LUTHER'S READING

I might be thought at this point to be heading in the direction of a lazy pluralism: texts have different senses according to the company (textual and human) that they keep; so the psalm means *x* in one company, *y* in another, and different interpretations can on that basis coexist without troubling one another. However, relationships between neighbors are

"Christological Interpretation of Psalm 1?" He was arguing against the NRSV's and NAB's adoption of the inclusive-language "Blessed are those" rather than "Blessed is the man," on the grounds that it cuts contemporary readers off from the christological sense that the psalm has had in the church for centuries. For more of the controversy, see Fessio, "'Blessed Is the Man'"; Jensen, "Inclusive Language and the Bible"; Clifford, "Bishops, the Bible"; Clifford and Waddell, "'Christological Interpretation of Psalm 1?'"; Jensen, "Watch Your Language."

15. *De doctrina christiana* 1.35(39); translation slightly altered. Cf. Williams, "Biblical Interpretation," 67–68.

often more fraught than that picture suggests. Somewhat later in the tradition of reading the psalm that flows through Augustine, for instance, we find Luther. He uses Psalm 1 in the preface to his first lectures on the Psalms, delivered when he was still a good Augustinian monk, as an example of the way that the Psalter can be interpreted literally and spiritually.

"Every prophecy and every prophet," he says, "must be understood as referring to Christ the Lord, except where it is clear from plain words that someone else is spoken of."[16] How much more so with David, that most intimately inspired of prophets.[17] Luther therefore rejects those who "explain very many psalms not prophetically but historically, following certain Hebrew rabbis who are falsifiers and inventors of Jewish vanities. No wonder, because they are far away from Christ (that is, from the truth)."[18] But

> Whatever is said literally concerning the Lord Jesus Christ as to his person must [also] be understood allegorically of a help that is like him, and . . . tropologically of any spiritual and inner man against his flesh and the outer man. Let this be made plain by means of examples. "Blessed is the man who walks not [in the way of sinners]" (Ps 1.1). Literally this means that the Lord Jesus Christ made no concessions to the designs of the Jews and of the evil and adulterous age that existed in his time. Allegorically it means that the holy church did not agree to the evil designs of persecutors, heretics, and ungodly Christians. Tropologically this means that the spirit of man did not accede to the persuasions and suggestions of the inimical flesh and of the ungodly stirrings of the body of sin.

When he gets to the commentary on Psalm 1 itself, Luther like Augustine takes it as an examination of the nature and sources of righteousness and

16. Luther, "Preface of Jesus Christ," 6.

17. The description of David in the Vulgate of 2 Sam 23:1 could be translated as "the man to whom it was appointed concerning the Christ of the God of Jacob"; the same passage gives, as David's final words, "The Spirit of the Lord has spoken by me, and his word by my tongue." For Luther, therefore, David (the author of the Psalter) is a prophet, one who had "some extremely intimate and friendly kind of inspiration. Other prophets confess that they spoke, but this one declares that in a unique way it was not he who spoke but the Spirit who spoke through him." Luther, "Preface to the Scholia," 9–10.

18. Ibid., 10.

of wickedness—particularly the latter; he takes verse 1 in particular as a scalpel-sharp anatomizing of temptation and sin.

However, the aspect of Luther's reading that stands out for a contemporary reader is the regularity with which he returns to the Jews as the paradigm of ungodliness, the exemplars of sin—and as the obvious, literal referent of the psalm's language about wickedness, sin, and scoffing.

In his somewhat later *Operationes in Psalmos*, the same theme appears—to even more chilling effect. In his explanation of "chaff that the wind blows away," Luther says:

> The Psalmist doesn't simply say "chaff," but rather "chaff that the wind blows away." . . . One should think, in the first instance, of the Jews. They are driven hither and yon in three ways. First . . . by the efforts and indignation of the people among whom they live, as we can see before our very eyes. . . . Secondly, they are spiritually driven hither and yon by the wind of diverse teachings of pernicious teachers. . . . Thirdly, on Judgement Day, they will be frightened away and scattered by the eternal storms of God's irresistible wrath . . .[19]

"[D]riven hither and yon . . . by the efforts and indignation of the people among whom they live." In Luther's hands, in other words, Psalm 1 becomes a mandate for pogroms.

Now, one could argue that this is simply Luther's all-too-well-known and all-too-regrettable anti-Semitism frothing up again, and suggest that however objectionable it is it shouldn't be allowed to taint the whole tradition of christological readings of this psalm. I'm not so sure. I think one could rather more convincingly argue that christological reading of this kind, even when it is dressed up in less offensive garb, is inherently supersessionist—and that Luther simply displays the logic of this supersessionism with frightening clarity. *If* the christological interpreter says (as we saw Augustine say), "This text is *really* about Jesus"—and so implicitly

19. Luther, *Selected Psalms III*, 189–90. This is discussed by Uwe F. W. Bauer in "Anti-Jewish Interpretations of Psalm 1." Bauer distinguishes three forms of anti-Jewish thought in the commentators he examines: (1) positive Christian appropriation of Psalm 1, with it seen as a condemnation of Judaism, as in Luther; (2) the psalm seen as the product of a degenerate form of late, legalistic Judaism—the kind of Judaism from which Jesus saved us; or (3) the psalm represented as a step in the evolution of religious life in history on the way to Christianity. "If one were to look," says Bauer, "for a common basis of the anti-Jewish statements of these exegetes, a decisive factor, in my opinion, is Christology, more specifically, the Reformation's justification-Christology with its exclusivistic, anti-Jewish configuration."

or explicitly says, "This text is *not* really about a *Torah*-righteousness for which Jesus is irrelevant or peripheral"—then he or she is saying that readers who do not find Christ here are kept from the psalm's proper meaning; they are outsiders to this text. In other words, ownership of the text is claimed, and previous owners are disinherited or superseded.[20] Jewish readers of the psalm are either condemned by it or they have not understood it; they are placed on the side of the wicked who do not *truly* meditate on the scriptures day and night, and are therefore those whose hermeneutical advice, whose interpretive path, whose exegetical seat will be shunned by the righteous—and whose un-Christed readings will blow away like chaff before the wind.[21]

Literally, then, the text for Luther, as it was for Augustine, is what it is in the context of the canon—but now it is clear that the rule of faith, the story of salvation, is one in which the contrast between law and grace, the superseded Jewish covenant and its Christian replacement, is basic. And his understanding of the special prophetic nature of this text means that this is as much a text of the covenant of grace as any you will find in the New Testament—and that the New Testament is this text's *only* proper context. This is, once again, not a matter of allegorical reading, for Luther: allegorical readings there might be, but in the end they all serve that basic exposition of grace and its opposition to law.

Of course, tropology still dominates: Luther is concerned with a reading that will be properly edifying (whether it be instructions on the obedience of an Augustinian monk in his first lectures on the Psalms, or more familiar Lutheran themes in his later lectures)—but the anagogy is

20. One could, of course, also say that there is a mirror image of supersessionism (infra-sessionism?) in some (and only some) forms of historical criticism. Later readers are denied access to the text: the text belongs in the contexts of its origin, and to those whose critical tools allow them access to those contexts. All other company that the text has kept is irrelevant, and meanings that the text acquired when it was used by people for whom it was part of a different canon are not simply different; they are mistakes.

21. Some of the ways in which God's authorship or inspiration of scripture is presented can contribute to this supersessionism. If the relation between divine and human causality in the production of a scriptural text is such that the web of secondary, creaturely causes involved in that production are overwhelmed by the primary, divine causality, then historical, contextual explanations of the text's original meaning will be radically incomplete *even in their own terms*: the words that appear here do so *not* because of the company that the human author kept, human or textual, *but* because God arranged it so or because the human author was given special insight that could not have come from the creaturely company that he kept.

slightly different in flavor, because the dominant accent falls on the separation of the righteous from the wicked, those under grace from those under law—those in Christ from those whose paradigmatic companions are the Jews. The eschatological vision is of the final purification of the elect and the condemnation of the wicked, and it guides an exegesis concerned to clutch the text to the breasts of those who are being saved, and keep it from the grasping hands of those on their way to damnation.

Is Psalm 1 a Christian text? Well, Luther may have answered with a resounding yes—but, after Luther, seeing what that answer entails, can we honestly go along with him? The company that this text keeps for him is a company defined, in significant part, *over against* another company; his plain reading gains its force by playing on the exclusion of that other company. Whose text is this? What company do we keep as we read? Once we've read Luther, these questions take on a sharper edge.

WHOSE COMPANY SHOULD ONE KEEP?

The Christian tradition of christological reading of this psalm raises the same question as the psalm itself: whose company should one keep? In whose company should one *read*?

On one side, there is a Christian tradition that effectively says: when one reads this text in company with Christians, in company with the Gospels, in company with Jesus, how can one do anything other than read the blessed man that the psalm describes as Jesus? No more than with Psalm 2 or the parable of the Good Samaritan can a Christian reader easily refuse this christological reading. On the other side, we have the suppressed voices of Jewish readers asking how Christians can say that without denying that Jews too are readers of this text. And standing beside them, for now, are the historical critics who ask what on earth a Jesus-focused reading could have to do with the contexts in which this text was produced and received. Can there be any kind of conversation, here? What would it look like for these companies not to read in opposition to one another, but together? And is such a conversation desirable?

The first move that I as a Christian theological reader of this psalm might take is one I have already demonstrated in the last chapter: it is to suggest that Jesus of Nazareth *is* a reading of Hebrew scripture. That is, his words and actions both make sense in the light of the Hebrew scriptures and are a way of making sense of those scriptures. Jesus' life is a commentary or gloss upon the Hebrew scriptures. When, for instance, we find a text in those Hebrew scriptures that say, "*This* is what righteousness means," a Christian reader cannot properly avoid asking, "Well, what do the stories of Jesus say about that?" I don't mean scanning the words attributed to Jesus to see whether he alludes to or quotes the passage in question; rather, the *life* of Jesus has been read by Christians as making a claim about the nature of that righteousness that belongs to and responds to the God of the Hebrew scriptures. With playful seriousness, therefore, it is quite proper to ask what happens when we take this text about righteousness and read it as applying to the life of the one who, for Christians, is the paradigm of righteousness. What happens, Christians can't but ask, if we take Psalm 1 to be about Jesus? What happens if we take the portrayals of Jesus in the New Testament as a commentary on the Hebrew Bible?

Well, what *does* happen if we take Psalm 1 to be about Jesus? Remember what I said in my so-called plain-sense reading: "The wicked at first sight seem to be substantial, to amount to something: they have a position, a path, a way of thinking. . . . The righteous, on the other hand, . . . at first sight seem less substantial than the wicked." Reading this with Jesus in mind, one thing that might happen is that we could find the rejection of the attractive stability of the ungodly sharpened. To the progression of metaphors from walking to standing to sitting we could add lying down, and note that Jesus was said to be one who had no place to lay his head.[22] The only way in which Jesus walks is the way of the cross (and the cross is a leafless, unwatered tree if ever there was one). His way looks like the way that leads to destruction, to the curse, to the end of prosperity. And yet Christians claim that this way of the cross is the way of life, the way that it is watched over by God, the only way that stands on the day of judgement. It is the wicked who *seem* to have a place to walk, stand, sit, and lie down, and the righteous who *seem* to have no place to stand—but Jesus and the psalm announce that appearances can be deceptive.

To head off in this direction is, of course, to pursue a trajectory of reading of the psalm that would already have been possible within the Hebrew canon. One could put Psalm 1 alongside, say, the book of Job and its critique of the Deuteronomic equation between obedience and prosperity. But one could also put it alongside any number of other psalms in which the prosperity of the righteous and the comeuppance of the wicked is hoped and prayed for, not seen—while the "prosperity of the wicked" (Ps 73:3) is all too evident. In fact, someone has *already* put it alongside

22. Matt 8:20 and parallels.

those other psalms: at some point, Psalm 1 *does* seem to have been pressed into action, or even composed, as a preface to the Psalter as a whole.[23] The christological reading of the psalm that I am suggesting simply twists the knife in a fissure already opened up by the placing of this psalm within the Psalter and the wider Hebrew Bible. In at least this way, the christological reading of the psalm need not necessarily remove the text from its existing company, but has the potential to send us deeper into the meanings that this psalm already possesses in its context within the Hebrew canon.

We can't stop there, however. Once we have got that far, we can't really avoid asking whether Jesus' righteousness, the way of the cross, can (contra Hilary of Poitiers) be understood as "delight . . . in the law of the Lord." We might find ourselves led to think of Jesus' claim that not one stroke of a letter will pass from the law until it is all accomplished (Matt 5:18) and that no one whose righteousness does not exceed that of the scribes and the Pharisees can enter the kingdom of heaven (Matt 5:20); we might also think of Jesus' claim that the whole of the law and the prophets hangs on the command to love God and to love neighbor (Matt 22:40). The commentary upon this psalm that Jesus' life offers is not a commentary that must deprecate its focus on *Torah* (it does not see delight in *Torah* as a Jewish doctrine that needs to be rejected or overcome); it accepts it and provides a contestable but serious interpretation of what delight in the law means. In the reading that Jesus provides or is, the way of righteousness is the way of the cross; the way of the cross is the way of love and justice; the way of love and justice is the way of obedience to and delight in the law.[24] The christological reading of this psalm has the potential to send us

23. It has been argued—in part on the basis of the difficulty of providing any kind of convincing metrical analysis of the Psalm (see Bullough, "Question of Metre")—that it was perhaps a prose preface written for the Psalter, or for some earlier version of the collection—and perhaps, therefore, that it was not originally counted as a psalm, so that our Psalm 2 would be the first; cf. n. 3.

24. Pursuing this line of inquiry further, we might find ourselves in the vicinity of a justification of my initial claim: that Jesus *is* a reading of or commentary upon the Hebrew scriptures—a commentary upon the law. And note that a *commentary* does not, or should not, replace the text upon which it comments; nor does it in and of itself render the existence of other commentaries unnecessary or impossible. To say that the circle of readers of this text includes those who cannot but ask this question—who cannot but look to see what happens if they take the text to be about Jesus, who cannot but see Jesus as *the* commentary upon the text—does not mean that the circle of readers, the human company that this text keeps, is or should be *reduced* to those Christian readers. Nor—as I shall be arguing more clearly in a moment—does it mean that those Christian readers themselves should *wish* for the circle of readers to be reduced to those who read as they do.

deeper into the New Testament portrayal of Jesus and of his relation to the law, making us ask about the nature of that relation in new ways.

I'm being too irenic, however, with my description of the first two steps in this proposed reading—the exploration of what the psalm says about prosperity and the exploration of Jesus' relationship to the law. A Jewish reader at this point might draw our attention to one of the elements that my exposition so far has ignored: the reference to the "congregation of the righteous." What this psalm opposes to the way of the ungodly, the Jewish reader might say, is obedience to God's law in the context of the people of Israel. It opposes to the false stability of the wicked a different kind of continuity and stability: the continuity and stability of *people and observance*. Holiness and blessing, in the psalm's terms, can't be detached from these things. And yes, these contrast with the stability of the ungodly (the history of the Jewish people over the last two and a half thousand years is enough to show us that), but we should not overdraw that contrast until it becomes a contrast between the purely material stability and prosperity of the ungodly and the purely spiritual stability and prosperity of the godly. In a Jewish reader's hands, therefore, the psalm might become a challenge to think about the material conditions of holiness in the Hebrew Bible: law, people, land. Isn't that what it really means, the Jewish reader might argue, to be in the congregation of the faithful, planted, watered, and in the deepest sense prosperous? Isn't it no accident that the stream and tree language in the psalm is redolent of land and of temple? To put it another way, hasn't the Christian reading too easily air-brushed out the full meaning of "*Torah*"?

The Christian reader might respond by arguing that the psalm is precisely part of a trajectory in the Hebrew Bible whereby land and temple are relativized or redefined in favor of delight in and obedience to *Torah*, and that the psalm is therefore representative of one of the shifts in the understanding of righteousness that made the Jesus movement possible as a Jewish righteousness movement in the first century. And at this point the Christian reader could reach for the weighty commentary by Hans-Joachim Kraus, who insists that the psalm's original setting is in post-exilic Israel where "the 'congregation of the righteous' is no longer all of Israel but a circle of those who have come out through decisions and separations, a group that thinks of itself as opposed to the mass of the ungodly";[25] it is the congregation of those for whom *Torah* is experienced

25. Kraus, *Psalms 1–59*, 115.

internally as revelation—for whom the heart of obedience, of observance, has moved inwards and (as von Rad says) the *Sitz im Leben* of *Torah* has become "more and more the heart of man."[26]

At this point the Jewish reader might interrupt to point to the end of Kraus's commentary on the psalm:

> The life-style of the [righteous person], especially his all-encompassing love and delight in the [*torah*], is sustained . . . by the Torah's own lively power to communicate and influence. . . . But everything that is stated in Psalm 1 about the [righteous person] basically entails a character that transcends any one individual. . . . The picture of the fortunate [righteous person] definitely bears the features of the super individual, the paradigmatic person. The "Pharisee," with his utmost rigoristic obedience to the Law, cannot fill out this picture. The New Testament declares that Jesus Christ, "whom God made our . . . righteousness" (1 Cor 1:30) is the fulfilment of this original picture that the Old Testament psalm had in mind and already joyously embraced.[27]

Our Jewish reader might well ask at this point ask whether Kraus's whole interpretation, his whole reading of the nature of *Torah* and its observance, his claim about the *Sitz im Leben* of this psalm, and von Rad's about the *Sitz im Leben* of *Torah*, have been secretly determined by this conclusion which is both christological and supersessionist, however dressed up it might be in a history-of-religions narrative about individualization and internalization. Once again, *Torah* has been too easily spiritualized by the Christian reader.

And so the argument might go on.

And that, I suggest, is part of the point. The psalm *could* become a source of productive disagreement, as it is read by people who look at it from within the differently constituted companies within which they sit, but who now read it in company with one another. It could lead to an ongoing argument that probes Christian and Jewish constructions of righteousness, challenging, for instance, simplistic binary construals (national-legal versus individual-spiritual) or simplistic narratives (internalization, individualization). The argument over the psalm could segue into a wider argument about the conditions for righteous life, forcing the conversation partners to work harder to sustain the positions they're defending, to be more aware of the ground on which their readings are

26. Von Rad, *Old Testament Theology*, 1:200.

27. Kraus, *Psalms 1–59*, 121.

erected, leading them into self-examination and an unexpected need to nuance.[28] Reading together could become a process in which the companies we keep are subjected to scrutiny, and in which the ways we have of defining those companies over against one another come in for attention and repair. The text could become not so much a trophy to be fought over, as a room to argue in.

SUPERSESSIONISM AND CON-SESSIONISM

I don't mean to bring my staged argument about the meaning of the psalm to any kind of closure. And I certainly am not claiming that there is any straightforward sense in which these meditations are *the* meaning of the psalm, nor any sense in which these are the meanings intended by the original author or understood by the original audience. The kind of ruminative, argumentative attention to the text that I am proposing does not lead to a decision about the one thing that this text really says; it does not close down our options in that way. It leads rather to attention to the different things that the text can say in different company, to the difficulties that are generated when one tries to read it in those different companies, and to the conversations or arguments that are generated between differing companies of readers, when we try to read the text in a company that includes all of them. What happens is not the discovery of an answer, but the opening up of a space for discussion and inquiry, for argument and exploration.

So then, literally or ontologically, in this view the psalm is what it is in all the company it keeps—not statically, as if it were simply the catalogue of all the differing readings that those companies make possible, but dynamically: the interaction, cross-fertilization, and argument of companies and readings, each holding on for a blessing from what is different, what is irritating, what is unassimilated in the other's reading. The text is what it is in all the conversations of the companies that it keeps

28. And good historical-critical reading could also be a real asset here, precisely because it can helps productively complicate simple pictures: the historical-critical debate about this text shows that it can be read as standing on the cusp of one of several transitions in Israelite/Jewish understandings of righteousness—king to *Torah* or temple to *Torah*; people to subgroup, corporate solidarity to wisdom; or even righteousness defined by cultic observance to righteousness defined by pure ethnic boundary. The community of historical critics can help dispel any remaining sense that there is a single, clearly defined, eternal Jewish meaning of righteousness or single, clearly defined, progressive history of that meaning.

because the text is what makes these conversations possible, and these conversations are the realization of the text.

Tropologically, this kind of reading only makes sense if the aim of reading is not correct knowledge of what the text means, but rather lives changed in the process of reading. The aim of this reading is neither historical reconstruction nor proof, but edification, righteousness, justice. This is a text embedded in the minds, desires, companies, and conflicts of differing religious companies, and reading it seriously cannot but be at the same time a reading, examination or testing of those companies and their conflicts.

Anagogically, and despite the tenor of Psalm 1 itself, the guiding vision of this kind of reading cannot be the triumph of the single correct reading, the separation of the pure from the impure, the blowing away like chaff of all mistaken readings. This kind of reading is, rather, about *enlarging the company* that this text keeps rather than about defining the one true company that owns it. The eschatological vision that guides interpretation is that of the full extension of that company—the *universal* extension, perhaps. More than that, though, this is a vision in which each part of that great company is brought into conversation with each other part.

Certainly, in pursuit of *that* vision, there are times when we have to say no, and refuse to walk, stand, or sit with some reading. Luther's reading, for instance, by violently suppressing other company that reads this text, must be resisted in pursuit of this vision, even if in his reading there is also much that can and should be heard. So I am not advocating reading without judgment—both the judgment inherent in the idea of conversation and the judgment involved in saying no to some whole tendencies—but the judgment involved grows out of charity, and makes for charity. In other words, the eschatological vision of a universal and harmoniously different company acts regulatively upon present reading: it shows that present reading to be as incomplete as the company in which we now read is incomplete. In pursuit of the unlimited extension of the conversational company that reading keeps, one may neither deny the text to any company, claiming exclusive ownership, nor abandon other companies in the false tolerance that agrees to differ: holding together in conversation and argument is the only way to do justice to all that this text is.[29]

29. Augustine has travelled most of this path before us: "For this reason, although I hear people say 'Moses meant this' or 'Moses meant that,' I think it more truly religious

Finally, what of allegory? Christians who participate in this conversation cannot but come back again and again to see what challenge or revision of the edification they are receiving here is posed by Jesus—not because Jesus presents them fully formed with the *answer* to the psalm (such that they have no need to hear what any other reader might say), but because Christian faith trusts that his company is hospitable enough to welcome and feed and, eschatologically, unite in harmonious difference the whole conversation of readings that gather around this text. So the Christian's constant return to Christ should not entail the repeated statement of an answer, nor the repeated claim to possess this text, but the repeated stating of a question of which Christians believe they have been made the bearers—a question the pursuit of which will disrupt both their present grasp on righteousness *and* their present grasp on Jesus' identity and significance.[30] For Christian readers, this constant return to Jesus should sustain this widening conversation, this extension of the company that our reading keeps—not shut it down. After all, it is their faith in Christ that is, for Christians, the proper ground of the trust that extending the conversation around this text *can* lead to peace: it is the ground on which Christians will resist the lazy pluralism that simply allows different companies to make of this text what they will in the privacy of their own enclaves, or of the exclusivisms that allow only one company to define the true meaning of the text; it is the ground on which Christians will reject the idea that their grappling with the text can survive without attentiveness to the voices of other readers. After all, faith in Christ is in

to say, 'Why should he not have had both meanings in mind, if both are true?' And if others see in the same words a third, or a fourth, or any number of true meanings, why should we not believe that Moses saw them all? There is only one God, who caused Moses to write the Holy Scriptures in the way best suited to the minds of great numbers of men who would see all truths in them, though not the same truths in each case. . . . As he wrote those words, [Moses] was aware of all that they implied. He was conscious of every truth that we can deduce from them and of others besides that we cannot, or cannot yet, find in them but are nevertheless there to be found. Finally, O Lord, since you are God and not flesh and blood, even if men have seen less in those words than there is to be seen, is it possible that anything should be concealed from your gracious Spirit . . . ? Could anything that you were to reveal by those words to readers in later times have been hidden from your Holy Spirit, even though the man through whom they were spoken may have had in mind only one of many true meanings? . . . [W]hether you disclose to us the one which your servant Moses had in mind or any other which can be extracted from the same words, we shall feed from your hand and not be deluded by error." Augustine, *Confessions* 12.31–32.

30. For Christians as bearers of a question, see Higton, *Difficult Gospel*, 68–71.

the end a faith that constant return to Christ, in the midst of conversation around his scriptures and in the midst of the unrestricted conversations with others in the world, is the way to truth, to love and justice, to peace.[31]

The Christian response to the supersessionism of some of their traditions of reading cannot be for them to abandon christological reading. If supersession was the act by which Christians evicted the previous readers of this psalm from their seats, the rupture between peoples caused by this act will not be repaired if Christians simply vacate that seat in turn, leaving it to its original owners. Rather, the evils of supersessionism can only be repaired by Jews and Christians sitting down together, around the text, with a commitment to read alongside, to read in conversation with, to read interrupted and needled and bewildered and delighted by one another—supersessionism overcome by con-sessionism.

Christian readers will have their own, Christian theological reasons for doing this, and for trusting that it will lead somewhere interesting—reasons distinct from (though possibly analogous to) Jewish reasons. Generically, Christians will say that it is in conversation with Christ that all things find their fullest meaning, but that it is only in conversation with all things that they themselves will understand Christ most fully. They have more of Christ still to receive, and as they don't own Christ, so they don't own any texts or the people through whom that "more" will be received. More specifically, though, Christian theology will say that the God of Jesus Christ is and remains the God of the Jewish people, and that the God of the Jewish people is the God of Jesus Christ, and that it is the dialectic between these two claims that is embodied in a commitment to read together, in conversation, holding on for a blessing.

This theoretical, theological commitment and hope is met and reinforced, however, by the discovery in practice that the text is indeed capacious enough for this expansive, argumentative conversation, that to read alongside those who read differently does indeed drive the participants deeper into the unexpected resources of their own traditions' wisdom, and that the debates and discussions involved need not always be a matter of earnest and agonized seriousness, but of friendship and of delight.

31. This is, of course, a sketch of a *Christian* justification for participation in a conversation with Jewish and other readers. It does not say anything about the Jewish justification for participation in such a conversation—whether there is one, or what form it takes. We will have more to say about this important point in the remainder of this part of the book.

When freed from our control and rediscovered in conversation, the text yields more abundant fruit. It becomes an arena for delighted, multi-voiced, sometimes cacophonous exploration; it becomes more uncontrollable, more surprising, more irrepressible. If it is, as Psalm 1 suggests, a stream of water, then it is not a slow, calm, and silent upwelling from which one may sip in a controllable, predictable way. It is something more like a garden hosepipe in the hands of unruly toddlers.

So yes, there is a sense in which Psalm 1 has to be for Christian readers a Christian text—but precisely because it is, it cannot be only or exclusively Christian.[32] To the question, "Is Psalm 1 about Jesus?" perhaps the proper Christian theological answer can only be, again and again, "Come on, let's find out . . ."

32. The form of christological reading I am suggesting is best thought of as a spiritual reading in part because (classically) spiritual reading does not *prove* doctrine. That is not because it is, as it were, evidence not quite strong enough to support doctrinal conclusion—i.e., not because it tries to prove doctrine but fails—but because spiritual reading is not a process intended to produce answers in the first place. It is about producing *people*, and it only proves doctrine in the sense that it tests it, explores it, and refines it.

9 What Is Scriptural Reasoning?

How Christians, Jews, and Muslims Can Read Together

Much of the material for this book emerged out of a particular practice that exemplifies and extends the "con-sessionism," the sitting together, advocated in the last chapter. It is a practice that has become known by the name Scriptural Reasoning, and it involves Jewish, Christian, and Islamic scholars meeting to read passages from their respective scriptures together. Characteristically, participants from the three traditions meet in small groups for significant periods of time (either intensively, at a Scriptural Reasoning conference, or in regular meetings over an extended period) to read and discuss passages from the Tanakh, the Bible, and the Qur'an. The texts will often relate to a common topic—debt, say, or prophecy, or the treatment of women, or the figure of Job. The participants discuss the content of the texts, and the variety of ways in which their traditions have worked with them and continue to work with them, and the ways in which those texts might shape their understanding of and engagement with a range of contemporary issues. A participant from any one religious tradition might therefore discuss with the other participants her own readings of the texts from her own tradition, and the other participants' attempts as outsiders to her tradition to make sense of those same texts, and in turn discuss with them the texts from their own traditions and their practices for making sense of them.

The diet of small group meetings is sometimes spiced with plenary sessions, which allow for larger-scale discussions of the practices of reasoning together that have emerged in the small group discussions, including discussion of how these practices might have something to offer to debates about tradition and reason in contemporary public life. Although these discussions have been generative of philosophical and theological accounts of what goes on in Scriptural Reasoning, those accounts are strictly secondary to the practice itself—a matter for discussion, development, and disagreement that might influence the practice, rather than the basis on which the practice was developed or on which new participants are expected to adopt the practice. The best way to understand the nature of Scriptural Reasoning, therefore, is to begin with description, and to move on to reflection.

A SESSION OF SCRIPTURAL REASONING

What goes on in a Scriptural Reasoning group does not lend itself easily to summary or report. The success of a Scriptural Reasoning discussion is not measured by the production of take-home conclusions, and even when a discussion generates ideas that seem to have legs, those ideas sometimes seem rather lame when taken out of the context that they temporarily powered. These difficulties of summary or report are not, of course, absolute: it is often possible to convey something of what has excited a group, even if such descriptions tend to work best when given to people who have studied the same texts in other groups. And it is similarly possible to generate interesting theoretical descriptions of the kinds of reasoning involved in Scriptural Reasoning discussions, even if, again, those descriptions have often worked better as aids to reflection for participants in Scriptural Reasoning than as clear explanations for others.

Nevertheless, summary or report is difficult, as anyone can discover by returning from a Scriptural Reasoning meeting and trying to explain to those who have never been involved what it was like, what good it did, and what came of it. In order to try to cross this barrier, therefore, I have produced the following fictionalized version of a real Scriptural Reasoning discussion, and then commented upon that fiction, trying to show what cannot easily be told.[1]

1. This account was "fictionalized" in the following way. Some time ago, and with the permission of the participants, I took detailed (though uneven) notes during one small group Scriptural Reasoning session. In writing up those notes, I have changed names; I have rearranged and redistributed comments, such that there is no one-to-one correspondence between the *dramatis personae* below and the original group members (Redha Ameur, Jeff Bailey, Gavin Flood, Tom Greggs, Martin Kavka, Catriona Laing, Susannah Ticciati, Umeyye Isra Yazicioglu, and William Young); I have borrowed some things I heard from other conversations on the same text; I have

Scriptural Reasoning groups differ widely, of course, and those differences are particularly marked when one moves between the different contexts in which Scriptural Reasoning is done: from academic to civic life, from long-term series to one-off events, and so on. Nevertheless, although what follows is a fictionalized version of a discussion from one very particular setting—a meeting of an academic Scriptural Reasoning group, largely involving people who were familiar with the practice and who had met in the same context before—I hope that it conveys something of the rhythm and progress of Scriptural Reasoning conversation more generally.

The participants in the fictional group are Aaliyah and Habib (Muslim), Morgan and Nathan (Jewish), and Brian, John, and Karen (Christian). Karen is acting as convenor. It so happens that in this session the group chooses to study a passage from the Qur'an; in other sessions, the group read texts from the Hebrew Bible and from the New Testament.

The group has been assembling and chatting for a couple of minutes already, exchanging greetings and questions about the journey to Cambridge. Karen has asked people which text they want to start with, and in the absence of a clear preference has suggested a brief snippet from the Qur'an—40:78.

KAREN: (*after a pause, reading slowly from the Arberry translation,*[2] *with the kind of tone and rhythm that might be used for a Bible reading in an Anglican church*) We sent Messengers before thee; of some We have related to thee, and some We have not related to thee. It was not for any Messenger to bring a sign, save by God's leave. When God's command comes, justly the issue shall be decided; then the vain-doers shall be lost.

(*There is silence, while the members of the group stare at the passage in front of them. After ten or fifteen seconds, Habib reaches into his bag and pulls out his Qur'an, flicking quickly through to the passage; his lips move slightly as he reads the Arabic.*)

---

neatened it all up, and tried to make it readable or followable, in a way that an unedited transcript would not be. The result is a fiction, even if it contains little of substance that was not said in the original session (though I admit that there were places where I couldn't help adding in something that I *would* have said, if only I'd thought of it at the time).

2. Arberry, *Koran Interpreted*.

BRIAN: The bit where it says "justly the issue shall be decided"—I looked at a translation online when preparing, and it had (*he refers to a sheet in front of him*) "it will be concluded in truth."[3] The translation we've been given seems to make more sense. The other one I have here (*he refers to the Penguin Classics Koran, which he has open in front of him*) says "And when God's will was done, justice prevailed."[4]

NATHAN: I have "When the command of Allah will come, matters will stand decided justly."[5] What does the Arabic say?

HABIB: (*somewhat hesitantly*) "Judgment was passed" or "Judgment was given, or made, with truth." "True judgment was passed."

BRIAN: So, is it: God's command comes by means of messengers; it comes when God chooses, and when it comes it executes true judgment?

HABIB: Yes. It passes or executes true judgment.

BRIAN: It sets things to rights, perhaps?

HABIB: Yes, yes. Perhaps.

(*Silence falls again for a few seconds.*)

MORGAN: So, who are the "vain-doers"? Are they, like, people consumed with vanity—all preening and posing?

HABIB: "Vain-doers"? They are those who deny God's revelation. They are the ones in the wrong, the ones who oppose God. You could translate it "falsifiers."

BRIAN: (*consulting his Penguin Classics Koran*) My translation has "disbelievers."

HABIB: Yes, yes—disbelievers.

MORGAN: Those who don't believe the message, or the messenger?

HABIB: Yes.

3. Saheeh International, *Qur'an*.
4. Dawood, *Koran*.
5. Usmani, *Meanings of the Noble Qur'an*.

(*Murmurs of assent lapse into another brief silence.*)

JOHN: "Of some we have related to thee . . ." That's "related" in the Qur'an, I assume?

HABIB: Yes, "related"—it is like saying, "We have given you information. We have told you stories about them." Yes, "We have told you some of the messengers' stories, and we have not told you others." It is not just in the Qur'an, though—

JOHN: Not just in the Qur'an?

AALIYAH: Mostly in the Qur'an. Some elsewhere, but mostly in the Qur'an.

HABIB: The Qur'an names twenty-seven messengers—but there are supposed to be 124,000 messengers in total.

JOHN: 124,000?

HABIB: Yes!

AALIYAH: Yes—(*then, animated, rapid-fire*) so it is like, "Don't think these are the only ones! There are many more. There's an abundance. More than you can count"—because 124,000 is not really fixing a clear limit, it is "thousands upon thousands." "I have sent you more messengers. Be open to them. Wherever you turn, there will be a messenger."

JOHN: And others—beyond the twenty-seven—are mentioned in the traditions?

AALIYAH: Some, yes, but not many. The point is not that there is any list of who they are. There couldn't be a list. There is an abundance of witnesses, more than you know, so many more than you might think. They are everywhere!

NATHAN: (*speaking at the same time as Morgan*) So, what makes someone a messenger?—

MORGAN: (*speaking at the same time as Nathan*) Who is the "We"? Is it Allah?

HABIB: Yes, it is one of the ways that Allah speaks of himself. There are different registers in the Qur'an. "We" is for God's greatness and "I" is more for God's nearness—

AALIYAH: (*interrupting*) Yes, like "I am near to them."

HABIB:—and "Thee" is Muhammad (peace be upon him).

(*yet another brief pause*)

KAREN: (*taking advantage of the lull*) What is the context for this verse?

HABIB: Allah is comforting Muhammad (peace be upon him). "You must tolerate the difficulties you have with your message, for there were many before you"—

AALIYAH: (*interrupting*) It's part of a longer discussion of messengers and signs. And there's a story of a believer in Pharaoh's household, who kept on trying to get Pharaoh to be open—to listen to the possibility that Moses was speaking the truth—

NATHAN: (*surprised*) Moses?

AALIYAH: Yes, Pharaoh wants to kill Moses because he does not believe his message.

MORGAN: So Pharaoh is a "vain-doer"?

AALIYAH: Yes, because he does not believe the message.

BRIAN: And so is this believer saying to Pharaoh, "Listen out for the message"? Is there something, then (*he pauses, searching for the right words*)—something about inculcating the right kind of attentiveness? Listen out for messengers, they're all around you! Look out for signs, they're everywhere! You need the right kind of attentiveness! Is that what it is saying? You need the right kind of eyes?

JOHN: But *is* that what this passage is saying? It's not really addressed to those who ought to receive the message, is it? It's addressed to the Prophet, and it tells him that he is not in charge of the message, but that when it comes, it will be effective.

BRIAN: Okay, yes, fair enough. So it's like: Don't worry if you can't produce the effect you want; this is not about you *producing* anything. You simply have to be obedient to the One who does produce, who can execute judgment when he chooses.

JOHN: Yes, I think so. I think that's right.

NATHAN: (*who has been waiting to say something for a little while, and now finds an opportunity*) So, looking around, could anyone be a messenger? Could you be—could you find that the people around you become messengers? Are messengers sent to everyone, to all peoples?

HABIB: In other parts of the Qur'an, it does talk about how there are messengers for each community . . .

BRIAN: Though that's not really in view in this text, is it?

AALIYAH: But this ayah does mean that the problem is not that Allah did not send enough messengers, because he has sent more than enough—he has sent thousands upon thousands. The problem is that you do not see them—

JOHN: You do not have eyes to see.

NATHAN: I guess what I was asking is whether a messenger is simply anyone through whom a sign is given, and whether a sign is simply anything that points you to God.

HABIB: Well . . . signs—miracles or recitations—they are in the permission of God, no? They cannot be demanded—"it was not for any messenger to bring a sign." God chooses when to make a sign, not the messenger. So God makes the sign and the sign makes the messenger. The sign is a revelation, and the messenger is one who transmits it. You need to keep God in the picture.

JOHN: The priority of divine action.

AALIYAH: The messenger is one who is given a sign, who believes the sign, and who proclaims it or presents it.

NATHAN: So the messenger has to believe?

AALIYAH: I think so, yes.

JOHN: If someone proclaims—if someone preaches truth about God, is that a sign? Does it make them a messenger?

AALIYAH: Well, like Habib was saying, the most important thing of all in this passage is that the messenger does not have disposal over the message. There is something in the context here: this ayah is part of a longer story where there have been demands for signs, for miraculous proofs. And Muhammad has been saying, "I'm only human. I do not have wonders, miracles, at my command." The only miracle he gives is the one he has been given: the recitation itself—the message itself. And he's not simply preaching: he's—like Habib said—he's transmitting what he's been given.

HABIB: Yes, "sign," *ayah*, can mean "miracle," or it can mean "verse," a verse of the Qur'an—

AALIYAH: (*interrupting*) They are both signs that point to God—to God's power.

HABIB:—and it is signs that confirm that a messenger is a messenger. That's really what miracles are for—they're secondary. They confirm a messenger's status as a messenger: they're signs pointing to signs.

BRIAN: So you might know you are in the presence of a messenger if there is a miracle, a dramatic sign—but this verse suggests that the real mark of a sign (the sign of a sign?) is that bit about deciding on truth. How did we say that should be translated?

KAREN: "When true judgment is passed" or "When God's true judgment is proclaimed."

BRIAN: Speaking with authority? The real mark of a sign is somehow its ability to speak authoritatively, decisively?

JOHN: So is recognition of a sign like the bit in the Gospels: "Were not our hearts burning within us . . ."?

AALIYAH: Where's that from?

JOHN: It's from one of the resurrection stories, where people at first don't realize that it is Jesus who is speaking to them until he reveals himself, but then realize that his words were having an impact on them even before they recognized him.

BRIAN: That would be a good passage to discuss one year, I think.

(*A brief pause*)

MORGAN: (*taking advantage of the lull, and speaking slowly*) I'm interested in the phenomenology of all this: the signs having this attention-grabbing power—

HABIB: But it's not just attention grabbing. The Qur'an speaks against signs simply as spectacle—things that attract attention to themselves, rather than to God—

MORGAN: Exactly: so there's this attention-grabbing power, and yet (*hunting for the right words*) a transparency, a transitiveness to signs?

HABIB: Yes, signs have to be transparent.

MORGAN: But in the Qur'an, isn't the whole world a sign?

AALIYAH: Yes, it points to God.

MORGAN: So the signs—specific signs—they have a kind of contagious transparency: your eye is drawn towards them and then beyond them, and if these signs do their work, then other things around them—whether that's other things that you might think these signs pointed to, or just the world around the sign—begins to become transparent too. The world's capacity to be a sign gets activated?

NATHAN: And messengers are there to help you read the world? They proclaim God, but in a way that's proclaiming the proper understanding of the world?

BRIAN: Passing true judgment on the world?

HABIB: Yes—and there is one messenger, there are twenty-seven messengers, there are 124,000 messengers—and this is a sequence that has a telos: when the whole world is a sign, the whole world becomes transparent.

MORGAN: So, the one, the twenty-seven, the 124,000—that's like an epidemiology of transparency?

(*A brief pause*)

BRIAN: Is there some kind of hermeneutics for the Qur'an itself here? If what Morgan says is right about contagious transparency (I love that phrase!) then does it work for the signs of the Qur'an? Are there central ayahs in the Qur'an that, as it were, activate the others—or some kind of mutual activation? So one ayah shows you God, but also shows you how to see God more truly in other ayahs, and vice versa?

(*John, Morgan, and Nathan nod—but nobody picks up the suggestion. There's a brief pause.*)

KAREN: When it says that the vain-doers are the losers, and the vain-doers are the ones who don't recognize or believe the signs, does that mean that we all have the capacity, the responsibility, to understand the signs?

BRIAN: Are we free to acknowledge or reject the signs, do you mean?

KAREN: Yes. Or is there anything like God hardening Pharaoh's heart in Exodus—

BRIAN: (*interrupting*) You mean, do the vain-doers become vain by rejecting a message they could have accepted—or are they people who have somehow been given over to vanity, and so are incapable of recognizing the message?

KAREN: Yes.

AALIYAH: Oh, I definitely think they are responsible. Yes, they are very much responsible. And Muhammad is like, "Why do you not listen? Why do you not understand? It has all been set before you so clearly!"

(*There's a pause. Karen, who is chairing, begins to shuffle her papers, wondering whether to suggest moving on to another text, but . . .*)

HABIB: The two meanings of "sign," of *ayah*: miracle and verse. I'm not sure—was it Aaliyah who said that Muhammad (peace be upon him) was not doing miracles, but simply gave the recitation, the message? But the Quran is both. When Moses gave miraculous signs, they made people look, or listen; they created a space that allowed him then to give his message and be attended to. And so the miracles and the message were separate, with the miracles making way for the message. But with Muhammad (peace be upon him), the recitation is also the miracle: its beauty, its power as language—it creates the space, and the attention, for its own message.

AALIYAH: Yes, it is itself miraculous.

HABIB: And the people to whom it was addressed, the Arabic people—they were people who would misunderstand other kinds of miracles, but they were a people for whom poetry was very important; it was central for them. So this sign, this recitation, is aimed right at them, to grab them and make them attend.

NATHAN: So, it is a message in their language, but which heightens, or disrupts, or breaks open that language to make it capable of pointing beyond itself?

BRIAN: In the Gospels, Jesus both heals and teaches—or heals, exorcizes, and teaches. But it's not that the healings and exorcisms are simply signs that make space for the teaching—

JOHN and KAREN: (*together*) No.

BRIAN: The teaching interprets the healing and exorcism, and makes those things signs of more than simply Jesus' power—

MORGAN: Contagious transparency, again?

KAREN: It goes the other way around, as well, though: the miracles interpret the teaching.

HABIB: How do you mean?

KAREN: Well, they show what Jesus means. They show what the kingdom of God looks like. It is release for captives, sight for the blind—

HABIB: Metaphorically, do you mean?

JOHN and KAREN: (*together*) No—

KAREN: Not *just* metaphorical—

AALIYAH: Is there anything like the Qur'an's recognition of the danger that miracles will not be understood, that they will not really be signs?

JOHN: There's the bit about this foolish generation demanding a sign—as if it were entertainment or titillation.

KAREN: And the demons—we discussed this last time, didn't we?—can't you say the demons as fixating upon the sign itself, the power of the miracle worker, but not seeing beyond it?

JOHN: Apart from that they do recognize Jesus' identity.

KAREN: I suppose so (*she pauses*), but we're getting away from the text in front of us. Unless—

BRIAN: Sorry, just one more thing on this. I don't think the right comparison is with Jesus' message and miracles, because the real sign in the Christian context is Jesus himself. And the teaching and the miracles are signs that interpret the sign that he is. I don't think, in Jesus' case, you could so easily say, "It was not for a Messenger to bring a sign."

JOHN: Well, Jesus says he only does what he sees the Father doing, so there's the same sense of dependence—

BRIAN: (*interrupting*) Yes, but the signs are not simply something that Jesus receives and transmits. That's all I mean.

MORGAN: Wouldn't Christians say—this is getting back to the contagious transparency thing again—wouldn't you say that Jesus is the one who makes all the other signs transparent?

BRIAN: Yes: he is the transparent one, and he makes other signs transparent.

JOHN: (*frowning*) I think you need a more dialectical picture than that, though: the teachings and the miracles are part of what makes Jesus transparent.

(*Brian nods, but doesn't respond. A pause for a few beats.*)

KAREN: (*taking advantage of the lull*) So we want to move on to a Christian text now, then? Our conversation seems to be heading that way?

BRIAN: Sorry, I didn't mean to derail our conversation.

NATHAN: Could we spend just a bit more time with this text, first, though?

KAREN: Sure, yes.

NATHAN: I wanted to come back to the point about the vain-doers' responsibility. Is there a sense in which the vain-doers have closed themselves off, so it's not simply a matter of a decision, in the moment when they are confronted by the sign, to reject that sign, but of that being a decision for which they have perversely prepared themselves? They've prepared themselves to ignore transparency . . .

BRIAN: They've immunized themselves against the contagion?

HABIB: The vain-doers are not simply all those who did not understand this particular sign (*he pauses to look at the Arabic again*).

KAREN: My translation has "the followers of falsehood,"[6] which sounds more like a pattern of life than a one-off decision.

AALIYAH: Yes, they are people who have told themselves that the world they see is all there is—

NATHAN: That there is only surface, and no depth?

AALIYAH: Yes—

6. Khan and al-Hilali, *The Noble Quran in the English Language*.

HABIB: But you shouldn't lose the sense of responsibility that remains at the time when the sign is actually given. Signs—in God's wisdom—they do really break through to people and confront them. God gives people signs that are fit for their context, fit to communicate to them. When a sign comes, it is powerful and active—

KAREN: It passes true judgment.

HABIB: Yes, but it also is not so overwhelming as to deprive you of responsibility. A sign comes close to you, but also leaves some distance; you will hear it, but you are responsible for acceptance or rejection. You're not deprived of your humanity in the process.

AALIYAH: And even Muhammad has to seek confirmation: the message he receives does not stop him from asking questions and doubting himself, or from knowing that he is human.

MORGAN: So a sign that comes to someone who has closed themselves off against the potential transparency of things—against the more-than-visible—is going to have to be something visible that nevertheless shakes them out of that—

NATHAN: Like the burning bush in the text we were looking at last time.

MORGAN: Yes.

BRIAN: Which also leaves Moses needing confirmation—leaves him human and questioning and unsure.

MORGAN: So the strangeness of a miraculous sign—it's miraculousness (is that a word?)—is not there simply to be a sign of God's arbitrary power ("Hey, look what I can do!"), but to make the sign a sign: something that actually breaks through and grabs the attention? Is that right?

NATHAN: But this thing about the messenger being left without complete certainty—left with questions—for both Moses, and even more for Muhammad (but not for Jesus), there's this sense of waiting on a message that is utterly beyond your control—

BRIAN: (*interrupting*) Jesus is waiting in Gethsemane, I think—

NATHAN: (*carrying on*) God says to Moses, "I will teach you what to say," and here Allah says, "It was not for any Messenger to bring a sign, except by God's leave." It's not in their control: they wait on it, and don't know if or when it will come again—

JOHN: Except that God has promised—

NATHAN: —except, yes, that God has promised. But that's trusting in someone else, trusting something outside yourself. It's not like simply being confident in your own right.

(*Pause. Karen is being more cautious about closing this part of the discussion down. She wants to be sure people have finished.*)

HABIB: Coming back to the "vain-doers"—

KAREN: Yes?

HABIB: Well, there are traditional discussions of people who can't be held responsible, who are not vain-doers even though they do not understand: if you are too young, or mentally unfit, or in some other way do not have the capacity—various different categories. But I think even those people are said to have been given signs that are fitted to their capacity, however limited.

JOHN: Accommodation—signs accommodated to their capacity?

HABIB: Yes.

NATHAN: Does that mean that, if they develop—someone who is at first too young getting older, perhaps—the signs that they are presented with grow with them, in some sense?

HABIB: Yes, I think you could say that. Until you reach the point where you are brought to the message of the Prophet, and submit explicitly to Allah.

NATHAN: But that submission builds on the preparation of the earlier signs?

HABIB: Yes.

BRIAN: There's a kind of pneumatology—

JOHN: Or doctrine of prevenient grace.

BRIAN: Yes, with the agency of the prophet—or of God through the Prophet—crowning that process?

MORGAN: And the vain-doer is not simply someone who says no to a sign given at one step of process, but is someone who has built up resistance?

BRIAN: Back to contagion again!

MORGAN: Yes, someone so acting as to make themselves go blind—

AALIYAH: Or maybe to keep their eyes from opening.

MORGAN: But it's a process, rather than a punctiliar thing.

JOHN: A *habitus*?

HABIB: Yes, although the supreme sign given through the Prophet (peace be upon him) is the Qur'an, you are still confronted by it with real responsibility, with a real decision.

(*Brief pause*)

MORGAN: When Brian said about the agency of God through the Prophet providing the central sign, the sign that sets all the others off—would Christians say the same about Jesus?

HABIB: It is different though. Muhammad (peace be upon him) is not with us, but his sign—the sign given through him—is. The focus is on the sign that is given through him.

MORGAN: So is the writing down of the Qur'an in Islam the analogue of the resurrection in Christianity—it is what prevents the sign dying away?

BRIAN: Would that make the act of copying the Qur'an like the Eucharist?

KAREN: Or would it be the act of recitation that was eucharistic?

BRIAN: Maybe. Maybe.

(*A longer pause*)

KAREN: (*looking around for confirmation*) Have we finished with this text for now, do you think?

(*With murmurs of assent, and shuffled papers, the session moves on.*)

REFLECTIONS

I am not going to offer a detailed commentary on the content of this discussion, nor at this point will I rehearse any more sophisticated theoretical discussion about the nature of Scriptural Reasoning. I simply want to offer a few low-key reflections on some facets of the practice that this dialogue displays.

Stuttering and motoring

The discussion begins with a stutter of clarifying questions, punctuated by pauses. After a while, it is as if the engine catches, and the stuttering gives way to motoring: conversation runs more or less smoothly, more or less energetically for a while, though eventually the engine does cut out, of course—and we're back to stuttering. No one knows when the engine will catch, when the stuttering will give way to motoring; it cannot be produced, only received. It is, perhaps, a matter of grace.

Hosting

This dialogue depicts the reading of an Islamic text, and there is an obvious sense in which the Muslim participants (particularly Habib, but also Aaliyah) function as hosts for some of the session: they answer questions about a text that is deeply familiar to them, welcoming in to that territory the other participants who are relative strangers there. But they are not only hosts, or not always hosts. They are most obviously hosts when the conversation is stuttering (when it is in question-answer form, with the hosts providing answers), least obviously hosts when the conversation is motoring.

Exegesis without exegesis

This dialogue is exegetical, but it is not as such *an* exegesis of the text. That is, it does not produce anything like a coherent, well-defended construal of the text as a whole. (A whole other level of reflection or commentary upon this dialogue would be needed to turn it into such an exegesis.) Rather, it is a series of playful explorations of the text. The pattern of stuttering and motoring makes this clear: to change the metaphor, it is as if the conversation is exploring a maze, not knowing which openings are going to lead to dead ends (stuttering), which to pathways to follow (motoring). The conversation finds its way—but finding a way and drawing a map are not the same thing.

With and Beyond the Plain Sense

What is the maze being explored, though? On the one hand, what is explored is not this text in the abstract: it is this text as the text of a religious community, hence the appropriateness of hosting, of the stutter of question and answer. On the other hand, this is not a session that consists simply in the group being told what Muslims have made of this text, hence the uneven presence of hosting, and the possibility of motoring. The exploration is a matter of the group playing together with and beyond the plain sense of the text—where the plain sense is the most obvious sense it has for the hosts.

Exploring the Penumbra

The exploration includes exploration of the penumbra of knowledge and assumptions that surrounds the faithful reading of this text. This is most obvious when specific questions for clarification are asked: "What is the context for this verse?" Karen asks; "Who is meant by 'We'? Is it Allah?" Morgan asks. But it sometimes involves longer detour, as when the conversation explores the relationship between signs and miracles—detours from the text, for the sake of the text, as now this, now that idea that has arisen in the course of explanation is explored.

Playfulness and Discipline

The exploration of the text and its conceptual penumbra frequently takes the form of experimentation: of the playful suggestion of possible construals. Could you read it this way? How about that way? "Can one read this text," Aaliyah suggests, "as being about Allah's condescension, sending appropriate messengers to all parts of humankind?" But these suggestions get tested, and sometimes rejected. "That's not really in view in this text, is it?" Brian answers Aaliyah. Both the discussion of the Islamic theological ideas that are in play when this text is read faithfully, and the experimental construals of the text offered, are from time to time disciplined by return to the specificities of the text.

Ambiguity of Voice

This experimentation often involves participants speaking in ambiguous voices. A Christian reader might playfully suggest a reading of part of this Qur'anic text—and it is in part an offering to the Islamic readers of a way in which *they* could read their text, a gift to the Muslims qua Muslims, from a non-Muslim who cannot but sit lightly to the gift. But sometimes, it seems to me, the suggestions made are as much suggestions to the Christians and the Jews: does the reading I am suggesting for this Qur'anic passage not suggest analogous readings of Christian and Jewish texts, or analogous theological ideas? Might it be an idea Christians or Jews can appropriately borrow or adapt, even if it turns out not to be a sustainable Islamic reading? Might it in fact be *more* a suggestion for Christian or Jewish participants than a suggestion for the Muslims? It is worth asking, for instance, who Brian is speaking to and for when he says, "So it's like: Don't worry if you can't produce the effect you want; this is not about you *producing* anything. You simply have to be obedient to the One who does produce, who can execute judgment when he chooses." And who is Morgan speaking to and for when he suggests the idea of "contagious transparency"?

Comparative Hypotheses

One of the way in which experimentation is conducted (and one of the ways in which ambiguities of voice are exacerbated) is by the explicit posing of comparative questions, or making of comparative suggestions. "Is the act of Qur'anic recitation in some sense eucharistic?" asks Karen. How does the relationship between messenger, message, and miracle work in the case of Jesus, or the case of Moses, and how does that differ from Muhammad's case? People sometimes make suggestions about Christian and Jewish parallels to help clarify the specificity of the Qur'anic text, sometimes to help suggest a new construal of the Qur'anic text, and sometimes simply to suggest ways in which the discussion might spiral into Christian or Jewish territory, if allowed.

Pick-and-Mix Vocabularies

To power and express their explorations, the participants draw on a variety of vocabularies, mostly quite unsystematically and playfully: most obviously the vocabularies of Christian and Jewish thought, but also (in this case quite briefly) clearly philosophical vocabularies. (Morgan mentions phenomenology, for instance, though that doesn't end up firing the conversational engine on this occasion.)

Conversational Momentum

Ideas or patterns of reasoning from previous sessions sometimes appear (acknowledged or unacknowledged), and help drive the conversation forward. There is a kind of momentum to Scriptural Reasoning groups over time—and that raises some interesting questions about how constant group membership needs to be in order to allow momentum to build, and how variable it should be in order to distribute the momentum achieved.

Running Jokes

Conversational motoring is powered in part by ideas that catch—and ideas that catch well can survive a conversation's descent from motoring to stuttering, and reappear. Motoring, momentum, and catching are not quite the same thing. Momentum is seen in the ways in which a conversation is informed by earlier conversations: it has to do with timescales longer than the individual conversation. Motoring is seen at a smaller scale, when a conversation flows for a single stretch of time, in some reasonably coherent way. Catching sits somewhere between the two: it is seen in the reappearance of concepts that you thought had gone away, or that refuse to go away—perhaps from one stretch of motoring to another, perhaps from one conversation to another. And sometimes the ideas that catch best in Scriptural Reasoning sessions are indistinguishable from running jokes.

WHAT IS SCRIPTURAL REASONING?

The description I have offered is not a neutral one. It was discussed at a 2009 meeting of the Scriptural Reasoning in the university group in Cambridge by a Muslim respondent, Rumee Ahmed, and a Jewish respondent, Shari Goldberg. Goldberg in particular noted that however recognizable it was as a description of a Scriptural Reasoning meeting, there was something distinctly Christian—even, at times, distinctly Anglican—about my presentation. Partly it was the words, ideas, and themes that I'd ended up emphasising, in which christological ideas were so prominent; partly it was my distinction in the "reflections" at the end between literal and spiritual—a distinction that I made in a way that someone steeped in rabbinic discussions might not. Partly it was a matter of notes briefly struck, like my mention of "grace" in my discussion of "stuttering and motoring." Ahmed pointed out that it was a description from a specific moment in the evolution of this one group: from a time when the group was sticking to fairly irenic texts, from a time when the group was perhaps less close-knit—and so on. In other words, I am not simply tipping my postmodern hat when I say that this is not a neutral description.

This is, however, itself an important point to make about the practice of Scriptural Reasoning. Its practitioners engage in it without an agreed account of why they do so, without an agreed account of what it is that they are doing, and without an agreed hermeneutic or theory of scripture. They do it without the sanction of a theory of argumentation structuring the neutral space within which their traditions can meet. But they do it nonetheless, and as they do so their differing patterns of religious reasoning mesh into something public: something in which participants' minds are changed by means of discussion and engagement. Muslims participate, at least in part, for a variety of Muslim reasons, Christians, at least in part, for a variety of Christian reasons, Jews, at least in part, for a variety of Jewish reasons; Muslims draw on and improvise on some existing Muslim practices, Christians on existing Christian practices, Jews on existing Jewish practices. And yet those reasons and those practices somehow make for a sustainable common practice. One can provide contestable Christian accounts, contestable Jewish accounts, contestable Muslim accounts—but any attempt to unify these into a general account cannot be anything other than a tentative post-hoc approximation, with an authority for the participants of the three traditions considerably less than the authority of the individual accounts produced from within their own traditions. Acceptance of such a general account could not meaningfully be offered to the members of religious traditions as a condition for the possibility of their participation in Scriptural Reasoning, nor as a recognizable account of the deepest patterns of reasoning in which they were engaged as participants. This is what is meant when it is said that Scriptural Reasoning is a practice more than it is a theory: Scriptural Reasoning is not the outworking of a prior theory of public discourse; instead, its practitioners "embrace the luck of the moment that enables them to read scripture together."[7]

Scriptural Reasoning's possibility seems to rely, for instance, on the accounts available in each tradition of the possibilities of relationship to those of the other two traditions. These are accounts with some overlaps and many differences, and it is possible after the event to investigate more fully the nature of those overlaps and differences as they are discovered in the act of pursuing the "luck" of the encounter. One might find, perhaps, that—with whatever differences and distinctions—each of the participating traditions already has some kind of expectation that it is possible to be called into deeper obedience to God by being called *out* of the current pattern of one's obedience. Whether that is in fact the case, whether the presence of some such structure in each of the participating traditions actually makes Scriptural Reasoning possible, how different the analogous structures are, how much those differences too make Scriptural Reasoning possible, and what would happen if Scriptural Reasoning were extended to traditions in which nothing quite analogous to this could be found—these are questions that can only be teased out patiently, attentively, ethnographically, by looking at what in fact happens.

7. Adams, *Habermas and Theology*, 105.

10 Patterns of Inter-faith Reading I

Scriptural Settlements

To understand Scriptural Reasoning more deeply, it will be helpful to take a detour by train.[1] I don't know whether it exists in the States or not, but in the UK most parents of small children will somewhere have a tub full of Brio train track: a set of wooden track sections—straights, curves, junctions, bridges—that can be fitted together into wonderful networks, around which one can then push trains. Now, most parents who have a tub of Brio have a pretty random collection of pieces—some inherited, some bought—and the attempt to make a coherent track from them all, a track that uses all the pieces and has no loose ends, is no easy business. You get a certain way through, and then realize that you do not have enough curves left to join the two remaining ends, so take a curve out here and a straight there in order to free up an extra piece—only to find that now you have a spare junction, and nowhere to put it. . . . Working towards a coherent layout is a matter of ongoing, iterative negotiation, and nothing can tell you in advance how deep the reworking of your existing layout will need to be as you face any particular inconsistency. Of course, when one has, with triumph, produced a workable network, with all pieces in place (and not too much strain on any of the joints), it inevitably happens that some small child (probably

1. I first presented a version of this material as part of a response to an American Academy of Religion session in memory of Daniel W. Hardy in November 2008; I was responding to Peter Ochs, Jacob Goodson, and Kristen Deede Johnson; Stanley Hauerwas was the other respondent. I am grateful to all of them, and to other participants in the session, for helping to shape what follows.

in revenge for the adult takeover of his or her playthings) will discover an extra piece of track from behind the sofa. And the finding of that extra piece will start the whole iterative process going again.

Now, we can use "settlement" as a noun to refer to a coherent track layout: a workable arrangement in which all the presently available pieces have been placed together, with no loose ends. However, we can also use "settle" as a verb, to denote the activity of *seeking* a settlement: the active process of iterative renegotiation and repair by which broken networks are remade in pursuit of coherence. And here is the first payoff of this elaborate metaphor: "reasoning" in this context is simply *the faculty of active settling*: the faculty by which one thinkingly pursues this kind of iterative, reparative renegotiation in search of a settlement.

In order, however, to move this in the direction of an account specifically of *Scriptural* Reasoning, there's another distinction that we need to put in place, because there are two different flavors of settlement for which the building of a Brio train track provides a useful metaphor. On the one hand, there is what I call an *individual settlement*. For instance, there's my own settlement. It seems clear that the way I read scripture shapes my theological ideas, and that my theological ideas shape how I read scripture; both are shaped by my negotiations with the Christian theological tradition, and in turn shape those negotiations; and all these negotiations are shaped by the practical, social contexts in which I find myself, and in turn shape the path that I take through those contexts. If I pursue some kind of coherence—some kind of a settlement in which these various things support one another—then I am involved in the process of individual settlement. My reason (my settlement-making faculty) works on scripture, on tradition, and on my context (or experience) in pursuit of a coherent life. That's an individual settlement.

On the other hand, there is what I call a *shared settlement*, which works rather differently—and does not simply resemble an individual settlement writ large. This is where the settlement sought is not the coherence of a single way of doing things, a single way of seeing, but the coherence of a corporate life in which the paths of people of *differing* ways of seeing and doing somehow mesh together in a sustainable whole. It is perhaps easier to imagine the static version of this, in which the way I act, on the basis of my own individual settlement, also happens to make enough sense to you, when received within your individual settlement, for you to respond meaningfully to that action; and the way you then act on the basis of your individual settlement makes enough sense when seem from within mine that I in turn can respond. We have a settlement of shared life whenever there is just enough such meshing between these two individual settlements to keep a conversation going, or to keep a sustainable common practice going—and it is worth stressing that it is a strictly secondary question whether that meshing is made possible by pockets of overlapping understanding, oases of consensus, or recognizable analogies between elements of our differing individual settlements. (The motors of a shared life might, after all, just as easily be patterns of consistent misrecognition between individual settlements.)

Of course, a more dynamic understanding of what a shared-life settlement is emerges when the individual settlements that interlock to produce common life are not finalized settlements, but ongoing activities of settling—where what mesh together to produce some kind of sustainable life are differing, interlocking practices of settling.

We can use the term "biblical reasoning" to name the activity of shared-life settlement by which Christians seek to make sense of themselves and their world in the light of the Bible, and of the Bible in the light of themselves and their world: the process by which they seek a biblical settlement in which there is at least a rough coherence between their ways of reading the Bible, their ways of living with each other, and their ways of living in the world. It is, indeed, a matter of *reasoning*—of the iterative, reparative making and remaking of sense, and it is *biblical* reasoning to the extent that settling with the Bible is a crucial part of what goes on. By analogy, we can use the phrases "qur'anic reasoning" and (for historical reasons)[2] "textual reasoning" to name, respectively, the Islamic and Jewish analogues of this biblical reasoning.

Finally, *Scriptural* Reasoning names a process of shared settlement that occurs when these three process of textual, biblical, and qur'anic reasoning are carried on in intensive dialogue with one another. It can be called a "settlement" just to the extent that this intensive dialogue turns out itself to be sustainable practice (such that there is an ongoing shared *life* of dialoguing), and just to the extent that interaction with the settlement of the other traditions makes a difference to the settling of each participating tradition (such that there is an ongoing *shared* life of dialoguing). And, once again, it is important to recognize that to call Scriptural Reasoning a "shared settlement" does *not* imply that this shared life is held together by consensus (by agreement between Jews,

2. For "textual reasoning" see the introductions in Ochs and Levene, *Textual Reasonings*, 2–27.

Christians, and Muslims on the authority of all their scriptures, perhaps, or even by particularly close analogies between, say, the way the Bible features in Christian settlements and the way the Qur'an features in Islamic settlements).[3] In fact, as we explained in the previous chapter, it turns out to be very hard to name what *does* make for the possibility of this sustainable practice (rather than to patiently describe how in fact it does sustain itself).

Nevertheless, in order to offer a tentative, partial glimpse to illustrate the logic of shared settlement exhibited by Scriptural Reasoning—and it *is* no more than an illustration, a diagrammatic representation of a reality that is very much messier and more varied on the ground—we turn in the next chapter to three very different texts, one from each tradition.

3. One of the slogans of Scriptural Reasoning is "not consensus but friendship" (Adams, *Habermas and Theology*, 243)—which we could temporarily and clumsily rewrite as "not consensus but shared settlement."

11 Patterns of Inter-faith Reading II

Digression, Kenosis, and Hospitality

THE DESCRIPTION IN THE previous chapter was entirely abstract. It provided a scaffolding of concepts that might be useful in describing more deeply what is going on in conversations like that reported in chapter 9. The scaffolding offered, however, was very bare—and, in particular, left it hard to imagine how the meshing of Jewish, Christian, and Muslim settlements in a shared settlement might work. This chapter offers a model—a vastly simplified one in which the complex patterns of the three individual settlements are represented by the patterns suggested in a single text read within each settlement—in order to give more food to the imagination. The next two chapters will offer much richer and more complex discussion of how the settling activity of Scriptural Reasoning might relate to the dynamics of particular traditions.

DIGRESSION: THE HOUSE OF BLESSING

[10]Jacob left Beer-sheba and went towards Haran. [11]He came to a certain place and stayed there for the night, because the sun had set. Taking one of the stones of the place, he put it under his head and lay down in that place. [12]And he dreamed that there was a ladder set up on the earth, the top of it reaching to heaven; and the angels of God were ascending and descending on it. [13]And the Lord stood beside him and said, "I am the Lord, the God of Abraham your father and the God of Isaac; the land on which you lie I will give to you and

to your offspring; [14]and your offspring shall be like the dust of the earth, and you shall spread abroad to the west and to the east and to the north and to the south; and all the families of the earth shall be blessed in you and in your offspring. [15]Know that I am with you and will keep you wherever you go, and will bring you back to this land; for I will not leave you until I have done what I have promised you." [16]Then Jacob woke from his sleep and said, "Surely the Lord is in this place—and I did not know it!" [17]And he was afraid, and said, "How awesome is this place! This is none other than the house of God, and this is the gate of heaven."

[18]So Jacob rose early in the morning, and he took the stone that he had put under his head and set it up for a pillar and poured oil on the top of it. [19]He called that place Bethel; but the name of the city was Luz at the first. [20]Then Jacob made a vow, saying, "If God will be with me, and will keep me in this way that I go, and will give me bread to eat and clothing to wear, [21]so that I come again to my father's house in peace, then the Lord shall be my God, [22]and this stone, which I have set up for a pillar, shall be God's house; and of all that you give me I will surely give one-tenth to you."

—GENESIS 28

Reading this passage, we might at first think that Jacob's dream occurs in an accidental place, or in no particular place—that Jacob simply stops fortuitously in a "certain place," caught there by the accident of a sinking sun, and a journey that happened to pass this way. When he sleeps, and dreams of a ladder, we might think that the stress falls on the fact that this ladder links heaven and "earth"—that is, heaven and places in general—not on the fact that it links heaven to this specific place; and when Jacob dreams of God, we might think that the stress falls not on the fact that he sees God in this specific place, but on the fact that he sees God already beside him, wherever he might be. Jacob, we might say, finds that there is an ongoing commerce between heaven and earth, and that God is already present—not because he has found the one place amongst others where this is true, but rather because in this accidental place he has been shown something of the general linkage between heaven and earth and, more particularly, something of the abiding presence of God "beside him."

Such an indifference to this specific place might find confirmation in Bethel's subsequent history. Yes, Jacob returns here (Genesis 35); yes,

Deborah judges here (Judges 4); yes, the ark of the covenant will later be kept here (Judges 20); yes, Samuel's circulating court will stop here (1 Samuel 7); and yes, there will be a school of prophets here (2 Kings 2)—but eventually Bethel will become a center not for blessing but for idolatry, for the worship of the golden calf (1 Kings 12), and Hosea will rename it Beth-aven, "House of Idols," and warn the people, "Do *not* go up to Beth-aven" (Hosea 4:15).

And yet, however much the emphasis at the beginning of the story of Jacob's dream, and in the story of the dream itself, does not fall on the specificity of that particular place, and however much later stories call into question that place's significance, Jacob's response to his dream is to say, "Surely the Lord is in *this* place!" and "How awesome is *this* place! *This* is none other than the house of God, and *this* is the gate of heaven." Jacob erects a monument *here*, as a marker of this specific place, and he gives this specific place a name, "House of God"—a name suggesting that this specific place is one where we might expect to find God.

If we look more closely, it turns out that the story of Jacob's dream itself sets out a complex mediation between the specificity of Bethel—this particular place—and the relativization of place. We see this in God's promise to Jacob—a promise that begins with this specific place ("the land on which you lie I will give to you and to your offspring") but quickly spreads ("abroad to the west and to the east and to the north and to the south") until it is universal ("all the families of the earth"). And the promise begins with Jacob in this specific place ("the land on which you lie") and returns to it ("I will bring you back to this land") but assumes that, in between, Jacob will not escape this promise even when he leaves this place ("I am with you and will keep you wherever you go"). Indeed, the implication is that Jacob will only return to this specific place once God has fulfilled his promise, by blessing all the families of the earth in him and his offspring; Jacob, we might say, will not return here until he and his offspring have been *everywhere* else. This specific place is both the first and the last place to be blessed; and in between, every place is to be blessed.

Jacob's response acknowledges this complexity: as we have noted, he certainly draws attention to the specificity of this particular place; he takes the stone which he happened to find in this unremarkable, accidental, fortuitous place—a place which appeared to be nowhere in particular—and sets it up as an immovable marker, as a monument testifying that this specific place is the gate of heaven; and he gives this specific place a name: Bethel. Yet the vow that he makes once he has set up that stone is curious: "*If* God will be with me, and will keep me in this way that I go . . . *then* the Lord shall be my God, and this stone which I have set up for a pillar, shall be God's house." The name Bethel will apply to this place, and the stone that Jacob sets up will be something other than a random rock, only *if* God is with Jacob elsewhere and everywhere. If Jacob finds God's blessing everywhere else, then he will know that he has found it here.

On the one hand, the story of Jacob's dream does not allow us to turn away from the specificity of Bethel, of a particular place of encounter with God; on the other hand, it does not allow us to think of that place without also thinking of all other places. And the logic by which it links this place and all other places is complex. On the one hand, a blessing appears in this particular place in order to spread to all other places—a logic of overflow. On the other hand, and more intriguingly, the blessing of this place is in some way dependent on the blessing of all other places: blessing must travel away and return in order to be complete—a logic of *digression*.

This digressive logic of blessing is present in the wider context of this story as well. Jacob's blessing (his calling down of God's blessing, the blessing given to Abraham for the blessing of all the families of the earth, Gen 12:3), intended for Esau, has been diverted by a ruse to Jacob. Jacob travels away from Esau, taking his blessing with him, and having that blessing renewed on the journey out (at Bethel) and back (at Peniel). Having been blessed with wives and children and flocks while away, Jacob brings a blessing back to Esau—only to find Esau already blessed, and to find God's blessing again in Esau's face (Gen 33:10). Blessings in Genesis do not travel in straight lines, or stay where they are put; they are always travelling by surprising digressions, and returning enriched from foreign lands.

Any attempt to construct an account of a specific religious tradition—a religious "house" in the jargon of Scriptural Reasoning—by reference to patterns of divine blessing focused entirely on the specificity of one place (even an attempt which added to that localization the sense of blessing's overflow to other places) is called into question in this text by the story of blessing's digression. And digressive blessing makes sense in the context of the wide promises of God: the digressions are ruses not of power, but of promise—ruses which divert blessing through the face of the other, even the face of the enemy, and bring it home enriched.

KENOSIS: THE MOUNTAIN OF GLORY

[28]Now about eight days after these sayings Jesus took with him Peter and John and James, and went up on the mountain to pray. [29]And while he was praying, the appearance of his face changed, and his clothes became dazzling white. [30]Suddenly they saw two men, Moses and Elijah, talking to him. [31]They appeared in glory and were speaking of his departure, which he was about to accomplish at Jerusalem. [32]Now Peter and his companions were weighed down with sleep; but since they had stayed awake, they saw his glory and the two men who stood with him. [33]Just as they were leaving him, Peter said to Jesus, "Master, it is good for us to be here; let us make three dwellings, one for you, one for Moses, and one for Elijah"—not knowing what he said.

[34]While he was saying this, a cloud came and overshadowed them; and they were terrified as they entered the cloud. [35]Then from the cloud came a voice that said, "This is my Son, my Chosen; listen to him!" [36]When the voice had spoken, Jesus was found alone. And they kept silent and in those days told no one any of the things they had seen.

—Luke 9

"Surely the Lord is in this place!" said Jacob. "How awesome is this place! This is none other than the house of God, and this is the gate of heaven." Peter might have said as much on the mountain of the transfiguration—before saying, "Master, it is good for us to be here." "Weighed down with sleep" but nevertheless—unlike Jacob—awake, Peter, James, and John have seen the glory of God in the face of Christ, and will soon be taken up into the terrifying cloud on the mountaintop and struck dumb by this God's speaking. These specific men have been led to a specific place (Jesus has chosen them, and has chosen their prominent destination); they have been led there at a specific time (we are told that this takes place eight days after the previous story, one day before the next—an unusual specificity in the Synoptic Gospels); and while there they have been shown a drama no less astonishing than the commerce of Jacob's angels, a drama that appears to authorize this specific place: they have seen Elijah and Moses, marking out this mountain as the successor of Elijah's Carmel and Moses' Sinai, and the voice in the cloud will speak to validate the place in which they find themselves, as if to say, "You are in the right place at the right time; stay here."

Yet, when Peter tries to build on this mountain (building not an altar but houses) his eagerness is marked by events, and by the Evangelist, as mistaken. The precise nature of his error is curious: he did not know what he was saying, we are told, and yet all he has done is to offer hospitality to those who have appeared on the mountaintop. Perhaps the subtext of his suggestion ("Let us make three booths") is: "We have now found the stable center; let us stay here." Perhaps even: "If others want to find this glory, they will have to travel here—and we will dispense the glory to others from this place. Glory has a location, a place where it is fixed—a place from which it might overflow to other places—and we will be its brokers." But there is to be no staying on this mountain; there is not even to be a final return to this mountain: the house of God, or gate of heaven in this case—the place marked out now by God—is Jesus' flesh. The voice from the cloud speaks not to designate this place as God's mountain, but Jesus as God's Son, God's Chosen; Elijah and Moses appear not in order to mark this mountain as a Jewish Valhalla, but in order to defer to Jesus—when the pressure of the overshadowing cloud finally releases them, Elijah and Moses vanish, so that Jesus is "found alone."

And, still more strikingly, this is a house or gate that is going to disappear: the "accomplishment" about which Moses and Elijah speak to Jesus is not his presence but his departure—and on closer inspection, the transfiguration story appears deftly woven into a series of pericopes in this gospel which set out an *economy of kenosis*, a series of moves in which glory, greatness, anointing, and salvation are tied to the trajectory into self-abnegation, betrayal, and death. The one who is picked out by God's light on the mountain is the one who eight days before the climb had announced to his disciples that he must suffer, be rejected, and be killed (9:22); a day after the climb, he will tell them again that he must be "delivered into the hands of men" (9:44).

In the story of Jacob's dream, blessing's direction is grounded in God's promise, and the note sounded is positive: God will accompany Jacob into foreign territory, and he will find blessing there too. Here, the note sounded is more somber: glory can only be pursued by heading away from the stabilities of the mountain top, into the loss of security, the loss of vision, the loss of self. "Foxes have holes, and birds of the air have nests; but the Son of Man has nowhere to lay his head" (9:58). The light that God shines falls not on a stable place, a place built up securely, a place to lay the head, but on a life moving swiftly towards death. And the passages immediately surrounding this mountaintop are filled with sayings in which Jesus' disciples are called to a similar kenosis, a similar handing over: "If any man would come after me, let him deny himself . . ." (9:23); "Whoever would save his life will lose it, whoever loses his life . . . will save it" (9:24); "He who is least among you all is the one who is great" (9:48).

This *kenotic economy* includes God, whose role in the story is to point those seeking him to Jesus of Nazareth—to hide himself, we might say, in Jesus of Nazareth, so that the disciples are reduced to silence, and find when Jesus explains this trajectory that they do not understand—"and it was concealed from them, that they should not perceive it" (9:45). This economy includes Jesus, on the way to the cross. It includes the disciples, who are asked to share that way. And it includes, in a story placed shortly after the transfiguration account, a random child: "He took a child and put him by his side, and said to them, 'Whoever receives this child in my name receives me, and whoever receives me receives him who sent me'" (9:47–48). Any attempt to construct an account of a religious "house" by reference to patterns of divine glory focused on the achievement of stability, the fixing of identity, are called into question in this text by this indication of the kenotic economy. If there are to be houses of God, this text suggests, then they must be houses of self-emptying, houses whose inhabitants follow Christ beyond their walls in utter vulnerability.

HOSPITALITY: THE MOSQUE OF TRUTH

[59]Indeed the example of Jesus to Allāh is like that of Adam. He created him from dust; then He said to him, "Be," and he was. [60]This truth is from your Lord, so do not be among the doubters. [61]Then whoever argues with you about it after [this] knowledge has come to you—say, "Come, let us call our sons and your sons, our women and your women, ourselves and yourselves, then supplicate earnestly [together] and invoke the curse of Allāh upon the liars [among us].

—Qur'an 3[1]

In the hadith, the passage from the Qur'an, 3:58–61, is given a particular context. Martin Lings provides a good summary:

1. Saheeh International, *Qur'an.*

> Deputations still continued to come as in the previous year, and one of these was from the Christians of Najran, who sought to make a testimony with the Prophet. They were of the Byzantine rite, and in the past had received rich subsidies from Constantinople. The delegates, sixty in number, were received by the Prophet in the Mosque, and when the time for their prayer came he allowed them to pray it there, which they did, facing towards the east.
>
> At the audiences which they had with him during their stay, many points of his doctrine were touched on, and there were some disagreements between him and them concerning the person of Jesus. Then came the Revelation. . . .
>
> The Prophet recited this Revelation to the Christians and invited them to meet with him and his family and to settle their dispute in the way here suggested. They said they would think about it, and the next day when they came to the Prophet . . . they said they were not prepared to carry their disagreement so far as imprecation; and the Prophet made with them a favourable treaty according to which, in return for the payment of taxes, they were to have the full protection of the Islamic state for themselves and their churches and other possessions.[2]

In this story we find a hospitable polity. The Najran delegation, invited to consider Islam, are welcomed, while still Christians within the walls of the Muslim house, to Medina; they are allowed "in the Mosque," in the presence of Muhammad—and even permitted to make their prayers there. They are invited within the mosque, however, not to demonstrate Muhammad's pluralism, but in order to engage in debate and confrontation concerning the truth of Islam and of Christianity. The hospitality, rather than smudging away the differences between the guests and their hosts, provides a context in which that difference can be seen starkly and honestly.

The confrontation centers on the most serious issue dividing Christians from the house of Islam: the Christians' continued worship of Jesus. From the Muslim point of view, this is a debate between true Islam and false Islam, and nothing is said which in any way softens that contrast. It is recognized that this is not a trivial difference, but a difference that cuts right down to bedrock: a difference that could quite rightly be made a cause for mutual cursing, for the breaking of all fellowship. There is no turning away from the seriousness of the difference, and Muhammad

2. Lings, *Muhammad*, 324–26.

receives a Qur'anic revelation during the Christians' stay, challenging them, as it were, to trial by mutual cursing. Muhammad's hospitality provides an arena within which the possibility of this mutual cursing can become visible.

Yet the debate is not pushed by either side all the way to the ignition of those curses. The Christians pull back from engaging in the trial by cursing, and Muhammad does not require their capitulation to true Islam but allows a "coming to terms." The same hospitality that has welcomed the Christians within the walls of the mosque, and allowed the true depth of the division between Islam and Christianity to become visible, now creates a polity within which that potential cursing can be contained—a polity nevertheless constructed in the light of the knowledge of this curse. The Christians are allowed to return to Najran, to remain Christians, and to receive protection from Muhammad in return for taxation—in return for becoming elements within a wider Islamic polity.

In all this it should not be forgotten that the hospitality and the confrontation it makes possible have become an occasion for revelation to Muhammad. The presence of those who must still be seen, by Islamic eyes, as teachers of a lie, debating the differences between their lie and Allah's truth, itself calls forth more of that truth. In other words, Muhammad's *hospitable polity* allows differences to be seen starkly, but nevertheless gratuitously relegates the curse of those differences to a secondary position—and this hospitality is not simply a concession by Islam, but becomes a blessing to Islam, an occasion for Allah's blessing, working by means of a strange digression.

Any attempt to construct an account of a religious "house" by reference to patterns of divine glory focused entirely on exclusion is called into question by this story of a hospitable polity—a polity strong enough to face the terrible curses that could divide it, strong enough to turn deliberately, knowingly and gratuitously aside from the full activation of those curses, and to discover blessing in life together, blessing in the very fact of confrontation.

ANALOGOUS LOGICS AND MESHING SETTLEMENTS

These three texts, with their different but somewhat analogous patterns, might help us to think about the nature of Scriptural Reasoning. My reading of each text tentatively suggests a facet that might be found in the logic of each tradition's own settling activity, and for the purposes of this chapter only I am taking that facet as if it were representative of the tradition as a whole.[3] If I now ask how these three logics—of digression, of kenotic economy, and of hospitable polity—might mesh together so as to allow a shared practice of dialogue, it is not in order to be able to claim that I have explained Scriptural Reasoning, but in order to offer one vastly simplified *model* of it, designed simply to aid description of the practice itself.

In the first place, then, we could simply say that Scriptural Reasoning's "tent" might be seen by Jewish participants as a staging post on the return of Jacob to Bethel. More concretely, Jacob finds that the promise of Bethel receives part of its fulfilment in the face of Esau, and the tent might be a location in which Jacob and Esau can meet. This need include no disavowal of the story of Jacob's election and Esau's rejection, but simply the recognition that the blessing promised to Jacob is not only a blessing *for* all, but a blessing *from* all, so that what Jacob receives from Esau is part of the covenant blessing Jacob was promised.

Somewhat similarly, the tent might be seen by Christian participants as a step on the journey of kenosis to which they are called. More concretely, the disciples of Jesus are called to discover him in the face of a child, rather than in the face of their own security—and the tent might be a location in which "children" (other "children of Abraham" in this case) may be encountered, and the face of Jesus discerned in their faces. Again, this need involve no rejection of the centrality of Jesus' name or of revelation in Christ, but the text suggests that it is only through finding Christ in these other faces, seen through these other eyes, that the whole Christ is found at all.

And finally, the tent might be seen by Muslim participants as an extension of Muhammad's hospitable polity. More concretely, Muhammad's hospitality provides an arena in which the faces of the Najran Christians can be seen, including their undisguised otherness, and blessing can emerge from the confrontation. The tent might be a location in which

3. All my caveats and disclaimers may be irritating to read, but I am all too aware in the abstract that a Christian theologian seeking to speak on behalf of his Jewish and Islamic colleagues is following some fairly unpleasant precedents, and in the concrete that making attempts of these kind in conversation with my Jewish and Islamic colleagues *never* leads to their unqualified approval of the proposals I have made. I am all too aware in this case that each of my three exegeses *sounds* (quite accurately) like I had written it: I've ended up giving my own accent to all three voices.

Muslim participants can hospitably confront Christian and Jewish faces from Najran and discover a Qur'anic blessing in the process.

To the extent that my descriptions of these three logics are recognizable within the three traditions, then Scriptural Reasoning itself can be construed as the practice in which these three logics mesh. At the simplest level, each logic is enough to hold the participants from the respective tradition in this practice of dialogue: it gives each a home-grown rationale for participation, and means that for the Jews participation in Scriptural Reasoning can be a Jewish practice, for the Christians it can be a Christian practice, for the Muslims a Muslim practice—and whilst those practices differ, they overlap just enough to make a common practice emerge. In each case, there is some sense to be made of the practice of spending time with outsiders to one's own house, seeing their faces *as* outsiders to one's own house but not therefore as irrelevant to the strange routes by which blessing, fulfillment or signs of God's glory arrive. In each case, there is some sense to be made of spending time with those outsiders *as* people with their own identity, not simply as defined by their membership of or exclusion from my own house; and so in each case there is some sense to be made of spending time with these people, and to spend time with them as they spend time with their scriptures, not because those scriptures are mine but because they are theirs.

That is enough; digression is not kenosis, not hospitality, and this meshing does not imply consensus. This is a practice of inter-faith study that requires no pluralist hypothesis: the three logics are not the same, and the meaning that this participation has within each tradition is different; the limits that will seem appropriate in each case are different; the patterns of connection between this practice and the existing practices of study and devotion within the tradition are different. Meshing is not consensus, and the fact that a sustainable practice turns out to be possible built from these overlapping agreements and disagreements is a gift, not a possession.

12 Why Inter-faith Reading Makes Christian Sense I

Hard Sayings

A SPECIFIC TRADITION

THE LAST CHAPTER OFFERED a "vastly simplified model" of Scriptural Reasoning, attempting to give a picture of the kinds of dynamic that might make it work by treating each of the three participating traditions as if it could be fairly represented by the logic of a single one of its texts. This chapter tries—as, indeed, do all the remaining chapters in this section—to deepen and complicate this model. Rather than asking whether and how Scriptural Reasoning makes sense from some generic Christian point of view (or Islamic or Jewish), I am going to investigate the sense that a specific piece of Scriptural Reasoning (an examination of some of Jesus' "hard sayings" in the Gospels) might make within a very particular kind of Christian culture.

I grew up within a specific kind of Christian tradition: evangelical, charismatic, and Anglican. In the terms established in chapter 10, it was a particular settlement or a particular ongoing activity of settling, with its own patterns of biblical reasoning. The generic term "settlement" however, which in chapter 10 chapter appeared as a general theory of religious traditions equally applicable to any of the participating traditions within Scriptural Reasoning, is applicable to this charismatic, evangelical Anglican tradition in a very specific way.[1] The "settlement" within which

1. Readers should take seriously the possibility that the general account of

I grew up involved at once a settled pattern of reading and, for very specific reasons, an ongoing activity of settling that potentially *un*settled that settled pattern. Let me explain.

The fact that my tradition was evangelical meant that study of the Bible played a central role. I grew up hearing regular expository preaching in which the sermon was addressed to the specific context and concerns of the congregation only by means of detailed, step-by-step examination of a connected biblical passage. I grew up attending a variety of small weekly Bible study groups often dedicated to working in sequence through particular books of the Bible. I grew up expected to engage in daily personal "quiet times," normally involving the use of published "Bible notes" inviting reflection on a new passage each day. These and other scriptural practices were woven deeply into the life of my church and the lives of each of its members.

As a community with a degree of recognizable stability over time, the life of this church necessarily involved some kind of settlement; with these practices so central in its life, it was unavoidably some kind of *biblical* settlement. The community had to have developed ways of making sense of, and of making use of, the scriptures that it read so intensively—and, indeed, it was a community with recognizable ways of handling certain kinds of scriptural text, a community where there was a degree of graspable hermeneutical stability.

Yet three things converged within this settlement to potentially unsettling effect. In the first place, the very seriousness about the Bible that I have sketched was supported by the idea that the church and its members could be *called to account* by the Bible. As God's Word, it was capable of convicting, challenging, upsetting, and provoking to repentance. Any claim to have finally settled with the Bible—any recognition that in practice one's community was living *as if* it had finally settled with the Bible—would have been deeply suspect: it would have sounded like a denial that the Bible was the living Word of God. And whilst the personal quiet time and the group Bible studies could be thought of fairly accurately as means by which the existing biblical settlement of this community was explored and inhabited by its members, expository preaching was held to be at its best when it had the potentially unsettling character of a challenge.

In the second place, that sense of potential disruption was amplified by my Protestant tradition's attitude to *law*. "Law" was a deeply

settlement offered in the previous two chapters is, in fact, a premature generalization from this one instance.

ambiguous term in relation to gospel, and that ambiguity gave rise not to any tendency to antinomianism but to a pervasive sense that the call to discipleship could not be exhausted by any collection of statable imperatives, any codified pattern of life. Discipleship was always potentially *more* than that: it was response to a personal, excessive *call*. No existing pattern of obedience, no existing understanding of one's responsibilities, however thoroughly inhabited, could eradicate the sense that there were still deeper levels of obedience to be reached.

In the third place, as charismatic, the tradition in which I grew up placed a strong emphasis on the expectation that, in particular moments of religious intensity, that deeper call to obedience that shadowed all one's settlements could and would break through in disruptive spiritual experiences—explicitly *liminal* experiences, experiences at the edge of one's existing settlement. I remember the impression made on me, as a teenager, by the biography of the Christian singer-songwriter Keith Green—aptly called *No Compromise*. In 1979, five years after he became a Christian and (along with his wife Melody) dedicated his life to evangelism and Christian ministry, he called a meeting in his Christian commune and made an announcement:

> You know I've been struggling with a lot of questions about my ministry and the Lord's will for my life. I've been really wanting God to be more real. I've wanted to be closer to him, to feel his presence more. Well, I was up all night in the Ark and God showed me so much sin in my life that I spent the whole night weeping and crying out to Jesus. I told the Lord I wasn't going to leave the Ark until I had a breakthrough—no matter how long it took. Finally it happened. I had a touch from the Lord like I've never had in my whole life, and, well . . . I know I just got saved—I just got saved last night.[2]

Whatever eccentricity there might have been (from the perspective of my tradition) in the way this was expressed, the sentiment was deeply familiar: all our settlements were shadowed by the knowledge that they would look like compromises in the light of the more radical call to obedience that could erupt at any moment. Serious, prayerful reading of the scriptures was always, potentially, the vehicle by which this call would be heard.

2. Green and Hazard, *No Compromise*, 267.

SETTLEMENTS AND HARD SAYINGS

[57]As they were going along the road, someone said to him, "I will follow you wherever you go." [58]And Jesus said to him, "Foxes have holes, and birds of the air have nests; but the Son of Man has nowhere to lay his head." [59]To another he said, "Follow me." But he said, "Lord, first let me go and bury my father." [60]But Jesus said to him, "Let the dead bury their own dead; but as for you, go and proclaim the kingdom of God." [61]Another said, "I will follow you, Lord; but let me first say farewell to those at my home." [62]Jesus said to him, "No one who puts a hand to the plough and looks back is fit for the kingdom of God."

—LUKE 9

The dual character of the settlement in which I grew up—a settlement *looking* for the unsettling—can be illustrated by examining the role played in it by the "hard sayings" of Jesus.[3] Some of the readings of that passage that I grew up with certainly have the already-settled air of belonging to readers who have discovered how to make peace with these passage, where "peace" means never having to be troubled again. The *NIV Study Bible* (one of the indispensable tools of my teenage bible studies) says, for instance, "*bury my father*. If his father had already died, the man would have been occupied with the burial then. But evidently he wanted to wait until after his father's death, which might have been years away. Jesus told him that the spiritually dead could bury the physically dead, and that the spiritually alive should be busy proclaiming the kingdom of God."[4] The bite of the saying is softened by means of the claim that the father is not dead, and by neat use of the spiritual/physical distinction—precisely the sorts of techniques that are always a necessary part of settlement building, but that here are used with a brusqueness that seems to neuter the text.

A more characteristic interpretation of the passage, from the point of view of the settlement I grew up in, is provided by a 1984 sermon by Andrew Davies to the Aberystwyth Conference of the Evangelical Movement of Wales.[5] The sermon exemplifies the attitude to the Word of

3. The category of "hard sayings" was indigenous in my tradition, thanks to books like F. F. Bruce's *Hard Sayings of Jesus*.

4. *The NIV Study Bible*, 1527; the note is apparently by Lewis Foster.

5. Davies, "Hand to the Plough." The church of which I was part as a teenager was a long way from Aberystwyth, and I never attended any conference of the Evangelical

God described above: the congregation are reminded that God has "sent his Spirit to speak to us through his Word" (3.55) and that they should therefore listen with a "sense of anticipation" (2.35), "wondering what God [is] going to do among us" (2.25). It quickly focuses on the nature of discipleship, asking, "How much of a follower of Jesus Christ *are* you?" (8.24) and, after a catalog of the *forms* of Christian obedience (scripture reading, faithful church attendance, and so on), the preacher repeats the refrain, "it's not enough!" (7.35). "Jesus wants us to *think* about what it really means to be a follower of his" (12.50); he wants "*real* disciples" (17.17).

When it comes to verses 59 and 60, the preacher says:

> Now we really do need to be clear about what this means. The real problem here of course was not that our Lord was somehow or another saying to the man you shouldn't care for your father. That could not be the case, could it . . . because we're told to honour our father and our mother, and in the Bible we read about those patriarchs who were buried with great honour. . . . Caring for and burying our parents is a very important human responsibility given to us by God. No, no. What our Lord really meant was this: *You*, however old you are, what you really want is this; you want to follow me, perhaps, but only after you've carried out your other responsibilities. . . . They come first. And this man was putting his parents first. The meaning could very well be construed in this way, that what the man was saying was Lord let me first go home and care for my father until he is dead and then I'll bury him, and after that's over I'll come and follow you. The real problem, you see, was his refusal to put Christ first. His family came first. His family was an excuse. Something came between him and Christ.[6]

A moment later he reiterates: "for a man or a woman to put his family first and to lavish time and attention upon them is honourable, and it's right, but families or friends should *never* come first, for this simple reason: that God is *always* first. *Always*."[7]

Movement of Wales. Nevertheless, in the absence of any recordings of the sermons that I *did* hear on this text as a teenager, this one makes a very good substitute: despite coming from a somewhat more conservative stream of evangelicalism than that in which I grew up, so recognizable are its idiom and cadences that listening to it effortlessly took me back to the hard plastic chairs and long services of my youth.

6. Davies, "Hand to the Plough," 23.52—25.35.

7. Ibid., 27.19.

Just as much as in the *NIV Study Bible*, there is here a stable settlement: a way of coming to terms with the passage that allows it to be woven in to a wider biblical pattern of texts about families, and that prevents it from disturbing settled convictions about the importance of families. "No, no," says Davies—don't think that the passage offends against that settlement. The assumption seems to be that, normally, one's duties—all the duties that obedience to God involves, including the duty to honor one's parents—will be compatible. It will be possible to fulfill them all, unless some disturbance has destroyed that compatibility and forced a choice.

Davies's sermon hints at two different kind of disturbance that might force just such a choice, however. On the one hand, it is possible that the fault lies in the objects of one's love. He provides the following example: "There's a young man in this conference who has had to experience the agony of having his parents criticise him in a most severe way because of his loyalty to his most dear and blessed saviour. It's been very hard for him. A gracious young man, who loves his parents, who wants to see them saved. Are you prepared for that?"[8]

On the other hand, it is possible that the fault lies in oneself. "Young man! Are you courting? Have you got a girlfriend, perhaps sitting next to you? Who comes first? Young woman! Have you got a young man you're intending to marry? Who comes first? Are you trying to be a Christian? Are you leading her, are you leading him with you? Or is she, or is he, leading you back, away? Who comes first?"[9] The disordering here is not due to some fundamental incompatibility between one's proper duties, but to the sinful human tendency to imbalance—the immoderate leanings of one's untended desires, backed by an ability to delude oneself about the true tendency of one's relationships.

This settlement contains the text: the impact is absorbed by the exotic possibilities of persecution and the more ordinary dynamics of inordinate desire.

And yet, characteristically for this settlement, however safe the exegesis has made the text, an unsettling question has been set loose. As the passionate and insistent rhetoric of later passages in the sermon attests, the demands that the gospel makes on believers are not to be tamed. There is no end to the process of self-examination, of self-questioning,

8. Ibid., 31.00. This is a familiar trope from such discussions: the reference to stories of persecution by the family of a believer (often a convert).

9. Davies, "Hand to the Plough," 29.40.

that they require. The answer to the question, "How much of a follower of Jesus Christ *are* you?" is one of those questions to which the answer can never properly be, "Enough."

WHERE DOES SCRIPTURAL REASONING FIT IN?

Bible study groups of one kind or another were a familiar part of the settlement in which I grew up: small groups of people reading through a text together, puzzling over the words in an effort to understand, but also hoping and expecting to be challenged. At the most visceral level, then, Scriptural Reasoning feels familiar to me: it is in its bare outline a recognizable practice. The continuities between that settlement and this new practice, however, go deeper than that.

At a Scriptural Reasoning conference in Cambridge in 2009, we discussed the same passage from Luke that fired Davies's sermon. The conversation took the form, in part, of a series of attempts by Christians—and by those playfully speaking on Christians' behalf, in the sense described in chapter 9—to offer an acceptable interpretation of the passage.

1

We began with a text expressive of a very similar settlement to the one with which I grew up. We were looking, however, not at the *NIV Study Bible* but at one of Augustine's sermons:[10]

> "Honour your father and mother": there's no doubt God said that. This young man, then, wished to obey God and to bury his father; but it is place, and time, and circumstance that is in this case to give way to place, and time, and circumstance. A father must be honoured, but God must be obeyed. He who begat us must be loved, but he who created us must be preferred. . . . There is a lesson written for us in the Song of Songs, when the Church says, "Set in order love in me" (Song 2.4, LXX).[11] What does it mean, "Set in order love in me"? Make the proper de-

10. Sermon 50 in Pusey's edition of *Sermons on Selected Lessons of the New Testament*; numbered as Sermon 100 in the Benedictine edition; translation slightly altered.

11. Song 2.4b is more familiar in translations based on the MT, as with the NIV's "his banner over me is love" (rendering *degel* as "banner" rather than, as in the NRSV and others, "intention"), but the LXX has an imperative: *taxate ep' eme agapēn*, "set love over me." In the Vulgate this becomes *ordinavit in me caritatem*.

> grees, and render to each his due. Do not put what should come before below that which should come after. Love your parents, but prefer God to them.

As someone who grew up with the settlement exemplified by Davies's sermon (or something very like it), it was unsettling to read Augustine's sermon in the company of others who did not automatically make the connections or fill in the gaps in the way that I did. They showed me, first of all, what Augustine did not say. His insistence that the duty to love God and the duty to love parents can conflict was not news; that much I knew already. What was more unsettling was that Augustine, unlike Davies, provided no hint that either the sin of the father or the sin of the young man is to be blamed. In this text, the incompatibility simply *happens*—thanks to "time, and place, and circumstance." God has issued two demands, and they cannot both be fulfilled—and it is not at all clear (unless one has already automatically filled in the gaps) that the choice of Jesus' command to follow over the law's command to honor parents should be described as a matter of preferring God to family. Isn't it, rather, a matter of preferring God *to God*?

Despite appearances, Augustine's sermon provides no answer to the text's question. What kind of "setting in order" can choose between divine command and divine command? Is it simply that Jesus' command is to be preferred because it is more direct? More recent? More personal? Is it to be preferred because it is issued by one who, in a specific time, place, and circumstance, has the power to set aside the more general commandment? Is it because Jesus' command is gospel, and the command to honour parents is law? [12] Precisely because he does not fill in the gaps (and because reading in company makes those gaps more visible), Augustine's sermon reveals the labor of settlement called for by this text.

2

Our group's discussion of the kinds of settlement possible with this text was driven onward by comparison with a passage from the Qur'an that we had read the day before. It is from the story of Noah, at the point when the ark has been built and the waters have started to rise.

12. A solution our group was particularly unwilling to countenance. One member of the group pointed out that since, famously, this command is the first to come with a promise (cf. Eph 6:1–3), it is clearly already "gospel."

> [41]And he said, "Embark therein; in the name of Allah is its course and its anchorage. Indeed, my Lord is forgiving and merciful. [42]And it sailed with them through waves like mountains, and Noah called out to his son who was apart, "O my son, come aboard with us and be not with the disbelievers." [43][But] he said, "I will take refuge on a mountain to protect me from the water." [44][Noah] said, "There is no protector today from the decree of Allah, except for whom He gives mercy." And the waves came between them, and he was among the drowned. . . . [45]And Noah called to his Lord and said, "My Lord, indeed my son is of my family; and indeed, Your promise is true; and You are the most just of judges. [46]He said, "O Noah, indeed he is not of your family; indeed, he is [one whose] work was other than righteous . . ."
>
> —Qur'an 11

Here the ties of family (and of the promises that go with them) are loosened not because the son was somehow demanding a form of attention from his parents that would have pulled *them* away from obedience to Allah. This is not a generational inversion of the story of the young man with the critical parents from Davies's sermon. The ties seem to be loosened because the son's own disobedience renders him (to true insight) *unrecognizable*.

Our group asked whether some such reading might make sense of the Lukan passage—if, perhaps, Jesus' reply to the man is to be read as telling him that his dying or father is *dead to him*: "He is not of your family." Resistant though I was to the suggestion, the conversation forced me to ask, "Can I make Christian sense of it? Can I settle with it?" Such an interpretation would take me in the direction of a starker eschatological separation between the living and the dead—the kind of stark separation that the flood brings about in the Qur'anic story. It would be a message of separation from unholiness—not the uncleanness of physical corpses, but the contagion of disobedience.

3

It was at this point that the third response to the passage, and to the readings we had been exploring, emerged. That response was one of *horror*, and it came primarily from one of the Jewish members of the group, whose own settlement was one in which love of God and love of family were so deeply entwined that the words of Jesus—not, for her, words that had been softened into a bearable settlement by long use—were deeply shocking, and not just shocking but dangerous and offensive.

Of course, within my own Christian settlement, it is acknowledged that Jesus' words are deliberately shocking, and the difficulty of the demand he makes is stressed rather than ignored. Nevertheless, within that settlement it has become all but impossible actually to *hear* the offense of the words, because they come ready wrapped in the soft tissue paper of the settlement, which has multiple strategies for getting beyond the sting to a challenging but positive message. My first reaction, on hearing my friend's offense, was to leap to the defense of the text, waving my settlement as I came. But her insistence on the shock of the text was relentless, and could not so easily be smoothed away. The text turns God against God, she insisted; it calls for a following of God that is an abandonment of family, and so of people, and so of land—the whole structure of God's ways with Israel abrogated in a shocking fiat. This was not, for her, a text to be settled with.

Reading in company can be uncomfortable. For me, I found that the knifepoints of my fellow group-members' questions and suggestions levered open the gap in my settlement between the stability of its existing strategies for living with this text and the openness to challenge that was an element of that stability. In a way that echoed the kind of question already posed *within* my settlement, the group's conversations forced me to ask whether my settlement was simply a way of making inoffensive a text that *should* offend—either because it contains a call to a more radical eschatological separation than I had thought (an obedience ready to turn away, for its sake, from all other ties) or because it is quite simply a text of terror, a text of God against God, and the dissolution of God's good order.

At their best, the conversations of Scriptural Reasoning have, in my experience, this capacity to give me back a familiar text as an unsettling question. They drive me to *wrestle* again with these texts, and in so doing bear a distant but unmistakable resemblance to the call issued repeatedly in all those passionate expository sermons I heard in my teens. Scriptural Reasoning is, of course, not unique; nor is it uniquely powerful as a means by which to rediscover the texts of one's settlement. There are other practices of reading, other conversations and relationships, that do the same. Nevertheless, precisely because of its unsettling power—precisely because it is a practice that sits on the edge of my existing settlement, itself questionable in the eyes of that settlement—it does have that unsettling power, and so makes deep sense to someone formed in that settlement. I do not participate in Scriptural Reasoning *despite* that, but *because* I grew up a charismatic evangelical Anglican.[13]

13. I *grew up* a charismatic evangelical Anglican. Whether that is the best way to describe the Christian settlement within which I live now is another question—and not a very interesting one, for the purposes of this book.

13 Why Inter-faith Reading Makes Christian Sense II

The Tent and the Net

[1]The Lord appeared to Abraham by the oaks of Mamre, as he sat at the entrance of his tent in the heat of the day. [2]He looked up and saw three men standing near him. When he saw them, he ran from the tent entrance to meet them, and bowed down to the ground. [3]He said, "My lord, if I find favour with you, do not pass by your servant. [4]Let a little water be brought, and wash your feet, and rest yourselves under the tree. [5]Let me bring a little bread, that you may refresh yourselves, and after that you may pass on—since you have come to your servant." So they said, "Do as you have said." [6]And Abraham hastened into the tent to Sarah, and said, "Make ready quickly three measures of choice flour, knead it, and make cakes." [7]Abraham ran to the herd, and took a calf, tender and good, and gave it to the servant, who hastened to prepare it. [8]Then he took curds and milk and the calf that he had prepared, and set it before them; and he stood by them under the tree while they ate.

—Genesis 18

Several influential descriptions of the practice of Scriptural Reasoning have used the image of the "tent of meeting," drawing on Genesis 18, to describe the imagined space in which Jews, Christians, and Muslims are gathered together to read one another's scriptural texts.[1] The

1. See, for example, Kepnes, "Handbook for Scriptural Reasoning," and Taylor, "How to Pitch a Tent."

"tent of meeting" is an imagined space that is the precondition for a real gathering together; its existence in imagination is the precondition for, rather than the denial of, its embodiment in practice.

In this chapter, I reflect on this imagined and real space of the "tent of meeting" from the perspective of the meeting house—that is, from my own continuing formation through worship and life in the Quaker tradition. Perhaps surprisingly—given the manifold differences between our contexts—I also, like Mike Higton in the preceding chapter, find numerous resonances in Scriptural Reasoning with the historical practices of biblical reasoning, and the forms of "biblical settlement" that I inherit. In what follows, I use specific reflections from Quaker contexts to illuminate aspects of the relationship between the Scriptural Reasoning "tent" and the "houses"—the particular traditions from which participants come and to which they remain faithful. The practices of Scriptural Reasoning, and the readings of Genesis 18 that are associated with them, both challenge and are challenged by the forms of communal life imagined in the meeting house.

BEING GATHERED

I begin with Francis Howgill's description, much beloved in Quaker circles, of the experience of the earliest Quaker communities.

> The Kingdom of Heaven did gather us, and catch us all, as in a net; and his heavenly power at one time drew many hundreds to land, that we came to know a place to stand in, and what to wait in; and the Lord appeared daily to us, to our astonishment, amazement, and great admiration, insomuch that we often said one unto another, with great joy of heart: "What, is the Kingdom of God come to be with men? And will he take up his tabernacle among the sons of men, as he did of old? Shall we, that were reckoned as the outcasts of Israel, have this honour of glory communicated among us . . . ?"[2]

The people to whom Francis Howgill's account refers—and it should be borne in mind that the piece was written many years after the events it describes—were among the "Seekers." In a time of intense religious conflict and confusion in mid-seventeenth-century England, they had for various reasons ceased to be members of Christian "houses" of worship.

2. Howgill, "Testimony Concerning the Life," preliminary leaf e3. Cf. the version in *Quaker Faith and Practice*, sec. 19.08.

Reflecting on the formation of one group of Seekers into a "people for [God's] praise,"[3] Howgill emphasizes the reversal of expectations and the confusion of agency. Having been scattered away from their various "houses," and thereby deprived of the contexts that made them possible agents within the divine covenant, these people find themselves caught and drawn in by the "kingdom of heaven," the inbreaking of the eschaton.

Howgill's "gathering net" and the Scriptural Reasoning "tent of meeting" are both imaginal bodies, in and from which bodies of people are formed; but the two images produce rather different understandings of who the gathered people are and how they relate to each other. I walk into a tent as, in some sense, the agent of my own "gathering," responding willingly to an invitation (and an invitation suggests the possibility of refusal: "My lord, *if* I have found favor in your sight, do not pass by your servant . . ."; Gen 18:3). The net, on the other hand, catches up whoever happens to be in its way—whether or not they seek it, whether or not they agree to it.

Those who practice Scriptural Reasoning do enter the tent of meeting by their own decision, but in doing so they also acknowledge a certain double compulsion, of a kind that is to the fore in Howgill's text. On the one hand, there is the compulsion felt by those who suffer, a compulsion to cry out and seek help—the compulsion that is, perhaps, reflected in the Israelites' cry in Exodus 2:23, a text to which frequent reference is made in accounts of the processes of Scriptural Reasoning.[4] Scriptural Reasoners, in their different ways, cry out at the sufferings of their own people and of other peoples, and in the pain of the disturbance of their own accustomed ways of reading and thinking. On the other hand, there is the compulsion of the gathering power of God, the compelling power that summons a response of "astonishment, amazement, and great admiration," "great joy of heart."

Mediating between these two compulsions is the work of imagining and reasoning, of re-membering scriptural texts—and the work of the Spirit of God, as God enacts God's re-membering of the people who suffer. As Peter Ochs notes in his discussion of Exodus 2:23, what turns the cry of the sufferer into a sign of redemption is in the first place God's

3. Howgill, "Testimony," preliminary leaf e4; *Quaker Faith and Practice*, 19.08.

4. See Ochs, *Peirce, Pragmatism*, 304–5.

act of hearing.[5] "Out of the slavery their cry for help rose up to God. God heard their groaning, and God remembered his covenant."

The piece of early Quaker "biblical reasoning" I have quoted raises particularly clearly the question of the possible separation of these works—the work of imagining and reasoning that constructs the new space, and the work of God to "gather and catch us all"—even as it draws them closer together. After all, to be caught in a net is not only involuntary—it is not necessarily an experience that affirms one's past or future agency (including one's agency as imaginer or reasoner).

Howgill has, in fact, taken up one of the more terrifying New Testament images of the kingdom of heaven: "The kingdom of heaven is like a net that was thrown into the sea and caught fish of every kind; when it was full, they drew it ashore, sat down, and put the good into baskets but threw out the bad. So it will be at the end of the age. The angels will come and separate the evil from the righteous, and throw them into the furnace of fire, where there will be weeping and gnashing of teeth" (Matt 13:47–50). Since Howgill places all of the Seekers together in the "net," he seems to place them at the point immediately before judgement—in a place "to wait in," where what is awaited is not necessarily a blessing. However, as the account progresses, the image of the net itself stretches and breaks with the load placed in it. What is received *is* a blessing, even though it has the fearful inevitability of a judgement. The net is superseded by the kingdom and the tabernacle, and none of these fully meet the case. It is as if the scriptural texts themselves do not bear the full weight of the reality they have to carry here. It is not merely that Howgill has to assemble a whole range of scriptural imagery here to speak about the imaginal/real space he entered, such that the deficiencies of one image are compensated for by another. It is, rather, I suspect, that the situation of which he speaks is in some way beyond his scriptural reimagining.

Why should this be so? The people of whom Howgill speaks were explicitly *not* members of any religious "house." They had walked out of, or been forced out of—or, as tends to be the case, something between the two—the Christian "houses" to which they belonged, because of (what they perceived as) both the failures of those houses to do what they claimed to do, and their own failures to fulfill what was required of them there.

5. Ochs, *Peirce, Pragmatism*, 305. For further discussion of this passage and the implications of God's act of hearing, see also Muers, *Keeping God's Silence*, 193–98.

The language Howgill uses to express this condition of "homelessness" is deeply problematic, in a way that discloses some of the basic issues confronting Scriptural Reasoning. He speaks of the people as "the outcasts of Israel." In appropriating this name for those who were cast out of *Christian* houses of worship, Howgill on one level simply repeats the assumption that the Christian community has superseded Israel. If we took his appropriation of this text to its logical conclusion, it would be saying that the only "outcasts" whom God now wishes to gather are the Christian outcasts. One might take this suspicious reading of Howgill's text (and the people to which it relates) further, and interpret it as a clear example of sectarian thinking. Have not these people done precisely what the visitors to the Scriptural Reasoning "tent" seek to avoid—withdrawing from the hospitable "houses" that shelter a wide variety of reasonings and conversations, claiming exclusive control over the texts and images that the "houses" contain, and making extravagant statements about the unmediated activity of God to support that claim? Is that what the "net" language is doing, and why it is so deeply problematic?

This is a real risk attached to the language of the "outcasts of Israel" in Christian, and particularly in "sectarian" Christian, mouths. The complexities of the move are, however, worth further consideration. In the King James Bible that Howgill read, the only references to the "outcasts of Israel" occur in the context of the promise or the celebration of God's act of "gathering." "The Lord builds up Jerusalem; he gathers the outcasts of Israel" (Ps 147:2). "He will raise a signal for the nations, and gather the outcasts of Israel" (Isa 11:12). "Thus says the Lord God, who gathers the outcasts of Israel, I will gather others to them, besides those already gathered" (Isa 56:8).

To write, in retrospect, of a community as those who *had been* "outcasts of Israel" was, then, to reflect on their situation as *now* "gathered by God." The Quakers were finding ways of imagining the place into which they had been brought, using the texts that they carried with them from the houses they left. In the *absence* of a "house," this rereading of scriptural texts constructs a precarious "tent" for shelter, a tent whose existence can only be spoken of at the time in the interrogative (or perhaps the subjunctive) mood—"Shall he take up his tabernacle again . . . ? Shall we, who were reckoned as the outcasts of Israel, have this honour and glory among us . . . ?" The precariousness of the structure—the ways in which its images break under the strain—is entirely appropriate to the situation;

for how can one even read these texts (other than literalistically or hyper-critically) without a "house," without an interpretive community?

Some might be inclined to take this further and say: surely the Seekers/Quakers deceived themselves; they were not "outcasts of Israel," they were simply outcasts, having abandoned the contexts that would give the specifically scriptural appellation its proper referent. I would suggest that the image of the "outcasts of Israel," if we recall its context in Isaiah 56, becomes in Howgill's text a way of gesturing towards the ambiguous position of those who find themselves both "outside" and "inside" a text and its community of readers—perhaps, then, those who most need to build tents:

> [6]And the foreigners who join themselves to the LORD,
> to minister to him, to love the name of the LORD,
> and to be his servants,
> all who keep the sabbath and do not profane it,
> and hold fast my covenant—
> [7]these I will bring to my holy mountain,
> and make them joyful in my house of prayer;
> their burnt-offerings and their sacrifices
> will be accepted on my altar;
> for my house shall be called a house of prayer
> for all peoples.
> [8]Thus says the Lord GOD,
> who gathers the outcasts of Israel:
> I will gather others to them,
> besides those already gathered.
>
> —ISAIAH 56

To speak of any *Gentile* people as the "outcasts of Israel" is also inevitably to recall that their capacity thus to speak of themselves depends on their having first been numbered among the "others . . . besides those," the "foreigners" whose gathering was by no means to be taken for granted—which was, perhaps, an overturning of expectations comparable to being caught in a net. The experience of those who became the Quakers points, in fact, to the ongoing need for Christians reading the Hebrew scriptures to recognize themselves as the outsiders who have been brought in.

We might say, further, that those who can only call themselves "outcasts of Israel" because they were and in some sense remain simply "outcasts" should for that reason have an acute and continuing awareness of the limited validity of their own houses, and of the experience of the "homeless." Perhaps they can learn to understand the "homeless" as those who may yet be gathered by God, in ways not necessarily commensurate with the modes of life or scriptural interpretation indigenous to any of the houses. An openness to this wider possibility is, it seems to me, integral from the start to the gathering of the "children of Abraham" in the tent of meeting. Abraham was, after all, himself a descendant of Noah, and hence already an inheritor, as are his children, of the enduring covenant of faithfulness God makes with *every* living thing.[6]

We do not, however, have to expect the whole work of "gathering" to happen at once; and both Howgill's account and the experience of Scriptural Reasoning can teach us something about waiting.

STANDING AND WAITING

The first response to "ingathering," to entry together with others into a space wherein the inception of God's reign is experienced, is, in Howgill's account, a curious one. The first response is to wait. What is given to the newly gathered people is "a place to stand in, and what to wait in." One might ask, what is the point of waiting if one is in already in the space associated with fulfilment?

If all that were given here were a "place to stand in," it might seem that the newly gathered community was simply setting itself in a bounded space apart from the complexities of the social world. It might look as if the community was being gathered *away from* the world and out of time, to a secure standpoint where no further exchange with others—perhaps no further reading—is necessary.

But the "place to stand in" is also a place "to wait in"—a place where people can await a future that was not previously possible. The community that is gathered is a community that waits. The Quaker practice of worship that draws on this text and the experience it describes is often

6. I discuss this further in chapter 17.

described as "silent," but is better understood as "unprogrammed." A Quaker meeting is framed and undertaken as "waiting upon God."[7]

This is what I recognize in the practice of Scriptural Reasoning. What happens in the "tent" of Scriptural Reasoning is, at its best, a practice of disciplined waiting upon God. I say "disciplined" to indicate that the kind of openness to the new that emerges from Scriptural Reasoning is not the same as the "openness to the new" forced upon those who have been unable to construct or find even a temporary home—even if they call upon God in their homelessness. It has a given shape and direction, a relation to an evolving set of shared rules, practices, and relationships. Both Quaker and Scriptural Reasoning's "waiting upon God" are the engagement of the whole person in learned and taught practices that align the person to God's future-directed involvement with the world, and to the world's corresponding transformation. In Quakerism, the ongoing practice of and reflection on historic "testimonies"—for example, nonviolence/pacifism/peace activism—is a part of this disciplined waiting alongside unprogrammed, silent worship.

"Waiting upon God" also, of course, recalls Abraham's hospitality in Genesis 18. Abraham *waits on* his visitors. He extends a welcome, shares what he has, and "stands by" them without (it would seem) any definite expectation of a specific outcome: "he took curds and milk and the calf that he had prepared, and set it before them; and he stood by them under the tree while they ate" (Gen 18:8). "Waiting upon God," in this text, is far from inactive. In fact, it is indistinguishable from hospitality and service to, and presence with, the neighbors and strangers whom one encounters.[8] Abraham receives his new blessing as he stands by the people he has welcomed.

Part of the waiting activity of Scriptural Reasoning—part of what it means to be gathered in the tent of meeting and to "stand by" neighbours and strangers there—is listening. Participants have to listen to their "own" scriptures, to "another's" scriptures, to other people. The various communal traditions from which the participants come have taught them, among other things, how to listen and how to wait. There are

7. This, incidentally, also applies to a meeting for the conduct of church business, which is less likely to have extended periods of silence. For more on the development and forms of Quaker worship, see Dandelion, *Liturgies of Quakerism*.

8. This recalls Dietrich Bonhoeffer's account of service to others as "penultimate" activity that "prepares the way" for the coming of Christ. See Bonhoeffer, *Ethics*, 163–64.

specific methods and techniques that Scriptural Reasoners use to discipline themselves in listening—the conversational structure of meetings, the commitment to close attention to scriptural texts over long periods, resisting the imposition of individual concerns on the group as a whole.

In this, Scriptural Reasoning perhaps recalls the academy—at least in the academic disciplines with which the participants in Scriptural Reasoning tend to have most to do—to its own best possibilities. Having called for "many voices" to be given speech, academic communities can fail to take seriously the difficulties of *listening*. It is surprisingly difficult—for academic Scriptural Reasoners, as well—to pay genuine attention to a multitude of voices.

Scriptural Reasoners can and should pay close attention to the various voices that speak, or even that fail to speak, in the scriptural texts we read. As we do so, I suggest, we learn that God is encountered in this text as a listener as well as a speaker—a listener, in particular, to what is barely speakable within the conversations currently being conducted: "And Sarah was listening at the tent entrance behind him. . . . Sarah laughed to herself, saying 'After I have grown old, and my husband is old, shall I have pleasure?' The Lord said to Abraham, 'Why did Sarah laugh . . . ?' But Sarah denied, saying 'I did not laugh'; for she was afraid. He said 'Oh yes, you did laugh'" (Gen 18:10, 12–13, 15). The position of Sarah within this text of hospitality deserves closer consideration from all the Scriptural Reasoning participants; she is both central to the text (the only one *within* the tent, and the focus of the divine promise) and most marginal to it (the listener at the edge of a conversation). When she laughs, the terms of the conversation are called into question; and when her laugh is *heard*, this calling into question is acknowledged together with the subjectivity of the one who has hitherto been only an object to be spoken about.

Whether the way in which Sarah's laugh is heard reassimilates her into the single narrative controlled by an authoritative voice, or whether it rather refuses to do so (by refusing to let her *deny* her laugh) is not an insignificant matter for Scriptural Reasoners. It points us back to all the inevitable acts of exclusion by which group identities are formed. Scriptural Reasoners talk *about* (for example) secularists, literalists, people of non-Abrahamic faiths. Quite often, as the biblical texts appear to allow them to do, Scriptural Reasoners end up talking *about* women—while identifying themselves with the men who dream visions of God, hold theological conversations, entertain strangers, and so forth.[9] So what does it mean for readers of scripture to be able to hear the laughs of others—not the cries of pain (of victims, objects of our pity), nor yet the words (which might render them fully commensurate with our dialogues), but the assertions of subjectivities and desires that simply do not fit into this particular conversation?

These questions have particular resonances in the Quaker meeting house, which (in Britain at least) is a space in the borderlands of Christianity. The people in the "house" from which I come position themselves in many different ways in relation to Christianity, Christian traditions, and the texts of Christian scriptures. I cannot responsibly ignore, co-opt, patronize, or condemn the laughter of people who are not going to sit and read with me. If nothing else, remembering this ought to teach Scriptural Reasoners something about the limits of their own importance.

9. On the double reading that this demands of *female* readers, see Schweickart, "Reading Ourselves."

14 Prophecy Heard and Unheard

A Christian Reads the Qur'an

[258]Have you not heard of that [king] who argued with Abraham about his Sustainer, [simply] because God had granted him kingship? Lo! Abraham said: "My Lord is He who grants life and deals death." [The king] replied: "I [too] grant life and deal death!" Said Abraham, "Verily, God causes the sun to rise in the east; cause it, then, to rise in the West!" Thereupon he who was bent on denying the truth remained dumbfounded: for God does not guide people who [deliberately] do wrong.

—QUR'AN 2

MUCH OF THE DESCRIPTION of Scriptural Reasoning offered so far in this book has focused on what happens when a participant from a particular tradition reads texts from her own tradition with the help of her fellow Scriptural Reasoners. Yet participants actually spend much of their time reading texts from the traditions of others. This chapter provides the results of just such a reading: a Christian theologian reading a Qur'anic text.

FIRST PASS

Reading this text in the company of Muslim (and Jewish) readers, I found myself asking, what (according to this text) is it to be a prophet, and what is it to hear prophecy? In this passage, Abraham most straightforwardly shows himself a prophet when, in response to questioning, he proclaims two truths about his Sustainer: that the Lord has power over life and death, and that the Lord is the one who makes the sun rise in the East. Yet this prophecy is not, apparently, heard. The king is not moved to acknowledgment of these truths, and to the praise that should take hold of his tongue as he contemplates them, but instead remains silent. Prophecy is, in this first pass, the giving of glad tidings, and to hear prophecy is to acknowledge those tidings as true.

SECOND PASS

Abraham's speech does not, however, simply deliver revealed information. His speech is, rather, prophecy as *performance*: it works on the king so as to bring him to a recognition of the true limitations of his kingship. And in this perspective, it is not so clear that the prophecy goes unheard. The king's silence suggests that even if he has not been moved to acknowledgment of the source of his kingship, his pride *has* been interrupted.

Abraham begins by declaring that his Lord is he who grants life and deals death. That claim, as it stands, is vague: it does not tell us what kind of power the Lord has, nor how it is exercised. As a delivery of information, it is incomplete. Yet by saying, "I too grant life and deal death," the king provides a specifying interpretation. Whether his claim is that he has this power *as well* as God or that he has it *instead* of God, he reads Abraham's message as claiming a power for God that is of fundamentally the same kind as the power that a human king might have. He reads Abraham's prophecy to be a declaration, perhaps, that God has the power to make specific interventions that break the order of things, just as the king can execute those who would otherwise live and can pardon those who would otherwise properly die. The king's claim is therefore not simply a claim about his usurpation of or independence of God's power, but more deeply a claim about the *nature* of God's power: that it is despotic. The king is claiming that he and God are in competition over the slices of the world's pie.

Abraham does not answer this claim directly, by addressing the nature, scope, or efficacy of God's power of life and death. It is Razi[1] who finds in this exchange between Abraham and the king a debate about pri-

1. Al-Razi, *Mafatih al-Ghayb*.

mary and secondary causality, and not the Qur'anic ayah itself. Indeed, Abraham appears at first to accept the terms that the king has established (the king's specification of Abraham's vagueness) and to raise the stakes within that game well beyond the king's ability to pay. The sun, Abraham says, rises in the East at God's command—can the king command such power? Of course not. The king is reduced to silence because he cannot exceed or even match God's bid. Game over.

In this second pass, the prophet is one who calls a sinner's attention to his presumption, and confronts him with a vision of God's immeasurable power. The hearer is one who learns the weakness of all his claims to strength and turns away from any hope of vying with God.

THIRD PASS

If this interpretation were complete, however, it would leave us with an uncomfortable conclusion. To declare a victory on these terms alone is to leave standing the king's contestation of God's power of life and death. It leaves that earlier claim as territory that Abraham has ceded in order to face the king on the larger battlefield, where more of God's force can be brought into play.

Three hints in the text suggest the inadequacy of this view, and push us toward a deeper interpretation. In the first place, God is referred to as "sustainer." In the second place, we are told that God is the one who had granted the king his kingship. The king's rule, his exercise of power, is only possible because he has been given that power by God, so that there is an ineradicable asymmetry between God and the king. And once we have spotted these two textual hints, we might note that they find a third echo in the narrative itself. After all, the arena in which the king is defeated is not simply one in which his despotic power is insufficient, it is one in which that kind of power is irrelevant. The king is shown that he has no power fundamentally to disorder the proper order of things, no power over the context in which his action is possible: the cosmos.

The king is not simply shown that God is stronger than he is. Rather, he is shown that his own strength comes from God, and that God's strength is not of the same order as his. The king's power and God's power cannot be understood if they are regarded as standing in competition. The king's strength can only be a following after, a working with what has been given—and God's strength does not have the character of power wielded against the world, but is the power that sustains and establishes the world. God's power over life and death is his power to allot the span and the limits within which human action is possible.

The silence of the king is, in this interpretation, ambivalent. It indicates, certainly, that he acknowledges defeat—but it does not tell us that he has understood the implications of that defeat. That the king does not turn to penitence and praise rather suggests that he has not truly heard the prophecy.

In this third pass, the prophet is one who points to God not as rival power, but as the source and sustainer of all things, or as the context in which all live and move and have their being. And the hearer of prophecy is one who learns to live his life as gift, in a world itself understood as gift.

FOURTH PASS

There is one more step that I think I can take—in the direction of a possibility left open by the text's recognition that God is specifically *Abraham's* Sustainer, and that Abraham is a prophet. That is, Abraham is not, here, someone who is simply allotted an ordered space in which to act. He is, rather, one who is given the words of God to speak—and (recognizing that his prophecy is not simply the delivery of information, but a performance) he is one whose life is conformed to the words that he is given to speak. The activity to which he is called is the appropriate performance of the words that he has been given.

What if the king's failure is not simply that he has not recognized the limits of his power, derived from the fact that this power is delegated to him by God—but that he has missed the fact that the power that he has been given as king is, broadly speaking, only and always the *power to prophesy*? That is, what if the king's power is not power to do as he will within limits set by God, but only and always power to hear and to embody the prophetic word of God?

The ayah finishes, after all, with the claim that "he who was bent on denying the truth remained dumbfounded, for God does not guide people who deliberately do wrong." The king has turned away from God's guidance, from living according to God's word; he remains dumbfounded not simply because he has lost an argument, but because he has been cut off from the true sources of his action. By turning away from the truth, the prophetic word, he has left himself with nothing to say: he has rendered himself incapable of prophecy.

Read in this way, the ayah teaches us the character of right action, guided action, in general. In the words of the Hebrew Bible, "Would that all the Lord's people were prophets!" To prophesy and to be a true hearer of prophecy are the same thing: to hear the word of God and to recognize that one is called to embody it, to become a communication of it to others.

CODA

Am I, a Christian theologian reading this ayah, one who hears this prophecy? In one sense, yes: reflecting on this text with the help of a Scriptural Reasoning group has sent me back to my own scriptures with insights that might prove illuminating. I am sent back to Genesis 3 with the recognition that the temptation to "be as God" is as much a misrecognition of the nature of God as it is a misrecognition of the nature of humanity. I am sent back to 1 Samuel 8 with new ideas about what is wrong with a "king like the kings of the Gentiles." I am sent back to 1 Samuel 10:9–12 to ask what it means for Saul also to be amongst the prophets. I am sent back to Numbers 11:29 with new ideas about what it might mean for all the Lord's people to be prophets. And I am sent back to 1 Corinthians 14 to see in a new light Paul's hope that all may prophesy. And I am sent back with a vision of the relationship between divine word and human action that asks to be traced through many texts from both Hebrew Bible and New Testament. Of course, I am sent back with more questions than answers—asking, for instance, what the prophecy-as-ecstasy of Numbers and 1 Samuel has to do with the Qur'an's prophecy-as-truth-telling (does the former perhaps *display* the dependence of one's agency upon God's that is *declared* in the latter?)—but I am certainly sent back to see differently, and perhaps more deeply, what is in my own scriptures.

In another sense, however, I am not a hearer of this prophecy. In addressing me, this prophecy comes to someone whose life is being shaped by other sources, other texts, and who can only hear the Qur'anic word as prophetic to the extent that it is confirmed and received by those other texts—my own scriptures. I remain, therefore, one who questions this Qur'anic Abraham about his Sustainer. I am not one who submits. Am I therefore one whom this God does not guide? After all, the combined definition of prophecy and of the hearing of prophecy with which I finished my fourth pass through the text had a degree of vagueness that I do not think the Qur'an as a whole will let me keep. The prophet and the true hearer of prophecy are not simply those who hear the "word of God"—they are those who hear and understand the *Qur'an*, and who recognize that they are called to embody it, to become a recitation of it to others. Whilst I might learn from this passage, and whilst I might hope to help my Muslim friends to understand this passage more deeply (just as they provoke me to deeper engagement with my own scriptures), the conversation in which we are engaged in no way involves the erasure of that difference between us.

15 Reading Within and Between Traditions I

It Takes At Least Two to Reproduce

[26]Then God said, "Let us make humankind in our image, according to our likeness. . . ." [27]So God created humankind in his image, in the image of God he created him; male and female he created them. [28]God blessed them, and God said to them, "Be fruitful and multiply . . ."

—Genesis 1

[1]Now the man knew his wife Eve, and she conceived and bore Cain, saying "I hav produced a man with the help of the LORD." [2]Next she bore his brother Abel.

—Genesis 4

[3]When Adam had lived for one hundred and thirty years, he became the father of a son in his likeness, according to his image, and named him Seth.

—Genesis 5

[23]Jesus was about thirty years old when he began his work. [24]He was the son (as was thought) of Joseph, son of Heli, son of Matthat . . . [38]son of Enos, son of Seth, son of Adam, son of God.

—Luke 3

All the chapters in this section so far have relied, more or less explicitly, on the idea that participants in Scriptural Reasoning belong to religious traditions. In this chapter and the next, the description we have been providing of Scriptural Reasoning is given a final layer of complication as we interrogate the notion of "tradition"—the notion of a settlement passed on (and worked on) from one generation to another, with all the metaphors that cluster around it: metaphors of reproduction, of paternity, of inheritance and legitimacy.

In 1991, the first occasion on which public attention in the UK was directed to the provision of artificial insemination to a woman without a male partner, a storm of controversy was provoked.[1] Feminist questions about female autonomy and the status of the "nuclear family" intersected with public understandings and misunderstandings of a developing reproductive technology, clearly framed (in the popular press) with a religious discourse that pointed to one or more accounts of divine agency in human production and reproduction. A woman threatened to produce a child without a paternal genealogy; or a scientist threatened to "play God" by changing the terms on which humanity could be fruitful and multiply; or wider society threatened to interfere with a parent's exclusive power to choose, name, and form a child. On any reading, what was at stake was (whether this was acknowledged or not) more than a single instance of the (re)production of a human being; it was the ways in which a society could (re)produce itself, understand its future, and form relationships of responsibility that would sustain it.

Theology has, it is clear, a major investment in the question of what modes of human reproduction are possible (not to mention desirable or normative). So, since its inception, does feminist thought; so do conspicuous contemporary discourses of ethics and politics, particularly in relation to new reproductive technologies. This chapter is concerned with how the thinking of modes of reproduction plays out in theology and ethics, and how feminist theologians can or should approach discourses of reproduction.

Jewish and Christian feminist theologians have concerned themselves extensively with the politics both of human reproduction and of its cultural representation. They have had particular reason to do so, not only because of the biblical, halakhic, and doctrinal significance accorded to reproduction (in its various modes), but also because of the ways

1. On which see Lawler, *Mothering the Self*, 150–52.

in which narratives of reproduction determine their problematic places as theologizing subjects. Christian feminist theologians are trained in *patristics*, and may seek to counter the influence of the *church fathers* by a search for their own *foremothers*; they might (as might their Jewish counterparts) define themselves as *dissident daughters*[2] or wonder what the *next generation* of theological thinkers will produce. Even when the language of reproduction, descent, parenthood, and childhood is not explicitly used, feminist thinkers have discerned the power of underlying structural assumptions about how "reproduction" works to shape how theology relates its past to its future. In particular, they have noted how dominant accounts of reproduction maintain the authorizing power of a male tradition.

There is a widespread, and not entirely unjustified, sense within wider feminist thought that Judaism and Christianity, as monotheistic faiths, are heavily invested in a monogenetic account of cultural reproduction.[3] Monogenesis is the belief that the activity of only one parent, namely the father, is crucial in the production of a child, with the mother functioning merely as the receptacle for the active or formative principle originating from the father—the father who thereby acquires *a son in his likeness, according to his image*.

In descriptions of human sexual reproduction, "monogenetic" belief might be signaled by imagery such as the sowing of seed in a field, or by biological accounts (Aristotelian or otherwise) depicting the sperm as giving "form" to the "matter" present in the female body. Even with accounts of sexual reproduction that admit the formative contribution of both parents, however, as feminist commentators have pointed out,[4] "monogenetic" patterns of thinking can persist at other levels. Male genealogies can be prioritized, so that children are members of their father's family, inheritors of their father's name and property, symbolic maintainers of his image. Cultural or intellectual history can be traced as the orderly and in some way inevitable succession of lines of "great men" whose heirs "we" are. And religious texts, biblical and traditional, can

2. The title of a collection of feminist liturgies edited by Teresa Berger.

3. For two feminist accounts of monogenesis and its relation to monotheism, from different disciplinary contexts, see Buell, *Making Christians*, and Delaney, "Meaning of Paternity."

4 Even at levels very close to the "scientific"; see Shildrick, *Leaky Bodies and Boundaries*, on the persistence in medical and popular literature of images of the maternal body that treat it as passive receptacle of the male seed.

trace this succession all the way back to the divine Father, who needs no other in order to beget his own image perfectly: *son of Joseph, son of Heli, son of Matthat . . . son of Seth, son of Adam, son of God.*

I want to acknowledge the strength of monogenetic thinking within theological accounts of tradition and practices of traditioning—theological relations to the past—and also within at least some theological accounts of relations to the future. At the same time, I want to follow a little way, in feminist and theological thought, the clues to another perspective given in the biblical texts I quoted at the beginning of this article. Adam might be said to have begotten *a son in his likeness, according to his image*, and with, apparently, no necessary reference to Eve as subject of reproductive work; but Eve had previously claimed to *have produced a man with the help of the LORD*, in the context of sexual relations with "the man," and in the aftermath of the command to male and female humanity to *be fruitful and multiply*. And then, of course, Jesus was only *supposed* to be the son of Joseph, the son of Heli, and so forth—Luke's text having previously, at the very least, opened the possibility that he was no such thing.[5]

So these texts do, I suggest, give the basis for a monogenetic account of reproduction to support a "master narrative"; but they also subvert that "master narrative" by an account of the appearance of human beings, and of the image of God, through *production from difference*. It is this second possibility that I want to trace here, because I believe it offers a way out of some dilemmas in thinking about (re)production that affect both feminist and theological thought.

THE MOTHER IN FEMINISM AND THEOLOGY

There is now a large body of feminist literature, from a very wide range of academic disciplines, about the denial or obscuring of the mother in accounts of human reproduction that in any way go beyond the family and the origins of the individual. So, for example, feminist sociologists observe the very long section in Marx's *Economic and Political Manuscripts* on

5. Delaney, "Meaning of Paternity," assumes that virgin birth and *paternal* monogenesis are closely linked—but this seems *prima facie* illogical. Rather more logical, in fact, is Sojourner Truth's approach: "Where did your Christ come from? From God and a woman! Man had nothing to do with him . . ." (Sojourner Truth, "Ain't I a Woman?," a speech to the 1851 Women's Convention in Akron, Ohio, as recalled by Frances Dana Gage in the *National Anti-Slavery Standard*).

"man's giving birth to himself." Feminist ethicists observe that significant strands in ethical theory (including some earlier feminist ethical theory, particularly that working within the traditions of political liberalism) assumes that everybody worthy of consideration is a fully rational adult, and shows relatively little interest in how they got to that point. Feminist scholars of patristics observe not only that the "church fathers" construct themselves as a monogenetic intellectual tradition, but also that their later commentators accept and reinforce this construction. Luce Irigaray is among those whose theoretical work draws together these various strands of critique, portraying the repeated *sacrifice* of women, and more specifically mothers, for the sake of the paternal genealogies that shape the West's master narratives.

In this context of feminist critique it is sometimes claimed, by feminist and non-feminist theologians, that religious traditions have the symbolic and textual resources to revalue maternal work and interrupt the monogenetic telling of human reproductive history. Theological reflection throughout the ages has not, of course, entirely ignored the fact that it takes two to reproduce. There has been ample feminist theological analysis of the extent to which, explicitly or implicitly, the question of the meaning of sexual difference has in the past been reduced to the question of the meaning of *woman*, and resolved to a greater or lesser extent in terms of reproductive capacity.[6] More recently, this thought on the fundamental significance of sexual difference for human being has been taken up alongside phenomenological accounts of "mothering" or of sexuality. The biblical "fruitfulness" of the male/female pair, and the valorization of mothers and the maternal within theological tradition, is seen as a significant counterbalance to masculinist accounts of the history of social and cultural reproduction.

As is well known, however, this approach has its own associated problems. "The fruitfulness of the male/female pair"—the claim that it takes *two* to reproduce—suggests a model of sexual complementarity that, literally and figuratively, domesticates sexual difference. The couple, or the family, may be internally differentiated but, as regards the wider social, political, or cultural context—as regards, then, the operation of many of

6 As, famously, in Aquinas' discussion in the *Summa Theologiae* (1a.92, 1) of why *another man* was not created as the "helpmate" for Adam: "It was absolutely necessary to make woman, for the reason scripture mentions, as a help for man; not indeed to help him in any other work, as some have maintained, because where most work is concerned man can get help more conveniently from another man than from a woman; but to help him in the work of procreation."

the powerful master narratives—it is for all intents and purposes a single and stable reproductive unit. Eve can, as it were, be recognized for her role as *the mother of all living*, but she can then be restricted to a sphere in which she does not affect the masculine story of the transmission of the image.

Importantly for our purposes, the male/female pair, and/or the parent with the child, has often been used theologically in discussions of what it means for humanity to bear the *image of God*.[7] For such readings, it is not merely that each human being can individually be called the "image of God"—it is that the relationships between human beings, including relationships of reproduction, are in some way constitutive of their imaging of God. Readings of the Genesis 1 and 3 texts can indeed scarcely avoid at least asking about the relationship between the image of God, the creation of humanity as male and female, and the instruction to be fruitful and multiply. The production/reproduction of human beings, linked in these texts to the image of God, already acquires a significance beyond the biological; the texts and the tradition set up a nexus within which images and concepts of human production and reproduction acquire great symbolic force. In what follows, I want to suggest a rereading of the theological-anthropological significance of "reproduction," which has as its correlate a different understanding of how the image of God is produced and reproduced in human life.

IMAGE OF GOD MALE AND FEMALE

There is a tension here between two well-established readings of the Genesis texts on the *image of God*, which goes to the heart of debates on how human (re)production is to be understood theologically. One reading locates the image of God in *male and female* existence, so that human orientation to transcendence is located primarily in ethical/erotic encounter with the other. The other locates the image of God, or human orientation to transcendence, in the capacity and summons to *be fruitful and multiply*, to produce and reproduce the human image that is also the image of God ("Adam . . . became the father of a son in his likeness, according to his image").[8] The former encourages accounts of sexual difference that pri-

7. For humanity, *male and female*, as "image of God" see (perhaps most influentially) Barth, *Church Dogmatics*, III/1:186–91.

8. See, for discussions of both of these alternatives, Kepnes, "Adam/Eve," and Richardson, "*Imago Dei*."

oritize the difference itself over any "productivity" that might arise from it; the latter, accounts that begin with "fruitfulness" as a characteristic of human being as a whole.

The tension between these two accounts of the human imaging of God has its feminist counterpart in debates over the significance that should be accorded to the maternal body and maternal "experience" in feminist politics. It is also the subject of several theological attempts at reconciliation—which, particularly when written from a male perspective, can find the double emphasis on difference and reproduction perfectly reflected in the double function of woman as wife and mother.[9] It is such conservative theological "reconciliations"—which end up *denying* woman's imaging of God by reducing her to a function of male self-transcendence—that lead me to hypothesize that feminist thought needs a different way out of the discussion, one that will prove theologically significant. Hence the title of this essay: it takes *at least* two to reproduce.

My hypothesis is that if non-eradicable, non-assimilable difference—discussed here in terms of sexual difference—is integral to human being in the image of God, it is also integral to the production and reproduction of the image of God, and *not* in a way that reduces to different functions within a single reproductive process, because that would amount to the *erasure* of significant difference. If breaking out of monogenetic thinking is possible when we are talking about gender and sexual reproduction, it might be possible to do so in wider theological, ethical, and political contexts.

I see the need for a view of cultural and social (re)production that would draw attention to the ways in which "products" themselves—not only persons, but also group identities and the narratives that shape them, religious and political systems and the artefacts that define them—carry with them traces of their differentiated and conflicted origins. In theological terms, this means seeing the image of God, even within the self—and certainly within the community that claims to image God—as appearing in and through the encounter with given and non-assimilable difference over time.[10] Being made "male and female" in the image of God is, on this reading, being made for a project of responsible encounter with, living with, and production of, different human being. This project is still

9. Katz, *Levinas, Judaism and the Feminine*, discusses the double significance of "the feminine" in Levinas's work in these terms. In Christian theology, Hans Urs von Balthasar's account (*Dramatis Personae*, §3) of the duality of "woman" is famous or notorious.

10. I am grateful to Susannah Ticciati for conversations about this idea.

one of production and reproduction, because the human future emerges from it; but the human future thus produced and reproduced is not simply the perpetuation of what is already given. It is a project that cannot be confined to the private or interpersonal sphere in the interests of human (national, cultural, religious) unity on another level; and it is also a project that cannot be short-circuited by declaring a return to some original state of harmony.[11]

Why talk about "at least two" in this context? The language and logic of *at least* is introduced by Irigaray and taken up (most significantly) by Elizabeth Grosz in work on the ethical and political significance of sexual difference. It is helpful in indicating, in the first instance, why an insistence on sexual specificity—talk about "female" bodily morphology, experiences, ethics, and so forth—need not lead to the kind of essentialism that closes off further sexually specific differentiation—differences among women, instabilities in the category "woman," perhaps most importantly a multiplicity in the woman's own self. Once there are *at least* two, in Irigaray's logic, there can be *more than* two; so the pair does not become a closed pair that can operate as a single unit for the purposes of sustaining a larger narrative of monogenetic production. An Irigarayan reading of Genesis 1:26–28, for example, might say that the image of God lies in the capacity of sexually differentiated humanity not only to "be fruitful" but to "multiply" through their fruitfulness, producing further differences that are not reincorporated into a single system.

I suggest that feminist and theological accounts of (re)production, and readings of narratives of (re)production, need to maintain an emphasis on "at least two"—and that readings of biblical texts on reproduction can help them do this. In the first place, the language of "at least two" can be introduced to call into question histories of how "we" (or anyone else) came to be where we are that project unitary and non-conflictual—monogenetic—lines of inheritance and succession.

Against readings of scriptures and traditions that emphasize the single narrative, a feminist hermeneutic of suspicion based on the insight that it takes *at least* two will direct attention both to aspects of the conditions of textual production and to characters within the narrative that have been

11. There is good theological sense here in the feminist riposte to Gal 3:28: "It may be the case that *in Christ* there is neither male nor female, but it is not true anywhere else." Read slightly against the grain, it prompts the recognition—already suggested in reading Genesis—that visions of unity achieved by ignoring, suppressing, or denying non-assimilable human difference are precisely *not* visions of the perfected *image of God*.

"sacrificed" to maintain the fiction of an undifferentiated past. The feminist theological reader can follow the signs in a text towards complexities in (re)productive agency—"the son, as was supposed, of Joseph," "I have produced a man with the help of the Lord"—as a way of drawing attention both to the suppressed complexities of present identity and the unrealized possibilities of the past that may still have a future.

REPETITION OF THE IMAGE

But what do we make, in this context, of the strong presence within this same tradition of what looks like a "monogenetic" pattern—*Adam . . . became the father of a son in his likeness, according to his image*? Here I want to suggest, more tentatively, that the logic of "at least two" can usefully be supplemented by attention to the logic of repetition. Paradoxically, the idea that the child is the exact likeness, the repetition, of the father, although at first it sounds like monogenesis, can already set up an instability within the line of transmission. True repetition, as opposed to similarity or conforming to a pattern, we have been reminded in many philosophical contexts, in fact implies the possibility of the new, the unique and the singular.[12] It calls into question chains of causes and effects, and narratives of progress—in which nothing can really *come back*, because each person or event only "fits" one place in the pattern. A narrative of historical progress tends to require a monogenetic logic, in which each event or person has an obvious predecessor and an equally obvious true successor, and whatever does not fit within this narrative cannot be taken into account. Repetitions, by contrast, open up the possibility of unconnected or non-systemized occurrences. Once there is a repetition, there are "at least two"; there are two in a way that necessarily makes room for more than two, and that makes apparent a context that transcends the two.

So there is a second way to read the plural production of *ʾadam* in the *image of God* as the basis of continuing responsibility for and to difference—*ʾadam* repeats, so *ʾadam* is each time singular. Hence, on this reading, sexual difference is not to be read simply in terms of two sets of characteristics that can be co-ordinated to each other (and that hence

12. The key discussion of "repetition" for recent philosophy is of course in the work of Deleuze; see his *Difference and Repetition*.

form a system that excludes any third, or different, possibility).[13] Hence, also, experiencing and living "common humanity" is perhaps not a matter of recognizing similarity—what fits the pattern, what is expected, another example of the "same sort of thing"—but of encountering otherness that cannot easily be kept away by assigning it a place in one's system of thought.

COMMUNITIES AND REPRODUCTIONS

How does any of this change feminist theological approaches to ethics and politics? In the context of feminist thought about reproduction, the most common challenge to individualistic ethics is the ethic of care, based on the primacy of particular relations of dependence and interdependence. Clearly relationships of care—maternal work and maternal thinking, the dependence of people on one another, and so forth—have ethical importance. In fact, all I have said about difference and its (re)production implies that ethics, including theological ethics, needs to have much to say about the ongoing work of production/reproduction—the "mothering" that monogenetic narratives take for granted, the multiple material and social prerequisites of the emergence of any new identity.

My concern, however, is about what happens when we extend a particularist "ethics of care" to an ethical and theological framework that starts from and prioritizes the existence of particular—perhaps family-like—communities with shared narratives of origin and defining characteristics. Again, the point is not to evade the claim that there is no view from nowhere and that the sovereign ethical "subject" is an abstraction. It is, rather, to problematize the "subject" of ethics still further, by drawing attention to the differentiation within the community identity that supposedly grounds his or her discourse. It is to refuse to treat the family, the locality, or even the religious community as a "black box" out of which the sovereign reasoning subject springs fully formed (as in the models of culture condemned by Irigaray, discussed earlier)—but also to refuse to treat it as a single harmonious whole that relates to "the other" as something *external* to its communal identity. A family or a group that knows

13. One of the significant moves made in Elizabeth Grosz's work (see above) is her placing of Deleuze alongside Irigaray to counter the former's neglect of (specifically) sexual difference and the latter's risks of essentialism. See for example Grosz, "Feminist Futures." One of the possibilities she does not explore is Irigaray's use of the "sensible transcendental" as a way of complicating Deleuze's rejection of "transcendence."

that "it takes at least two" to reproduce and is constituted *as* a project in living with difference is formed from the beginning for openness to the other.

And that brings us, once again, to Scriptural Reasoning. One of the significant correlations I see between the inter-faith work of Scriptural Reasoning, on the one hand, and feminist theological thought, on the other, is that both problematize for ethical and theological reasons the concept of the group representative (with its implication that the voices of a community can be summarized without remainder in the voice of one of its—properly selected—members, and that therefore internal difference or conflict must be resolved or suppressed before the exercise of dialogue can begin). Both feminist theologians and Scriptural Reasoners recognize that to reveal the life of a community—the way in which the image of God dwells within it—is to reveal its multiple origins, its present differences, and the many possible futures that are taking shape out of those differences. The inter-faith work conducted in Scriptural Reasoning is at the same time work that affects "Jewish," "Christian," and "Muslim" identities.

There is scope here, then, for a significant feminist contribution to the theorizing of a range of issues around traditions and their perpetuation, "intercultural" and "inter-faith" exchange and its possibilities—and none of this in abstraction from the material and social conditions of such (re)productive processes.

16 Reading Within and Between Traditions II

Tradition, Invention, Recognition

THIS CHAPTER WILL DISCUSS many of the same themes as the last, but in a somewhat different idiom, prompted by engagement with a different set of texts. I found myself forced to re-examine questions about the legitimate and illegitimate reproduction of a tradition when reading through the first chapter of Mark. At several points in that first chapter, the reader is faced with an interplay or tension between continuity and discontinuity, faithfulness and innovation. Working through the passages ruminatively and playfully,[1] I realized that I lacked a good language for describing what I was reading—specifically, I realized that the assumption of a simple opposition between discontinuity and continuity or between faithfulness and innovation was making it hard to speak coherently about the dynamics of Mark's story.

In what follows, I first highlight some of the passages that drove me to pose the question, and then (in a series of aphorisms) present the attempt to rethink the nature of tradition and faithfulness to which I was driven.[2] At the end I return to Scriptural Reasoning, to ask what might

1. My rambling explorations of these texts can be found at the blog *Kai euthus* in irregular entries from April 2005 to September 2007.

2. The connection between the exegetical and the aphoristic sections of the chapter might seem tenuous, at times—but that is not because they have been arbitrarily stitched together for the purposes of presentation. Those with a high enough boredom threshold to read through the blog entries cited in the previous note can watch the aphoristic reflections on tradition emerging as a detour in my journey to make sense of Mark 1.

happen to the attempt to describe it as a dialogue between traditions if my aphorisms are taken seriously.

BEGINNING IN THE MIDDLE

Mark

[1:1]The beginning of the good news of Jesus Christ, the Son of God. [2]As it is written in the prophet Isaiah . . .

Mark's Gospel begins with a gesture of discontinuity, a brushing away of the past: *archē*, "the beginning." And yet in the very next sentence it takes that fresh start away: *kathōs gegraptai*, "as it is written."[3] Mark makes a fresh beginning on an avowedly new text, and then as his first step acknowledges that he is following a traditional script. What kind of faithfulness is involved in this "beginning"?

The Disciples

[1:16]As Jesus passed along the Sea of Galilee, he saw Simon and his brother Andrew casting a net into the sea—for they were fishermen. [17]And Jesus said to them, "Follow me, and I will make you fish for people." [18]And immediately, they left their nets and followed him. [19]As he went a little farther, he saw James son of Zebedee and his brother John, who were in their boat mending the nets. [20]Immediately he called them; and they left their father Zebedee in the boat with the hired men, and followed him.

The call of Simon and Andrew and the call of James and John both begin with *seeing*: not with the disciples' seeing (these are not stories of their insight, nor of a light that suddenly dawns for them), but with the four fishermen being seen by Jesus. Having been seen, they are called—but the two call narratives are subtly different. Simon and Andrew are called to a strange fulfillment of what Jesus has seen that they already are. They *are* fishermen, and besides their names and their current activity, that is all that the text tells us about their identity; Jesus calls them to *become*

3. For my purposes, it does not matter whether this is how Mark has always begun, or whether it is a result of some process of mutilation. See, for example, Croy, *Mutilation of Mark's Gospel*.

fishermen. This calling is certainly to a process where Jesus is a maker ("I will make you fish for people"), but that making is not simply an imposition, a creation *ex nihilo*. Jesus works with what lies ready to hand.

James and John, on the other hand, are called to the abandonment of what Jesus has seen them to be. They leave their nets in the boat, and they leave their father, and in this leaving they abandon the only markers we have been given of their identities: they are, after all, simply the net-mending sons of Zebedee. What Jesus will make of them he will make by calling them *away* from what he has seen.

In other words, if we ask what discipleship will involve for these four men, there's an ambivalence between continuity and discontinuity—an ambivalence about whether the following to which they are called is a wholly new beginning, or a rereading of what they already are. And it is worth noting that the relationship between the future to which they are beckoned and the past from which they are called is not in these narratives presented as a relationship between sin and salvation; their response to Jesus' call is not in any direct way presented as a matter of repentance. We are simply presented with Simon, Andrew, James, and John as people with existing names, existing occupations, existing family relations, existing economic roles—as people with an existing place and identity, an existing pattern of life. And we are presented with the bare question, what does the call they hear from Jesus do with that existing pattern?

Jesus

[1:21]They went to Capernaum; and when the Sabbath came, he entered the synagogue and taught. [22]They were astounded at his teaching, for he taught them as one having authority, and not as the scribes. [23]Just then there was in their synagogue a man with an unclean spirit, [24]and he cried out, "What have you to do with us, Jesus of Nazareth? Have you come to destroy us? I know who you are, the Holy One of God." [25]But Jesus rebuked him, saying, "Be silent, and come out of him!" [26]And the unclean spirit, throwing him into convulsions and crying with a loud voice, came out of him. [27]They were all amazed, and they kept on asking one another, "What is this? A new teaching—with authority! He commands even the unclean spirits, and they obey him."

Jesus teaches in a synagogue. His teaching has a specific context: in the midst of an already-formed people. Yet Mark tells us at this stage very little about the *content* of Jesus' teaching, giving us instead three substitutes: the repeated astonishment of the people, their recognition of a contrast with the scribes, and the effect of Jesus' teaching on the unclean spirit.

The third of these is most fully elaborated. On the one hand, the man with the unclean spirit marks Jesus out as dangerous, as one who will not let him alone, as he has (apparently) been let alone by what has happened before in this synagogue—and the incident as a whole marks Jesus' ministry out as an eruption of something new, so that it is when faced with this exorcism the people cry that they have heard "a *new* teaching." On the other hand, this clash gains its shape from the contrast of uncleanness and holiness, so that its content (the only real content that this passage gives to Jesus' teaching) is provided by a key code in the structure of identity that the synagogue upholds. Similarly, the recognition that Jesus' teaching is *authoritative* is voiced by the synagogue: it is an authority that they, formed by their synagogue's tradition, recognize.

Is this teacher an upholder of the traditional order, a faithful son of the synagogue—or is he "new"?

John the Baptist

[1:2]As it is written in the prophet Isaiah, "See, I am sending my messenger ahead of you, who will prepare your way; [3]the voice of one crying out in the wilderness: 'Prepare the way of the Lord, make his paths straight,'" [4]John the baptizer appeared in the wilderness, proclaiming a baptism of repentance for the forgiveness of sins. [5]And people from the whole Judean countryside and all the people of Jerusalem were going out to him, and were baptized by him in the river Jordan, confessing their sins. [6]Now John was clothed with camel's hair, with a leather belt around his waist, and he ate locusts and wild honey. [7]He proclaimed, "The one who is more powerful than I is coming after me; I am not worthy to stoop down and untie the thong of his sandals. [8]I have baptized you with water; but he will baptize you with the Holy Spirit."

When John the Baptist appears, he is clothed in the words of the Hebrew Bible. He is presented as a continuation, a form of faithfulness to the text—and the people go out to him because they recognize him: he makes some sense within their existing patterns of thought. But John is not simply the projection of their existing understanding: there is a specificity, an unexpectedness about him, such that he *exceeds* their current understanding of the text, making a new text of it. The desert setting, the raw food, the strange clothing, the asceticism—they seem to indicate that John stands explicitly for liminality, for a reality that stands at an angle to, or on the edges of, the present established order.

John is recognized as a prophet, a messenger of the Lord: the new reading he provides is a divinely authored reading. John is, one might say, understood by the people to be God's rereading of God's own text. He stands for, announces, or represents a call to continuity (to faithfulness, to holiness—to the tradition) that is at the same time a call to discontinuity (to repentance, to something new, to one who is coming). John announces a new beginning, in the middle. What is going on?

APHORISMS ON TRADITION AND PROPHECY

Aphorism 1: All action is the action of our past.

My attempt to think through what tradition and faithfulness mean begins with this aphorism because tradition and faithfulness are normally (and rightly) thought to have *something* to do with the indebtedness of our present action, our present pattern of life, to the past.

This first aphorism points to the fact that one always and inevitably acts in a way that is thoroughly beholden to one's past. One always and inevitably acts *from* what one has been given, what one has heard, what one has inherited. To put this in more theological terms, action is simply one form that a person's utter dependency takes. Sometimes theologians might want to talk about that dependency in terms of the power of sin, sometimes in terms of grace; sometimes in terms of constriction, sometimes in terms of liberation, sometimes (and perhaps most fundamentally) simply in terms of creatureliness—but dependency it remains.

Yet to say that James and John, Simon and Andrew cannot help but respond to Jesus *as* the people who have been formed in a particular Galilean past tells us nothing interesting, unless we can specify more closely the ways in which that past impinges on their present and future. This barely stated indebtedness of present action on the past is too general, too much a characteristic of *all* action, to be useful in picking out specifically "traditional" action, and so it tells us nothing about what "faithfulness" means. We are going to need a somewhat more sophisticated conceptual machinery to enable us to talk about tradition. So, on to . . .

Aphorism 2: Every action tells a story.

A person acts as one formed by her past, and there is nothing she can do to cease being the person who inherited a certain set of genes, who had those genes expressed in a certain environment, who was brought up in a certain way, and who had a whole stream of particular experiences. There is no way in which she can cease to act as the person who has been formed by that history, even if it should turn out to be a history that leads her into some form of disintegration or amnesia.

Yet one of the specific ways in which the person who has been so formed might act is as one who actively *construes* the past, one who tells a story about it. To say this involves shifting to a different level of description of our action from that employed in the first aphorism. It involves talking about one of the contingent forms that might be taken by the action that is, on that first level of description, always and inevitably the action of one's past.

Now, obviously there are times when one tells such a story about the past quite explicitly. I put up the Christmas tree on Christmas Eve because that's when we've *always* done it, and I've been brought up to recognize as barbarians those who put it up any earlier. I tell my children this, explaining our present action by telling some kind of story about the past.

Such story telling can also be implicit, however. This morning, I went with colleagues from the Department of Theology to the common room in our building for a cup of coffee. That action made sense to me, and perhaps a certain amount of sense to those around me, because of a mostly unconscious set of stories we tell about what this department is, about how we do things here, about the background against which we do them. *Sotto voce*, that action was telling or reinforcing a story not all that different in form to the story I tell my children about the proper timing of Christmas tree installation.

One can imagine a Simon or an Andrew, not simply acting as those who have been formed by a particular history, but acting as those who have learnt to *see themselves* as men who have been called, and who have responded to that call. Their subsequent actions indicate the nature of the narrative they were telling about themselves. Or when, in Mark 10, James and John ask to sit on Jesus' right and left hands in his glory, their action clearly proclaims the kind of construal they are working with of their journey so far.

It turns out, however, that this level of description too is going to prove to be too general to capture what is meant by "faithfulness" or "tradition." My second aphorism, after all, makes the claim that *all* action tells such stories (or, at least, is bound up with such stories—reinforcing them, helping to shape them, passing them on). And that is because, for something to count as an action at all, rather than simply as random behaviour, it must be *meaningful*—it must speak some kind of (actually or potentially) recognizable language. It cannot therefore avoid drawing on, reinforcing, perhaps subtly reshaping, and passing on, the language that it speaks. As soon as one is dealing with units of action above the microscopic (something fairly complex, like "going to coffee," rather than something fairly simple, like "moving one's hand slightly so as to tip one's cup") one's action is bound to be drawing on, reinforcing, reshaping, and passing on quite complex stories about who one is, how one relates to certain others, and so on. (That, incidentally, is why the critical reading of even everyday action is possible: nothing is inherently beyond the reach of various forms of ideology critique.)

So, in the loosest and least technical sense of the word "story," to act is to *tell a story* (or a set of stories) about the past, and to act so as to continue that story. Or, to put it another way:

Aphorism 3: All our action plots, abducts, and divides the spoils of the past.

First, to act is to plot the past. I say, "We always go to coffee" just as another story might say "For a long time, I used to go to bed early"—and as soon as I do, I already have the barest beginnings of a plot. Second, all action is therefore bound up with the identification by abductive reasoning (an unnecessarily technical term in this context, but irresistible for the sake of the pun) of some *structure* to the past; the great mass of disordered data is read or construed as meaningful. Third, as with all identification of plot, this abduction involves dividing the past into the salient and the peripheral. All action, one might say, involves deciding what precedent to ignore. Plotting, abducting, and dividing— that's what one does to the past as one construes it, and *all* action construes the past.

This is still very general, however. I'm still talking about *all* action rather than succeeding in distinguishing traditional action from other kinds. But I think that the conceptual machinery we need to start talking about tradition is now nearly in place. We need one more ingredient, though:

Aphorism 4: The past cannot be changed, but those who live from the past can.

Let me briefly make this more theological again. As a Christian theologian, I believe in the possibility of various kinds of forgiveness or healing—and I live with narratives like the story of the Jesus' healing of the demoniac in the synagogue. That means that (without needing at this point to say anything about possible *mechanisms* for such transformation) I believe in the possibility that someone can come to construe the past *differently*, to tell a *different* story in their action about who they are and where they come from. You were a fisherman; you are now becoming a fisher of people.

People can, in that sense at least, live differently out of the same past. The past is present in one's action not just automatically, at the level of basic creaturely determinism, but in this second, more malleable form.

And with that, finally, we can get to tradition.

Aphorism 5: Tradition is that activity in which the past is construed as the proper context for action.

My decoration of the Christmas tree with my children on Christmas Eve is an example of traditional action: it is (explicitly and implicitly) bound up with the telling of stories about the past, about how things are done. And in this activity, those particular stories are presented as making for *proper* Christmas activity; and the activity fairly explicitly works not only to decorate the tree but to reinforce and pass on the stories, and so to pass on the construal of the past that is involved.

Of course, "proper" is a rather vague word. As this example might suggest, we could take it in the "prim and proper" direction, and this definition would be about the past as corset. Tradition would then be that activity in which I so act as to tell a story about the past that says, "But of course this is how we should act. Anything else is just *not done*. People who do differently are not to be countenanced."

But I'm assuming for now that at least some proponents of some traditions want to say something more positive than that, and to think of tradition as that activity in which the past is construed as an *enabling* context for action—that activity in which the past is construed as giving us what is necessary for well-constructed action to be possible. One acts in some way not only because it is what one has always done, not only because it is in some prim sense "proper," but because one takes it that acting in that way is to be who one is, and creates possibilities for one's life that would otherwise be lost. Tradition can be understood to involve action in which the past is construed not as a prison to be broken free from, nor as a childhood to be grown out of, but as an enabling context for ongoing action—and therefore as a context to be deliberately preserved to enable the action of future generations. If all action draws on, reshapes, and passes on something like a language, tradition in this most benign sense passes on a particular language because of all that it enables one to say.

Something like this appears to be going on when Mark says, "As it is written . . ." He is providing the beginning of the story he tells with a backdrop against which it makes sense. The written tradition that he passes on is not, in his hands, a bar to innovation: it is the foundation upon which the new thing—the gospel of Jesus Christ—is built.

Aphorism 6: There is no past in theology.

This aphorism is not mine, but Karl Barth's. He once said, "Augustine, Thomas Aquinas, Luther, Schleiermacher, and all the rest are not dead but living . . . they and we belong together in the Church. . . . Our responsibility is not only to God, to ourselves, to the men of today, to other living theologians, but to them. There is no past in the Church, so there is no past in theology."[4]

Now, it is not of course that the past does not exist, nor is Barth denying that at least some of it happened quite a long time ago. But the past is not, he insists, "past" in the sense of over and done with, and the past is not "dead" in the sense of inert and available for our manipulation.

One could, perhaps, put Barth's aphorism differently:

Aphorism 7: All tradition is in danger of betraying the past.

It is easy to think that tradition involves one seeking to preserve and hand on one's past, and so focus on the problems that might be created by an unduly constricting imprisonment of future action by the past. But the definition of tradition that I have offered suggests that traditioned action has another facet: it is a picking up as well as a handing on. If one can sin in the handing on, Barth's aphorism suggests that one might also sin in the picking up. To act traditionally in the sense that I am describing is

4. Barth, *Protestant Theology*, 17.

to be faced with the temptation to treat the past as dead, and as at one's disposal—as something that is there to be forced into use in one's hands. To use the past without acknowledging simultaneously its resistance to use is to betray its *life*. (That is the sort of question that Mark's quotation of "Isaiah" most readily raises: has Mark distorted what he has picked up, manipulating it for his own purpose?)

Barth is able to make the point he does because Christian theology, specifically ecclesiology, provides one way of naming this possible betrayal *as* violence, as a failure in the love one owes to one's brothers and sisters. If Augustine, Aquinas, and the rest—and Isaiah and John the Baptist—are "not dead but living," then the notion that one is responsible to them makes sense. That yields:

Aphorism 8: The past gets in the way of tradition.

If all tradition involves a construal of the past, and if the past is not dead, or over and done with, then there will always be a possibility (perhaps well hidden) of remembering *against* the tradition—of remembering that which resists and exceeds the construals one has made as one makes use of the past. If one is responsible to Augustine, Aquinas, and the rest, then such *remembering against the tradition* is a perpetual Christian responsibility. If we take "traditional*ism*" to be the name of the kind of use of the past that denies its life, Aphorism 8 yields as a corollary:

Aphorism 9: Having a short memory is a necessary condition of being a traditionalist.

However, in order to take this discussion in the direction that my attempt to read Mark 1 requires, we need to take a different turning here.

Aphorism 10: If nothing ever changed, there would be no such thing as tradition.

I have been stressing that tradition is not simply an attempt to hand on the past; it also involves the *active construal* of the past. Aphorism 10 points out something about the context for this action.

A world where nothing ever changed would be a world where there was no use for the word "tradition"; there would *be* no identifiable reality called “tradition,” only life. Nobody would need to work (consciously or unconsciously) to preserve anything, because there would be nothing to preserve it from. We only talk about “tradition” when there is something to contrast it with: something against which we can preserve that about the past that is construed as enabling, some reality or possibility of change that calls forth the attempt to preserve the past. To inhabit anything worth calling a “tradition,” we might say, is therefore bound to involve construing the past in a changed situation, for that changed situation, because of that changed situation.

Aphorism 11: All tradition is invented as a response to change.

If tradition inherently involves the construal of the past *in* a new situation, *for* a new situation, it inherently involves construing the past differently. The act of passing on a tradition is the act of reinventing it.

The phrase “invention of tradition” is sometimes used to name a particular process by which modern patterns of life are, sometimes quite deliberately, provided with fictive, nostalgic backstories. (My parents-in-law, for instance, used to tell of seeing a sign while at the University of Montana in the 60s that said something like, “Traditionally, students do not walk on the grass in this courtyard. This tradition will come into force on the first of June.”) I’m claiming something more generalized than that: that *all* tradition is always, necessarily, invented and constantly reinvented. The act of construal that is at the heart of tradition is a creative act, which cannot help but make something new out of the past. The mere fact that Mark does something *new* with the texts of the Hebrew Bible that he quotes, and the mere fact that Jesus does something *new* in the synagogue, does not tell us that their action is thereby not traditional, not faithful to a tradition. Innovation is the form that passing on a tradition necessarily takes.[5]

However, any necessarily creative construal will only count as a continuation of a tradition if it is recognized by others as a faithful and authoritative construal of their past. Therefore:

5. Here, I think, is another place where the excess, the resistance of the past to tradition, becomes important again. The past does not simply get in the way of tradition, as I suggested in Aphorism 8; it can always be *re*read for the reinvention of tradition. The excess of the past is potentially as much resource as resistance. Tradition involves the constant revisiting of the past in order to construe it differently for a different context.

Aphorism 12: Tradition shall live by recognition alone.

All the construals that constitute tradition are social proposals about the proper way forward, and they only succeed in constituting an actual tradition if they are recognized socially as appropriate proposals. The people go out to John; the members of the synagogue are astonished at the authority of Jesus' teaching.

The conditions for my department's coffee breaks are constantly changing—available members of staff, available venues, teaching timetables, available drinks, and so on. Departmental coffee time is therefore necessarily an evolving tradition (such that one could, in principle, write a history of it). And when things change, there's sometimes a quite explicit, sometimes an implicit process of proposal and response—"Shall we go to the plush Business School coffee shop, instead?" These proposals only succeed in keeping the tradition going to the extent that they are recognized: to the extent that enough other people see them as an appropriate continuation of what we have done in the past, or an appropriate way of meeting what they take to be the same goals. And it is quite possible to imagine failed proposals—"Shall we organize a formal rota to govern who pays for coffee?"

What we normally think of as "tradition" is simply the form of this process of proposal and recognition that happens when both proposal and recognition are tacit, when they "go without saying." But proposal and recognition are still always part of the process of tradition.

If we translate the term "proposal" into more obviously theological terms, we get the following:

Aphorism 13: Tradition cannot exist without prophecy.

I have said that tradition is inherently and unavoidably marked by speaking *out* of the construed past, *into* a changed situation, proposing a way forward—and speaking in such a way that the faithfulness and authority of this proposal is recognized. You could therefore say that tradition is impossible without prophecy: without authoritative and faithful forth-telling. And so, for the Christian tradition, the making of proposals (the activity of construal that is at the heart of tradition) can be understood as the prophesying of the members of the body of Christ. The prophecy is a gift from God to the prophet (and remember that I said that the creative act of construal is not itself an act which somehow escapes the utter dependency that characterizes all our acts); the prophecy becomes a gift from the prophet to the body.

We have finally reached the point at which it becomes possible to address the awkwardnesses of my readings from Mark 1, because we have a vocabulary in which tradition, the "as it is written," and the eruption of a prophetic word (a new "beginning") stand next to one another. The process by which something is made from what Simon and Andrew already are, their pasts reread, is of the same form as the process by which James and John are summoned to a new obedience (but recognize and respond to that summons). Jesus, speaking "a new teaching—with authority" in the synagogue, is doing what *always* happens in the synagogue, if the synagogue is a context for the faithful continuing of devout life. And John the Baptist is God's reading of God's own text. He stands for, announces, or represents a call to faithfulness, announcing the new thing that faithfulness means *now*. Without him, the text suggests the people would not have known how to go on faithfully: true obedience to their tradition would have been impossible for them. For Mark, John's ministry represents, in its eschatological immediacy and its liminality, the starkest version of the equation between faithful continuity and prophetic challenge—but in doing so he simply dramatizes what is always and everywhere the necessary nature of tradition.

APHORISMS ON TRADITION AND THE CHARISMATIC BODY

We have not yet finished, however. I began with questions about the meaning of "tradition" in Scriptural Reasoning, and to answer that question requires a little further playing with the idea of tradition that has been emerging in my aphorisms. That further playing becomes possible if we seek a translation of "recognition" to parallel the translation of "proposal" as "prophecy" that drove Aphorism 13. The translation that suggests itself is "discernment of spirits"—though that is a translation that pushes us away from Mark's world of discourse, and towards Paul's:

> [4]Now there are varieties of gifts, but the same Spirit; [5]and there are varieties of services, but the same Lord; [6]and there are varieties of activities, but it is the same God who activates all of them in everyone. [7]To each is given the manifestation of the Spirit for the common good. [8]To one is given through the Spirit the utterance of wisdom, and to another the utterance of knowledge according to the same Spirit, [9]to another faith by the same Spirit, to another gifts

of healing by the one Spirit, [10]to another the working of miracles, to another prophecy, to another the discernment of spirits, to another various kinds of tongues, to another the interpretation of tongues. [11]All these are activated by one and the same Spirit, who allots to each one individually just as the Spirit chooses.

[12]For just as the body is one and has many members, and all the members of the body, though many, are one body, so it is with Christ. [13]For in the one Spirit we were all baptized into one body—Jews or Greeks, slaves or free—and we were all made to drink of one Spirit.

—1 Corinthians 12

[1]Pursue love and strive for the spiritual gifts, and especially that you may prophesy. . . . [3][T]hose who prophesy speak to other people for their building up and encouragement and consolation. [4]Those who speak in a tongue build up themselves, but those who prophesy build up the church. [5]Now I would like all of you to speak in tongues, but even more to prophesy . . .

[26]What should be done then, my friends? When you come together, each one has a hymn, a lesson, a revelation, a tongue, or an interpretation. Let all things be done for building up. . . . [29]Let two or three prophets speak, and let the others weigh what is said. [30]If a revelation is made to someone else sitting nearby, let the first person be silent. [31]For you can all prophesy one by one, so that all may learn and all be encouraged. [32]And the spirits of prophets are subject to the prophets, [33]for God is a God not of disorder but of peace.

—1 Corinthians 14

Aphorism 14: Tradition cannot exist without the discernment of spirits.

Christian tradition is impossible without the discernment of spirits, in the sense of a process by which prophecy is weighed and recognized as authoritative—or rejected. Prophecy and the discernment of spirits *together* are the form that the continuity of Christian tradition takes. Without them, there could be no such thing as a Christian tradition.

Yet this charismatic language of gifts of prophecy and discernment leads on to the suggestion that, for Christian theology, to talk about tradition is to talk about the church as an *economy of gift*—an economy in which the life of the body of Christ is *constituted* by the offering of Spirit-given gifts by members of the body and their discerning reception by that same body—prophets subject to prophets. For there to be an ongoing tradition, there will need to be a constant stream of proposal and recognition, of prophecy and discernment, of giving and receiving: there is no other way that the tradition can persist.

To speak about tradition is therefore to speak about recognition, and therefore to speak about tradition is therefore to speak in the loosest sense about politics: about the ways in which proposal and recognition form a polity. And to speak about those things in a Christian theological context is to speak about *the church*.

I'd go so far as to say that something *analogous* to the church, something analogous to the body of Christ understood as a charismatic body and as an economy of gift, is therefore necessary to the functioning of *any* tradition *as* a tradition, unless tradition is to be simply a matter of violent constraint. In an earlier version of this chapter, I allowed myself, at this point, the aphorism, "*Extra ecclesiam, nulla traditio*, outside the church there is no tradition," which rather over-egged this point, but you can perhaps see how I was tempted to put it that way. One way of understanding these aphorisms is to see them as a machine for transmuting questions about tradition into questions about ecclesiology. It turns out that there is not a question about the faithful handing on of the past that can be separated from questions about how the body of Christ is formed by gift and reception, and about how it conducts itself as a charismatic body.

What, though, of *failures* of recognition?

Aphorism 15: Tradition cannot exist without repentance.

If a constant stream of giving and receiving is a condition for the operation of tradition, then tradition as I have been sketching it so far is clearly an eschatological concept, and repentance and reconciliation—processes for responding to fractures in the body, to failures of prophecy and discernment—will be *de facto* necessary conditions for any partial existence of tradition on this side of the eschaton.

This means, however, that if the concept of tradition *in principle* marks out a kind of unified social space, a space of consensual and free exchange, then *actual* tradition will take place in a considerably messier space, in which there is a more uneven fizz of differing construals in play. It is important, therefore, to note that, against Aphorism 12, we have:

Aphorism 16: Tradition shall not live by recognition alone.

Paul's depiction of the body of Christ to the Corinthian church is not a description: it is a *call*. It does not, therefore, describe life as it actually functions in Corinth, but depicts it as it *should*—as it would if the body were one in heart and mind. Yet this does not mean that a real tradition cannot exist this side of the eschaton (though it comes close). A tradition of sorts can exist and persist in this time between the times provided that there is *just enough* recognition for an ongoing shared life to function.

The existence and persistence of a living tradition of sorts does not therefore require the kingdom come, the body of Christ fully realized in the midst of the world, but a space of jostling construals held together by their overlaps and interlocks—a shared settlement, to use the language of an earlier chapter.

The space marked out by tradition will therefore be a space that is bound both to have fuzzier edges and to be more of a site for argument than any eschatological space of pure giving and receiving. As I said, it will be a space in which there is an uneven fizz of differing construals in play.

Rather than simply talking about proposal and recognition, therefore, we need to talk about traditions functioning in an economy of recognition, non-recognition, and *mis*recognition. The work of Timothy Jenkins is helpful here, and specifically his account of what he calls the "economy of fantasies" in his *Religion in English Everyday Life*. In his ethnographic work, Jenkins describes the ways in which different groups of people in a given context employ differing ways of making sense of the world, differing ways of making distinctions between themselves and other groups, differing assessments of appropriate and inappropriate behavior, and, we might say, differing construals of the past. Social life can be carried on not because these ways of making sense *agree*, but because there is an extent to which they interlock: they are like cogs with imperfectly meshing teeth that nevertheless work together just sufficiently to keep the social machine moving. The passing on of these ways of making sense from generation to generation is, therefore, complex for Jenkins: new generations learn to conduct themselves appropriately in the spaces opened up by the matches and mismatches between the previous generations' ways of making sense, in such a way that they themselves come to perpetuate those matching and mismatching ways of making sense.

You can imagine, for instance, at a very broad brush level, suggesting that English Anglicanism survives as a tradition *precisely because of* the partial recognition and misrecognition between (say) evangelicals, liberals, and Anglo Catholics; that it is only if you account for the way in which the patterns of interaction and mutual incomprehension between these three are reproduced that you can account for the reproduction of any one of them.

With something like this view in hand, one can move away from the idealized or eschatological picture of a single unified tradition, and towards a more complex layering and overlapping of spaces in which it is difficult or impossible to delimit individual traditions, and in which the reproduction of traditions depends as much upon the disagreements and confusions between these spaces as upon explicit recognition and agreement.

Let me try and illustrate that. When I talk to my parents about Christianity, there are times when we *can* really talk: when we're clearly having a conversation in terms that make sense to all of us, clearly either agreeing or disagreeing about something. Some of the time, however, we don't *quite* manage to have such a conversation: the terms in which we're speaking don't match up, and we're aware of some *labor of translation* involved in speaking to each other, and some dissatisfaction with the results. At other times, we find we simply talk past one another: we're each speaking languages we don't yet know how to translate into terms that the other will recognize. But here's the thing: although I find this to be particularly true with my parents (with whom I have a history of explicit theological agreement and disagreement) it's also true for every single other person I've ever managed to talk to about Christianity. If I've managed to talk at all, it will be because there are some areas of at least partial recognition; but given even moderate time to explore, that recognition always turns out to be mottled, to give out in places, to have unexpected points of contact surrounded by deserts of incomprehension. This is not (I think) because there's something wrong with me, but because this is what traditions look like: mottled maps of partial recognition. You recognize the existence of some kind of tradition where some kind of conversation is possible—some kind of argument, even some kind of real disagreement. You could in principle create a model of tradition by mapping those possibilities of conversation, provided one construed "conversation" broadly: tradition is not simply a matter of ways of *talking*, but involves mottled possibilities of meaningful cooperative action, or meaningful interaction; patterns of activity that succeed in meshing together sufficiently to sustain something that, at least temporarily, looks like a common life. But if one does map these possibilities, the map is going to be a bewildering and multidimensional network, a fractal that bears a lacy complexity at every level of magnification.

APHORISMS ON TRADITION AND SCRIPTURAL REASONING

After these long, long detours through Mark and through Paul, I am ready to return to the questions that started the chapter: What does it *mean* to say that participants in Scriptural Reasoning do so as people who belong to different traditions, and who make Scriptural Reasoning possible precisely by remaining faithful to their traditions in the process?

Aphorism 17: A tradition is not best represented by consensus.

If proposal and recognition or prophecy and discernment constitute a tradition, then a tradition cannot be represented by one person calmly setting forth achieved consensual content, but only by two people engaged in conversation, demonstrating the processes by which proposals are made and by which they are tested. (In the terms used in earlier chapters, this means two people engaged in the activity of settlement.) If, then, Scriptural Reasoning is supposed to bring together the reasoning practices of the three participating traditions, the theoretical minimum size of a viable group is not three people but six.[6]

Aphorism 18: Participants in Scriptural Reasoning are not representatives of their traditions, but agents in them.

If proposal and recognition, prophecy and discernment, are the processes by which a tradition is constituted, the participants in Scriptural Reasoning are not representatives of the tradition (as if the tradition were going on elsewhere, and they simply brought reports of it); they are engaged in the activity by which the tradition lives. The desideratum for participation

6. Note that I have slipped here from talking about the meaning of "tradition" in a Christian context (or at least one *construal* of what "tradition" means in a Christian context, which I offer for the recognition primarily of Christian readers) to using the term in the same way for Judaism and Islam as well. Implicitly, I am offering this construal of the meaning of "tradition" to Jewish and Islamic readers in the hope that they will recognize that an analogous construal is possible for their religious houses—without any certainty of success.

in Scriptural Reasoning is not, therefore, that one has participants who can somehow *speak authoritatively for* their home traditions, but at least some who are engaged (or who are learning to be engaged) in the processes of conversation, of argument, of disagreement that are the life of their traditions. Reading, proposing interpretations, and criticizing those interpretations—that activity, going on at all sorts of scales, in all sorts of places—*is* the tradition.

Aphorism 19: Scriptural Reasoning is a resource for the faithful continuation of the traditions.

So, in principle, the participants in Scriptural Reasoning are agents in the processes of textual, biblical, qur'anic settlement that constitute their "home" traditions, attempting faithfulness in the only way that faithfulness is possible: by going back to the sources of their tradition (to their inheritance) and looking at them again with fresh eyes. And therefore that there need be no "despite" in the claim that participants in Scriptural Reasoning pursue faithfulness to their own traditions while engaging deeply with those of other traditions. The engagement is one that can prompt them to read their own scriptures differently, and so it is potentially a *driver* of faithfulness to their own traditions—a seedbed of prophecy. Of course, the recognition or discernment possible within a Scriptural Reasoning group can only be provisional and small-scale, but that simply means that a question remains about the ways in which those engaged in Scriptural Reasoning are bound into the wider patterns of exchange that constitute their own tradition, and therefore about the ways in which the reinventions of each tradition brewed in the bubbling vat of Scriptural Reasoning might be recognized and welcomed—or challenged and rejected—as proposals for the renewal of those traditions. In principle, however, Scriptural Reasoning is a laboratory for experiments in faithfulness.

part three

Reading the Book of Nature

17 Reading the Rainbow

Playing with the Text and Living in the World

A Biblical Reasoning group met in Cambridge in 2002 to discuss Jonah, and found themselves captivated by the links between the story of Jonah and the story of Noah.

> The book of Jonah retells and reverses [the story of Noah]—such that the logic of the covenant with Noah is rediscovered through the text and used to re-read its events. The book begins, as does Noah's story, with God's resolve to destroy the wicked, and the word of the Lord to the righteous man (see Genesis 6:11–21). It seems that the story of Noah may be repeated; but the Lord has promised never to repeat that story (Genesis 8:21: ". . . nor will I ever again destroy every living creature as I have done") and has made a covenant with "all flesh that is on the earth" (9:16). So, instead of being repeated, the story is inverted: the call of the Lord is refused, the wicked are saved, and the one called by God—who is also the *dove*, the meaning of his name—is submerged in the waters.[1]

These striking textual links call for further reflection on the relationship between the stories. Jonah is *after* Noah; but he, like his reader, is turned back to reread the story of Noah.

The covenant with Noah is a covenant with "all flesh," and it centers on a change in God's heart (Gen 8:21). From this point onwards, God has determined Godself for patience with, and faithfulness to, *everything*

1. Muers, "Sign of Jonah." The meeting included Jon Cooley, David Ford, Dan Hardy, Jason Lam, Rachel Muers, and Chad Pecknold.

living—a covenant whose scope is unimaginable, taking in as it does not only "all generations" of humanity but the vast numbers of living creatures. The rainbow, the very first sign God makes, is established to remind *God* of this covenant (Gen 9:15). God declares how it is to be read by other readers—as a sign for God of God's own faithfulness to "every living creature of all flesh that is on the earth." God is, in this story, a reader of signs who draws others into the process of reading.

In the book of Jonah, I suggest, we see God teaching Jonah to read the signs of God's faithfulness and steadfast love, *as God reads them*. The point is not the continuing need of humanity to be reminded that God is faithful and "abounding in steadfast love"—Jonah knows that already (Jonah 4:2)—but rather the need to learn to read the *signs* of God's faithfulness. The natural world in the book of Jonah is full of signs of God's faithfulness to "all flesh"—the fish that "the Lord appointed," the bush, the people and animals in Nineveh—which are repeatedly misread by Jonah.

What explains the tension between Jonah's acknowledgement that the Lord "made the sea and the dry land" and his seemingly futile attempt to flee from God by going to sea? Perhaps it can be explored in terms of the tension between an assertion of God's "global" concern and the practices of exclusion that such an assertion can often mask. It is one thing to say, "God has made a covenant with all flesh," and another to say, "God has made a covenant with both me and my enemy." The former requires no new readings; the latter only comes about when one is taught by God to read the signs. Jonah learns to read the fish, the bush, and finally Nineveh itself. We might see this as part of the ongoing encounter between God and all the children of Abraham through which they, as (also) children of Noah, learn to "read the rainbow."

The "reading" of the rainbow (and it must be noted here that the rainbow itself is not a "word" of God, not quite the same as a text; *davar* does not appear in Genesis until chapter 11) occurs in connection with the reading of texts that convey and interpret the divine sign. Noah is silent until after the flood and the declaration of God's covenant.[2] After Noah, people enter conversation with one another and with God. The very fact that Jonah can call on God (for the first time in this story, although the sailors have addressed God already) from the belly of the

2. See on this Neher, *Exile of the Word*, 99–109. It is noteworthy, however, that the qur'anic account of Noah focuses on his preaching before the deluge (Surah 71), and that rabbinic commentaries describe him praying in the ark.

fish serves as a reminder that his life is located in the aftermath of the covenant with Noah, in the time in which the natural and human worlds are full of signs.

Jonah, then, knows that God is "slow to anger and abiding in steadfast love" because he is of the people within which that particular naming of God by Godself is recorded and reflected on—because he is, as he says, a Hebrew (1:9). Being a child of Abraham as well as a child of Noah means, perhaps, not only being taught *to* read the rainbow, each time in each particular situation, but being taught *how* to read the rainbow. The readers of these texts are made into "readers of the rainbow" by being given a further set of signs—signs that bring them into practices and ways of relating appropriate to readers of the sign of God's faithfulness.

Also remembered in the book of Jonah, however, is the threat of destruction—without which the contexts in which the divine promise of faithfulness is relearnt make no sense. The waters that Jonah enters do not destroy him; and his liturgy from the depths points back to a puzzle in the story of Noah. God's words in Genesis 8:21 suggest that God *has* destroyed "all flesh," this once and never again; so what is the status of Noah and those with him, with whom the covenant is made? (There is an interesting comparison with Jonah's declaration that he speaks from "the land whose bars closed upon me for ever," 2:6—how would it really be possible to speak from this place?) A deep question seems to remain about the nature of the resolve God makes—compounded by the close association between that resolve and God's recognition of the "evil intention" of the human heart. The rainbow is obviously an "open sign," perhaps the open sign that opens all the divine signs; less obviously, it seems *at the same time* to be a sign of something hidden.

As the Christian scriptures reread the story of Noah, these tensions in interpretation, far from being resolved, become even more apparent—together with words concerning the "one greater than Jonah," who is also greater than Noah. First Peter 3:18–20 speaks of God's patience *before* the flood, "during the building of the ark," hence for the sake of the salvation of the few. On one reading of this passage, what is spoken of here in connection with Christ is a repetition of *that* patience, which consigns those outside (that is, outside the group reading this letter and owning these words) to the deluge. That is the repetition of divine patience that Jonah seems to seek, or assume God seeks. For Jonah, God will wait until the right time to destroy those excluded from God's future—that must be either Jonah or the Ninevites.

However, Jonah's story takes a different turn, and 1 Peter 3:18–20 takes a very different turn. Christ's preaching is to "*the spirits in prison, who were disobedient during the days of Noah.*" Part of the point about Noah's story, it seems, is that it cannot be repeated; God has sworn never again to destroy all flesh. Its "non-repetition" in the book of Jonah is directed at the relearning, within the order established by the covenant with Noah, of the scope of God's faithfulness. Its non-repetition in 1 Peter seems to be about a further reinterpretation even of the "change in God's heart"—somehow to include the "spirits in prison."

Reading these texts, and learning to read the signs to which they point, involves learning to read the scope of God's mercy—a mercy that stretches further than we might think. And so this brief exposition serves as an appropriate overture to the third section of this book because it opens up a set of questions that broaden the scope of our experimentation still further, without in any sense finishing with the experiments started in the first two sections. It is a playful exposition, in the sense explored in Part One: it is an exposition in which the relationship between Hebrew Bible texts and New Testament texts begs for further exploration, of the kind explored in Part Two. But it is also a text in which those hermeneutical questions are joined by two others. What does it mean for the readers of these texts to find themselves in the natural world—the world of rainbows, bushes, and fish, the world of "all flesh" (and more)—and to know that world as the world of God's mercy? And what does it mean for them to find their reading of these texts mixed up with their readings of the God-given signs of that natural world? The connections between all these questions have only just begun to become visible in this chapter, and they may as yet seem tenuous. In the next two chapters, however, we will see just how substantial they are.

18 Literal Reading and Other Animals I

Setting Free the Mother Bird

[6]If you come on a bird's nest, in any tree or on the ground, with fledglings or eggs with the mother sitting on the fledglings or on the eggs, you shall not take the mother with the young. [7]Let the mother go, taking only the young for yourself, in order that it may go well with you and you may live long.

—Deuteronomy 22

In this chapter I pursue ethical and theological questions about reading a biblical text at several levels, and demonstrate that the connections lightly sketched in the previous chapter are unavoidable. First, I reread a text that has been used in the development of Christian and Jewish ideas about "all flesh"—specifically, Jewish and Christian responses to the environmental movement and to debates about the moral status of animals—in the hope of deepening and complexifying existing readings, and thereby in a small way (this is a small text, after all) contributing to Christian theological work in these interconnected areas. Second, this leads me in to reflections on *how* to read biblical texts for engagement with contemporary issues—whether and how such reading can be ethical (sustainable, respectful, compassionate, and so forth) and what the ethics of reading itself has to do with theology and with the text I am discussing. Third, this process engages me in an inter- and intratraditional conversation about interpretation, the right conduct of which is also not irrelevant to the reading of this specific text.[1]

In recent decades, there has been a small but not negligible upsurge of interest in the "bird's-nest precept" among ethicists and theologians, both Jewish and Christian.[2] The two interconnected areas of contemporary discussion to which it is most often linked—sustainability and environmental ethics on the one hand, and the ethical status of animals on the other—can draw on distinct, if again interconnected, strands in the earlier history of the text's interpretation.[3] Very broadly speaking, to read this as a text about environmental ethics is to focus on the ethical principle of *sustainability*; to read it as a text about the status and welfare of nonhuman animals is to focus on *respect* and/or *compassion*. Although these look, at face value, like the equivalent in theological ethics of motherhood and apple pie, in the context of the reading of a text like this they become, potentially, conflicting demands. The interpretation of the bird's-nest precept involves a careful thinking through of the relationship between them.

These two directions of contemporary interpretation can easily be seen to originate in the text itself—in the duality of the response of the addressee of the precept to what she *finds*. The bird's nest is something "come upon," found accidentally (not previously created or claimed by the addressee of the precept). The instruction is that what is "found" is to be treated in two different ways: one part of the find is to be set free, or sent away, and the other may be taken "for yourself."

If we start from this division of the nest in the precept, it becomes clear how two emphases can develop in its interpretation. To interpret this passage in terms of *sustainability* is, I suggest, to begin from the "taking" of the young. Whatever else it is, the nest is a food source, a resource for use. To send the mother bird away is to preserve the "breeding stock" and hence to manage the food source responsibly. The nest, that which is found, is available for *use* of some sort; right interaction with it is beneficial, or even necessary, for the one who finds it. Environmental "sustainability"

1. I am grateful to the many people who have helped in the preparation of this article, and in particular to Susannah Ticciati, Chad Pecknold, David Horrell, and two anonymous readers for *Modern Theology* for their comments on earlier drafts. Some of the material discussed here was presented in a paper for the Cambridge Systematics Seminar on January 26, 2005.

2. In addition to the sources cited below, see Olley, "Mixed Blessings for Animals," 134.

3. For another brief overview of the range of interpretations of the text, see Segal, "Justice, Mercy," 176–77.

interpretations of Deuteronomy 22:6–7, which have a longer history than that of recent "green" theology,[4] acknowledge the dependence of humanity on the continuing life and fruitfulness of nonhuman creation.

Thus, Wendell Berry calls Deuteronomy 22:6–7 "a perfect paradigm of ecological and agricultural discipline, in which the idea of inheritance is necessarily paramount. The inflexible rule is that the source must be preserved. You may take the young, but you must save the breeding stock. You may eat the harvest, but you must save seed, and you must preserve the fertility of the fields."[5] For contemporary interpreters who take this line, there is an obvious link with Deuteronomy 20:19–20, and the injunction not to destroy trees that produce fruit, even in situations of (supposed) military necessity. For one commentator, these two laws are "examples of early environmental protection regulations";[6] in an evangelical text on environmental ethics they both teach "the ethical principle of *sustainability*."[7]

Berry also, however, somewhat elliptically relates the bird's-nest precept to a principle of indefinitely extended "charity."[8] It seems that a "sustainability" interpretation that treats the bird's nest *entirely* as managed resource fails fully to engage with the central action enjoined by the precept: the *sending away or letting go* of part of what has been found. Something must be allowed to persist as *un*available for use—perhaps possessing value or moral significance not dependent on its value—for the one who found it. The "animal welfare" interpretation of the bird's-nest precept begins from what seemed obvious (as we shall see) to most of the earliest interpreters of the passage, however non-obvious it seems to most contemporary commentators; if this precept has a meaning or a reason, it is to be found in the relationship (of compassion or respect) to the bird that is freed, not in the relationship (of use or profit) to the birds that are taken. So, for example, for Dan Cohn-Sherbok, drawing on Maimonides (whose interpretation I shall discuss further), the bird's-nest precept becomes an important text for a Jewish ethical critique of cruelty towards,

4. As Jeremy Benstein notes in "The Earth's Reward," Isaac Abrabanel in the fifteenth century noted the contribution of "freeing the mother bird" to the perpetuation of creation "so that we will be able to partake of it again in the future." See further on this Segal, "Justice, Mercy," 193.

5. Berry, *Gift of Good Land*, 273.

6. Miller, *Deuteronomy*, 171; and note the similar observations in McConville, *Deuteronomy*; Clifford, *Deuteronomy*, 118; and Craigie, *Book of Deuteronomy*, 288–89.

7. Bouma-Prediger, *For the Beauty of the Earth*, 149.

8. Berry, *Gift of Good Land*, 273.

and exploitation of, non-human animals.[9] It is, of course, not surprising that this interpretation has puzzled many commentators; if the guiding principle is found in the "sending away," what of the young birds that are taken?[10]

These twenty-first-century rereadings of the bird's-nest precept represent, I would suggest, attempts to bridge the perceived divide between environmental ethics on the one hand and theological ethics on the other. They might succeed in that attempt: that is, in conjunction with readings of other texts they might help to persuade (at least some) Christian or Jewish readers that concern for sustainability and/or the compassionate treatment of animals form part of a "biblical ethic"; and they might help to persuade (at least some) secular environmentalists or animal rights campaigners that the Christian or Jewish traditions are not necessarily inimical to their cause. In neither case, however, would the reading help to resolve a wider question in which I am interested here: about how readings of biblical texts should be developed and used in debates like this.[11]

This wider question is not only, I would suggest, a meta-ethical question; it is also an ethical question, because there are ethical issues at stake when people decide how to read and use texts. Thus, we should not be surprised that the two areas of discussion described above, when analysed more closely, draw attention not only to different guiding principles of *interaction with nonhuman nature* but also to different guiding principles of, or emphases in, *reading*. These different principles of reading, in turn, are brought out within the interpretive tradition. In other words, this text has at several points in its history been interpreted as a text about how to interpret, and similar differences of emphasis appear when it is read in this way as appear when it is read in terms of its plain-sense referent: how to behave in relation to (a particular part of) the nonhuman/animal creation. To sketch the direction of the argument that will be developed in more detail later, I observe at this point the possible comparison between the biblical text itself, qua scripture, and the bird's nest. The text, as scripture, is not the creature or the possession of the reader, but is "found" as part of

9. Linzey and Cohn-Sherbok, *After Noah*, 45–48.

10. Those familiar with recent debates in environmental ethics will observe the parallels between these two poles of interpretation, on the one hand, and "anthropocentric" and "biocentric" accounts of the value of nonhuman nature, on the other.

11. David Horrell, Cherryl Hunt, Christopher Southgate, and Francesca Stavrakopoulou's work on the use of the Bible in environmental ethics (see their *Ecological Hermeneutics*) is clarifying further the range of possibilities currently available in that field.

the already-existing environment of her activity. It is found both as something to be *used*—beneficial or necessary—and as something that should escape or resist use.

The route I am taking into a complexified twenty-first-century reading of this passage leads me through a group of readings that have very little (save obliquely) to do with environmental concerns, and rather little (save obliquely) to do with relations to nonhuman nature in general. Medieval Christian interpretations of the bird's-nest precept do, however, enable us to see within a Christian theological framework the connections between approaches to reading texts and other questions of ethics and politics.

INTERPRETATION ON THE WAY

Interpreters for many centuries were able to find in the bird's-nest precept an account in miniature of the Christian life—its direction, conduct, and end. The beginning of our text in the Vulgate locates the interpretations I am about to discuss: *si ambulans per viam*. In medieval Christian commentaries the precept was read as addressed to humanity as *viator*, on a journey towards its final end in God. Of course, the verse itself, for these interpreters, journeys towards this final end—the promise that "it will go well for you and you will live long" is read (as indeed some of the rabbinic commentators read it)[12] as a reference to *eternal* life, the end and goal of the *via*. The beginning and end of the text, their spatial and temporal terms read within an overarching story, thus set out the location and the direction of the act of interpretation itself—the interpreters read *ambulans per viam*, looking towards *longo vivas tempore*. Where the midrash in *Deuteronomy Rabbah* treats the location of the bird's-nest precept "on the way" as a sign of the *extent* of the precepts—"Even if you are not engaged on any particular work but are merely journeying on the road, the precepts accompany you"[13]—the interpreters I discuss here treat it as a sign of their *intent*.

We would, then, expect the interpretation of the bird, her nest and young, and the actions performed, to focus on how the action performed

12. R. Joseph (quoting the earlier statement of R. Jacob) concludes that "the verse, *That it may go well with thee*, refers to the world that is wholly good, and that the verse, *That thy days may be prolonged*, refers to the world that is wholly long." *Bavli Hullin* 142c, in Epstein, ed., *Babylonian Talmud*.

13. *Midrash Rabbah*, 123.

brings about or aids the movement through time towards eternal life. Thus Bede's brief account: "The way indicates this world, the tree pride, the earth carnal desire, the nest conduct, the mother the sinful flesh of each person, the long time the future age."[14] Bruno of Segni, much later, likewise focuses his interpretation on what is needed "as we go on the way, leading to our homeland and to God."[15]

Of course, one of the consequences of interpreting within the *homo viator* theological framework is that not only the eggs and the young, but the mother bird—and even the tree and the earth—become features of the *human* "landscape," the space of the human soul. The interpretation is, to use an anachronistic term, anthropocentric—not in the sense of regarding the literal referents of the text (birds nesting in trees or on the earth, and by extension the animal and plant realms more generally) as at the disposal of humanity, but in the sense of regarding *the text itself* as addressed to human well-being in the fullest sense.[16] The text is read rightly, according to the true intention of its divine author, if it is read for salvation.

Now, these *in via* interpretations should not be confused with the suggestion that the *bird and her nest* are to be interpreted anthropocentrically—that is, that real birds and their eggs (and by extension nonhuman nature) are primarily resources for human disposal. Nonetheless, it is important to note what is emphasized when the texts, or the actions they command, are thus viewed. These readings speak of the duration of life as opposed to the single right action—the formation of habits, the acquisition of virtues—and to an ongoing interaction between humanity and world in which the aim is the transformation of humanity towards their proper and final end. "Sustainability" interpretations (of the real birds and their eggs) likewise read into the text the duration of human

14. Bede, *In Pentateuchum Commentarii: Explanatio in quintum librum Mosis*, in PL 91:390B.

15. Bruno of Segni, *Expositio in Pentateuchum: Expositio in Deuteronomium*, in PL 164:522B.

16. Nachmanides' view that the laws are given not to express and enact divine compassion for animals but to teach compassion to humanity is in some ways comparable; I discuss this further below. In Nachmanides' interpretation, not the *text* but the *action to which it refers* is interpreted anthropocentrically: "The benefit from the commandments is not derived by the Holy One Himself, exalted be He. Rather, the advantage is to man himself. . . . [T]hese commandments with respect to cattle and fowl are not [a result of] compassion upon them, but they are decrees upon us to guide us and to teach us traits of good character." Nachmanides, *Commentary on the Torah*, 5:268, 271.

life. Moreover, in both of these modes of interpretation there is an inherent connection between the action (setting free the mother bird, taking the young) and the reward (long life): the setting free of the bird and/or the taking of the young makes "long life" possible. The connection between action and reward is given not simply in the status of the action as obedience to divine command, but in the sense it makes within the sphere of action within which it is located (what difference it makes to ecosystems, human character or the state of the soul). Of course, in such a reading the reward of long life can still be interpreted as a reward "from God"—either insofar as the entire sphere of action (the material creation and/or the course of the soul's journey) and the enduring constraints and possibilities it contains are themselves determined by God, or insofar as God rewards behavior that "makes sense" within this sphere of action.

Seeing possible parallels between the approach to the text and the approach to the bird's nest prepares us for the next point. A significant strand of medieval Christian interpretation of this passage makes an explicit connection between the mother bird and the *literal sense of the scriptural text*, and between the young and the eggs and the spiritual senses of the same text. I intend, in what follows, to take up this approach and turn it in directions not anticipated by the commentators I discuss. First, however, I examine some of their texts.

THE BIRD AND THE TEXT

The earliest instance I have been able to trace of a Christian commentator reading the bird's-nest precept as a text about interpretation is the extended discussion in Rabanus Maurus's commentary on Deuteronomy (which was included, together with Bede's one-sentence reading cited above, in the *Glossa Ordinaria*).[17] His interpretation begins with a straightforward remapping of the way, the tree and the earth onto the way of the soul with the contemplative life (the tree) and the active life (the earth). In both active and contemplative life the mother bird is read as the scriptural text, specifically the text of the Old Testament—thus in the contemplative life she is primarily the *historia* (producing knowledge), in the active life primarily law (producing action or disposition). In both cases she produces, first, eggs—spiritual things perceived in riddles, good works

17. Rabanus Maurus, *Enarratio super Deuteronomium* 2.30, in PL 108:923B; *Glossa ordinaria*, loc. cit., in PL 113:475D.

done through fear—that subsequently hatch into chicks—spiritual things seen according to their true nature, the works of love. Particularly in the case of the reading of *verba historiae*, the instruction to those proceeding *per viam* is clear; the mother bird, the literal sense of the text, is to be sent away so that her young can be consumed. "Therefore, sending away the mother, we eat the young, when . . . we retain the allegorical sense in our minds . . . for not the mother, but the understanding of the spiritual senses, satisfies us." "Sending away the mother bird," as a way of depicting the relationship between literal and spiritual senses, is used much later by Bruno of Segni in the context of the interpretation of another passage altogether; the bird's-nest precept is appealed to in a digression, as a way of drawing attention to the interpretive process in which he is engaged. As Bruno describes it, the bird is the "letter" of the text, which hides the spiritual senses under its wings—either in a tree or on the ground, that is, either in a more difficult or a more straightforward scriptural *locus*. The *via* here is the scriptural text itself, which the interpreters (Bruno and his readers) traverse in search of whatever gives life—and in order to gain this, they must send away the letter that kills. Bruno emphasizes that the spiritual sense is the *child* of the letter—but the contrast between them (life-giving/killing) is emphasized far more in this text than is the closeness of their connection.[18]

Now it should be noted that neither Rabanus Maurus nor Bruno says much about what happens to the mother bird—the letter of the text—after it has been sent away. The mother bird is not killed, and these commentaries—even when they refer to the letter that kills—preserve an implicit reference to the work she does in laying and then protecting the eggs. The literal sense, these interpretive texts remember even if they do not emphasize, is necessary as the means for bringing the spiritual into the world; no eggs and no young would be found were it not for the mother bird. I shall say more about this aspect of the commentaries below. Before doing so, however, we should pay attention to a more extended medieval discussion of the bird's-nest precept, which both finds in this text a deeper theological reason for reading in this way and, in doing so, exposes a nexus of interpretive possibilities and risks to which Christian theological readings should still pay careful attention.

Rupert of Deutz develops an explicit and extended allegorical treatment of the bird's-nest precept in *De sancta Trinitate et operibus*

18. PL 164:543A.

eius.[19] He takes as the first key to the interpretation of this text Jeremiah 17:11—"Like the partridge hatching what it did not lay / so are all who amass wealth unjustly." Thus it is possible to say that the "mother bird" has no right to the eggs or birds on which she sits, and sending her away is the restoration of justice. So, in the first interpretation Rupert presents, the mother bird becomes the devil, making humanity into his children when they were created as the children of God; and Christ, as the "unique hearer and doer of the law" (*singularis auditor et factor legis*), on his passage through the world takes the "children" to himself and abandons the devil to his eventual destruction. The nests in the tree and on the earth are interpreted respectively as the people of Israel (still subject to the devil, but exalted by their relation to the law and to the faith of Abraham) and the Gentiles; and the "doing of the law" by Christ when he takes the children to himself refers to his taking up of *both* groups, "Jews and Greeks without distinction."

In the second part of Rupert's interpretation, he adopts the by-now-familiar spiritual/literal reading, drawing directly on Rabanus Maurus's interpretation but developing it significantly. The mother bird is identified here, not only as "the letter" and "the letter of the law," but as *littera Synagogae*, which cannot be "taken up" by Christ. The parting of mother and chicks is used to read the "parting of the ways" between Jews and Christians.[20] Having again (as in his previous chapter) established the mother bird as a problem—"the letter of the law that kills"—Rupert again faces the question of why she is not killed but merely "allowed to go." The answer is found, repeating a familiar Augustinian trope and its proof-text, in Psalm 59:11—"Do not kill them, or my people may forget." The "wandering Jew"—dispersed throughout the world as a perpetual sign, for Christians, of divine judgement—the Jew "having only the letter of the law," is invoked in the flight of the mother bird. This is, then, not only a textbook case *of* supersessionist reading—it provides the textbook *for* supersessionist reading.[21] In a final move, the reader can be enjoined and

19. *De sancta Trinitate et operibus eius: In Deuteronmium* 1.14, in PL 167:933A. On this work and on Rupert's approach to biblical interpretation more generally, see Van Engen, *Rupert of Deutz*, 81–94.

20. An interpretation recorded by Rabanus Maurus in *De Universo* 8.6 also reads the "mother bird" as the Jewish people—and also uses the text to read the "parting of the ways." The chicks are the apostles, the "children" of the Jewish people taken up by Christ. PL 111:242B.

21. On Rupert's anti-Jewish biblical interpretation more generally, see Timmer, "Biblical Exegesis"; Cohen, *Living Letters*, 271–72.

enabled to perform the birds-nest precept for himself—in a repetition of Rabanus Maurus's call to send away the *historiae exempla* and retain *allegorarium sensus*.

What is happening here? In the first place, Rupert's initial reading of the text makes explicit the starting point for any subsequent reading—the law is fulfilled in Christ and this transforms its significance. Law is reread as and through prophecy; the eschatological redirection of the bird's-nest precept (so that its reward becomes eternal life) is grounded in this reorientation of the law to Christ as its fulfilment (the one who is and gives eternal life). Although he does not make this connection between his two readings explicit, Rupert has used this passage to show, first, *why and on what basis one should read*, and second, *how one should read*; it is a move from allegory to tropology, but with the added complication that the tropological reading is about practices of interpretation.

The problem, I suggest, is that the first, christological reading sets up a pattern of thinking about Christ in relation to the world that causes problems when it is transferred to an account of how to read. It is a reading that makes it difficult to find space—in or around the "way"—for the continued significance of the literal sense of the text. The saved (the chicks and the eggs) are taken *from* the nest and from the way—from "this world"—and all that remains in "this world" (the mother bird) is abandoned to destruction. The division of the nest is mapped onto the ultimate conflict between Christ and the devil, and this dichotomy is repeated in the interpretations that affect life "on the way." There is rather little space in this reading for attention to the persistence of the world and the continuing relations of interdependence within it—the penultimate in relation to the ultimate, to use Bonhoeffer's terms. We could note, for example, the assertion, in the first section and by implication also in the second, that the eggs and young are badly off as long as they are in the nest—they would do better if only they could be freed completely from their current material dependence.

In this Rupert's reading, of course, directly *opposes* the popular contemporary interpretation—for which this text is precisely about the durability of relations of material dependence, that is, the need to preserve the natural environment. More than this, as we have seen, this reading reduces to a minimum any Christian responsibility for a continuing relationship to Jewish readers of the text—or to any of the interpretive approaches they pursue.[22]

Now, for both of these reasons a contemporary Christian reader might be inclined to drive these interpretations away in the hope that, like the mother bird, they will disappear quietly. Why be concerned with them? Simply, I suggest, because they have *not* succeeded in killing the text—and nor have they exhausted the potential fruitfulness of the connection between bird and text. They have, in fact, directed our attention to a basic tension in the reading of strange texts as scripture—between, on the one hand, the need to see past or beyond the strangeness of the text, and, on the other hand, the obligation to preserve it. If a sense of *care for strangeness*, or of the demands that arise from encountering what is unassimilable, is missing from the interpretations of "bird as text" that I have discussed, there is no reason *a priori* why alternative readings cannot be developed that do manifest a care for the strangeness of texts.

What the medieval readings of "bird as text" do present, in contrast to at least some later readings, is the recognition that the scriptural text *is* being encountered *in via* (so, from some particular historical context) and approached with a view to finding food; and that the acquisition of such food implies at least some relation to whatever in the text resists conversion into resources for use. In this they may help subsequent readers to note and avoid the temptation—especially in a reading "for ethics"—to suppress whatever in the text fails to fit the agenda of the reader. They may also help subsequent readers to note and avoid the temptation to claim justification in the literal reading without remainder ("this is what the text is really about, so any other interpretation is clearly erroneous") for a thinly veiled theological appropriation. Rupert of Deutz's reading, in particular, draws attention to the need for a Christian reader who searches this text for "ethics" not to neglect the fact that it is read as Old Testament, that is, it is interpreted in relation to Christ.

I am interested in the possibilities that arise in the interaction between these medieval readings and a range of other interpretations of the bird's-nest precept—interpretations that take the freeing of the mother bird as seriously as the appropriation of her eggs and young. First, then, what happens if the literal sense is taken seriously as the *source* of whatever

22. The correlation in medieval Christian thought between negative or dismissive attitudes to the durability of the world—to what I, following Bonhoeffer, term here the "penultimate"—and anti-Jewish thought is identified and illustrated in Cohen, *Living Letters*, esp. 69.

reading we might require to provide nutrition "on the way"—and/or as commanding respect in itself? At minimum, thinking about the "sustainability" interpretations sketched above, this would presumably mean that the literal sense has to be *allowed to live*. Either taking the literal interpretation as food (assuming a "literal" reading is the only reading that does people good) or killing the literal interpretation (presenting a single spiritual interpretation as the only one that the text will ever produce) constitutes an unsustainable interaction with the text. I have suggested that this is not unconnected with an attitude that tends to disregard the duration of the world—and that this in turn can be linked with failure to allow time and space to other readers of the text.[23]

But how might we understand, in a theological context, the relationship between the response of compassion or respect for the mother bird, on the one hand, and the preservation of a food source, on the other? And how might the negotiation of this relationship affect our reading of the precept as a precept *about* reading? In what follows, I seek answers to this question through a wider range of conversations about interpretation—beginning with a closer consideration, firstly, of readings of the literal sense, and secondly, of how and on what basis the precept can be read as concerned with respect or compassion.

IN THE CONTEXT OF WAR

Calum M. Carmichael's commentaries on the bird's-nest precept link it, as do many others, to Deuteronomy 20:19: "If you besiege a town for a long time, making war against it in order to take it, you must not destroy its trees by wielding an axe against them. Although you may take food from them, you must not cut them down. Are trees in the field human beings, that they should come under siege from you?" Several features of Carmichael's analysis, which is one of the most extended discussions of the bird's-nest precept in recent commentaries, are of interest for our purposes. First, there is his simple admission: "the bird law, no matter

23. What I am suggesting here relates closely to various recent evaluations of the Augustinian "witness doctrine" and its historical effects—evaluations that draw attention, for example, to Bernard of Clairvaux's demand that Jews be *protected* as Jews because of their essential continuing role as "witnesses." See for example Cohen, *Living Letters*; Fredriksen, "Augustine and Israel" and *Augustine and the Jews*. I am very grateful to Chad Pecknold for discussions of his ongoing work on the theological reappropriation of Augustinian thought for contemporary Christian-Jewish relations.

how one looks at it, reads strangely."[24] Proposing a range of possible interpretive contexts for the precept, as he does, cannot abrogate its strangeness. Of more substantive interest is the fact that he shows warfare, or the response to the enemy, to be a plausible interpretive framework for the bird's-nest precept. Not only is "the mother with the children" a form of words associated elsewhere with the total destruction of enemy populations and cities,[25] but the verb translated "come upon," according to Carmichael, frequently connotes an *adverse* encounter.[26] It should be noted that midrashic tradition makes this connection strongly—less in the comments on the bird's-nest precept than in other instances in which the "mother with the children" appears. God is said to obey God's own precept by allowing the "mothers" of Egypt to live, even though Pharaoh violates it (*Exod. Rab.* 20:4); the enemies of Israel transgressed the Torah when "mothers were dashed in pieces with their children" (Hos 10:14; *Lam. Rabb.* 1.9.37).[27]

Together with the links to the fruit-trees precept, Carmichael's analysis of the warfare connotations of the bird's-nest precept builds up a powerful interpretive nexus within which to situate other readings of the text. How might this shape our reading of the bird's-nest precept? Firstly, I suggest, it would shed light on the interpretations discussed above in which the mother bird appeared as a "threat," and in which the possibility of violence on the part of, or within, the interpretive community was apparent. Reading this as a text about warfare draws attention to the violence done to the bird's nest in its division, to nonhuman nature in its use for human purposes, and potentially to the text in its interpretation. As Carmichael notes, refraining from harming the fruit trees is commanded in the first instance because they are *not* human beings; they are, rather, part of the whole context that sustains human beings, in peace or war.[28] The interhuman conflict is not all-embracing, and not everything reduces to a useful weapon for either side.

24. Carmichael, *Laws of Deuteronomy*, 153.

25. The texts in question are Hos 10:14—"as Shalman destroyed Beth-arbel on the day of battle / when mothers were dashed in pieces with their children"—and Jacob's prayer in Gen 32:11—"Deliver me, please, from the hand of my brother, from the hand of Esau, for I am afraid of him; he may come and kill us all, the mothers with the children."

26. Carmichael, *Laws of Deuteronomy*, 154.

27. See Johnston, "'Least of the Commandments,'" 210.

28. Carmichael, *Laws of Deuteronomy*, 153.

To spare the fruit trees and to spare the mother bird could be said to express a political hope—for "long life" beyond the time of conflict. These precepts express this hope, moreover, not by a simple appeal to expediency on the expectation of victory or continued power ("save them because you might need them later"; Carmichael describes the law as "soberly practical"[29]), but by locating the sustaining context of human action—nonhuman nature—implicitly within the scope of divine care and provision. The durability of the world—and not merely the "wild natural" world, but the cultivated world, the world of the planting and tending of fruit trees, and, we might add, the keeping and interpretation of precepts—is not a matter of indifference.

Placing the bird's-nest precept alongside the fruit-trees precept, besides pointing to environmental preservation, can, I have suggested, point to questions about the right conduct of "battles"—and in connection with this to battles conducted with or around the biblical text. We often, as the interpretive texts I have discussed here make abundantly clear, interpret in the context of religious battles that are not unconnected from physical violence. In fact, twenty-first century interpreters read in a world in which many have declared religious battles to the death—the deaths of entire cultures and traditions, as well as of the children of these traditions. Violence against the sustaining contexts on which both sides rely—not merely nonhuman nature, but political and religious institutions, texts and communities that read them—is a constant risk in this situation.

Thinking about how readings of texts are mobilized in ethics and politics, we might suggest that it is particularly in the situation of an inter- or intratraditional "battle" that the temptation to destroy the literal sense of the text, along with or as part of the destruction of one's opponent's arguments, appears—just as the fruit trees are liable to be cut down, or the mother killed with the children, in times of war. The present purposes for which the text is to be put to use are absolutized—the text becomes "prooftext"[30]—and are thereby allowed to damage or destroy the inter- or intratraditional context within which different relationships could be

29. Ibid.

30. It should be noted that the prooftext is not solely the province of theologians. Anti-religious prooftexting also has a long history—"How can anyone possibly take seriously a book that says things like *this*?" or "that contradicts itself like *this*?" Some of the best modern examples of this reverse literalism can be found online at http://www.infidels.org.

formed or new readings developed. A medieval example relevant to the bird's-nest precept is found in Guibert of Nogent's treatise "Against the Jews,"—written in the context of the Crusades—where he uses (what he assumes to be) the literal sense of the bird's-nest precept as proof of the folly and blindness of Jewish reading and religious practice.[31]

Carmichael's work, then, invites a consideration of what it means to preserve, through limitations on the exploitation of texts and contexts, livable worlds that endure beyond a given struggle. It also draws attention, at least potentially, to the ethical demand not only for restraint in exploitation (sustainability) but also for respect or compassion. Carmichael himself discounts (without entirely eliminating) the possibility that the bird's-nest precept "reveals any humane consideration."[32] I would argue, however, that when we hear the echoes of the other "mother with the children" texts, to which he draws attention—the texts that speak of slaughters in war—the bird's-nest precept does draw attention to the human capacity for excessive and unchecked destruction, destruction that exceeds reason or necessity. In the context of unchecked violence, it confronts interpreters with the vulnerability of the bird—like the vulnerability of children and their mothers in times of war. Like the face of the other in Levinas's work,[33] the mother bird encountered "on the way" issues the injunction against violence—in a context in which violence is already being done.

All of this draws us towards the idea that the first call of the bird's-nest precept is not to the pragmatic maintenance of sources of food, but, as a long (mainly but not exclusively Jewish) tradition of interpretation suggests, to *compassion*. Alongside that, I suggest, the bird's-nest precept also summons *respect* for the other, in which—or in whom—God is encountered as interrupting and redirecting the "use" of the world.

"WHOSE MERCY EXTENDS TO A BIRD'S NEST"[34]

The discussion of the bird's-nest precept in *Deuteronomy Rabbah* is introduced by a series of reflections on divine compassion and its

31. Guibert of Nogent, *De Incarnatione contra Iudaeos* 3.8, in PL 156:524A.

32. Carmichael, *Laws of Deuteronomy*, 156.

33. Levinas, *Totality and Infinity*, esp. 35–62.

34. For further discussion of the history of the interpretation of the Talmudic texts referred to here, see Segal, "Justice, Mercy."

extent—ending with the claim that God has mercy on the birds. In the Talmud (Bavli *Berakoth* 33b) the prayer "whose mercy extends to a bird's nest" clearly refers to our text (although this prayer is regarded as unacceptable). The "compassion" interpretation has been so widely discussed in past centuries that one contemporary Jewish commentator can refer to it as "the obvious reading."[35]

In the first instance, however, as several commentators besides Carmichael (discussed above) are keen to note, the compassion expressed or enacted in the bird's-nest precept is oddly restricted. The young birds are, after all, identified as legitimate spoils. We might say, anachronistically, that the bird's-nest precept, like the fruit-trees precept, is about the just war rather than nonviolence. One (Christian) interpreter, in fact, goes so far as to say that it is about the *necessity* of sacrificing some in order to save others.[36]

Maimonides' reading of the bird's-nest precept, and a tradition of reflection on it, however, suggests that the dynamic of compassion that the command establishes is supposed to reach beyond the mother bird. Famously, Maimonides argues that nobody would want to eat the young and the (nearly-hatched) eggs—so to command the sparing of the mother bird will in fact lead to the sparing of the entire nest. For Maimonides, the command can be linked to the Torah's many instructions about methods of slaughter, the intention of all of which (in a context in which meat-eating is assumed to be necessary for survival) is to enact divine compassion for nonhuman animals.[37] In other words, the sparing of the mother bird is the starting point of compassion, not the mark of its limit; or, better, the claim that compassion extends as far as the bird gives compassion the *broadest* possible scope. It should be noted here that one of the reasons given in the Talmud for rejecting the prayer

35. Weiss, "Maimonides on *shilluah ha-qen*," 346.

36. And thus to provide a handy christological punch-line (and an excellent example of what Girard refers to as the logic of redemptive violence): "According to the Gospel account, Jesus died that we might live." Christensen, *Deuteronomy* 21:10—34:12, 500. I have not found other commentators who make the same theological move; the christological reading I develop below contradicts it directly.

37. For a survey of commentary on Maimonides' interpretation, and for a more detailed exposition of the reading I assume here, see Weiss, "Maimonides on *shilluah ha-qen*." Maimonides in *Mishneh Torah*, beginning from Berakhot 33b, classified the bird's-nest precept as a command for which there was *no* reason; Weiss offers a plausible explanation for his shift of opinion. On the idea that the command has no reason, see below.

". . . whose mercy extends to a bird's nest" is that this risks suggesting that the mercy of God *only* extends to a bird's nest, and not to other creatures. The implication is that this is an inversion of the intention of the precept—if indeed its "intention" can be thus discerned.

Where for Maimonides the extension of compassion beyond the mother bird is given in the unwilled consequences of the commanded action (the fact that you will be left with inedible eggs and/or fledglings), for Nachmanides in his response to Maimonides' interpretation the extension of compassion comes about through the learning of compassionate habits. In either case, the mother bird, and the command to spare her, comes in the first place to interrupt the use and abuse of everything and everyone in the environment, and in the second place, at least potentially, to transform the practices of use and abuse. It should be noted that the act of sparing the bird's nest is, for Nachmanides, performed in the first instance simply to fulfill a precept and *not* to instantiate a general principle of mercy. Respect is granted not to the bird *per se* but to the precept, as itself the sign of the divine other in relation to whom humanity exists. At the same time, in its very performance the bird's-nest precept transforms relations to the nonhuman other. In Nachmanides' terms, the precept is given "that we should not have a cruel heart . . . for cruelty proliferates in man's soul"; and it is also "so that His creatures be refined and purified."[38]

The idea that compassion, divine or human, extends from the mother bird outwards—perhaps even to the human enemy or stranger who is "come upon"—relies on her being a possible, even if minimally important, object of compassion (a point discussed by both Maimonides and Nachmanides). The minimal, but non-negligible, importance of both the mother bird and the precept that relates to her is itself a significant feature of interpretations of our text, and one with important New Testament resonances. In fact, as I shall now suggest, it provides the starting point for a Christian reinterpretation of the bird's-nest precept—a reinterpretation that should (following Rupert and other medieval interpreters) be christological in focus but should also (following my critique

38. In a similar way, and referring to the pacifism/just war analogy above, it could be argued that Christian pacifism (especially as found in the historic peace churches, Anabaptist and Quaker) has had at its center, for most of its history, not the general *claim* that warfare is wrong or contrary to the nature of God but the *act* of refusing, under pressure, to take up arms or to contribute to a state's war effort. In recent years the peace churches, at least in the West, have placed much less emphasis on refusal and much more on "positive" peacemaking; the possible reappraisal of the refusal tradition, to which my argument points, is beyond the scope of this article.

of the medieval interpreters and the subsequent discussion) reflect and perform the ethical imperatives of the bird's-nest precept.

THE LIGHTEST PRECEPT AND THE LEAST VALUABLE CREATURE

[19]Therefore, whoever breaks one of the least of these commandments, and teaches others to do the same, will be called least in the kingdom of heaven; but whoever does them and teaches them will be called great in the kingdom of heaven.

—MATTHEW 5

One of the few extended treatments of the bird's-nest precept in relation to Christian traditions begins from the observation that it is only *this* precept that is referred to as "the least of the precepts" in the rabbinic literature. The author, Robert Johnston, argues on this basis that the most obvious resonance of Matthew 5:19 in its original context was with discussions of Deuteronomy 22:6–7.[39] This association, as Johnston notes and as I shall explore later, points to further connections between the "bird sayings" of Jesus (especially Matt 10:29) and rabbinic discourse. The "lightness" of the bird's-nest precept, particularly combined with its association with the promise of reward,[40] led in the rabbinic literature to reflections on the greater importance of other commands (such as, by way of contrast, the honoring of father and mother—the "weightiest" precept)—and *how much more* they will merit reward.[41] A look at one example of this rabbinic literature will help us to see the implications of calling the bird's-nest precept the "least of these commandments," and then to see what this might imply for a Christian rereading of the precept.

39. Johnston, "'Least of the Commandments.'"

40. This was, presumably, why it attracted attention in the first place in discussions about the relative "weight" of precepts. The reward is mentioned in relation to three precepts: the bird's nest; the honoring of father and mother (Exod 20:12, Deut 5:16)—regarded as the "weightiest" precept; and, less often discussed but interesting in terms of the "weighing" of precepts, fair weights and measures (Deut 25:15). See *M. Rab. Deut.* 122 and, for a recent discussion that does discuss (briefly) the "weights and measures" precept, Benstein, "Earth's Reward."

41. See, in addition to the passage discussed below, the conclusion to the discussion in *Bavli Hullin* 12, 5b. The literature is discussed further by Johnston, "'Least of the Commandments,'" 207–8.

In *Midrash Rabbah Deuteronomy* a parable told in relation to this passage suggests that the connection between the *specific* command and the reward is deliberately obscured, lest the observance of the *entire Torah* be neglected. The parable describes a king who calls workers into his garden and instructs them to harvest the fruit of the trees, without informing them of the rates of payment. At the end of the day, he asks each worker to which tree he has attended; only at that point are the workers informed of the value of the trees and hence of the payment for the work done in tending them. "What did God do? He did not reveal to His creatures the reward for each separate precept, so that they may perform all the precepts without questioning. . . . So God did not reveal the reward of the precepts, except of two, the weightiest [i.e. honoring of parents] and the least weighty [i.e., the setting free of the mother bird]."[42]

We might say, reasoning beyond this passage, that what is encountered in the mother-bird precept is law that approaches the zero-point of content but still bears all the characteristics of the legal. This would allow another possible, and in many ways very attractive, reading of the connection between action and reward: that *lawfulness as such*—the very existence of laws that are recognized as given and intergenerationally binding—is what makes possible sustainable existence. On this reading, the setting free of the mother bird would again be about the safeguarding of social "resources"—but in particular about the maintenance of law.

The problem with this reading is that if it is simply (as I have suggested so far) that the "rule of law," the maintenance of stable social and cultural institutions, is a good thing, it does not matter whose law or what law rules. It would return us to the idea that the setting free of the mother bird, or the sparing of fruit trees, is purely practical, a matter of survival; and when this is applied to laws it can become a mandate for preserving more or less *any* law, any system of social and cultural institutions. Even if the "rule of law" is necessary for the continuation of life on earth, this principle supplies nothing that would ever give the laws content beyond securing survival. There are many laws that would ensure "that you may live long," but this says nothing about the kinds of laws and institutions that ensure "that it may go well with you."

If a Christian interpreter, in particular, is tempted to read a straightforwardly conservative attitude to law in general from of the bird's-nest precept and/or the midrash and/or Matthew 5:19, she is pulled up short both in the midrashic parable and in the New Testament. The midrashic

42. *Midrash Rabbah*, 121–22.

parable, first, is clear about reading the setting free of the mother bird as "work for God"—the work done by the laborers in the king's garden, expecting their pay from the king, who sets values on the work (and who also, moving to Matt 5:19, establishes orders of priority in the kingdom of heaven).[43] Thus, the bird's-nest precept has its importance not as simply law but as *divine* law.

Second, having begun by referring the work and its reward to God, the discussion in the midrash then undermines the (apparent) logic of the parable, together with any attempt to establish a one-to-one correlation between human and divine evaluations of laws, when in the citation of the relevant texts it becomes clear that God, unlike the king in the parable, gives the same reward—"length of days"—for the most and the least "weighty" precepts, that is, for the honoring of parents and the setting free of the mother bird. Jesus' words in Matthew 5:19 repeat this undermining move. By pronouncing not a generalized significance for all law nor a comprehensible scale of relative significance for laws, but the ultimate significance of a particular and obviously trivial law, the midrash and Matthew 5:19 point *this specific* law back to its basis—in the "kingdom of heaven" and God's call of particular "laborers" into it; and they make it impossible to avoid the particularity of the call by calculating in advance the relative importance of its different aspects.[44] The law matters because of the relationship to God it enacts; but precisely for this reason even the "lightest" precepts matter.

If this is a fair reading of the midrashic parable and discussion, and at least a plausible reading of Matthew 5:19, what is a Christian interpreter to make of the "lightest precept" and the eschatological reward linked to it? One possible answer, I suggest, can be developed through a further intertextual reading—concerned not with the significance of the precept but with the significance of the bird.

43. Compare the New Testament parable of the "workers in the vineyard" (Matt 20:1–16); and for discussion of the "economics of the kingdom" in relation to this parable, see Hardy, "Societal Economics."

44. For the account of the relationship between law and election developed by Susannah Ticciati, on which I have drawn for this discussion, see her *Job and the Disruption of Identity*.

[29]Are not two sparrows sold for a penny? Yet not one of them will fall to the ground unperceived by your Father. . . . [31]So do not be afraid; you are of more value than many sparrows.

—Matthew 10

Johnston argues that for the rabbinic thinkers and for Jesus "the commandment, not the sparrow" and "the human being, not the sparrow" is important—and that this (the importance of the commandment and of the human being) is a locus of reflection on the bird's-nest precept that they share. Persuaded of the importance of Johnston's intertextual connections, I am less persuaded by the conclusions he draws from them. The bird *has* to be important, in at least two senses, for the whole chain of reasoning in the Matthean texts and in (at least) Maimonides' reflections on rabbinic texts to work: it has to be a creature of God and within the scope of God's knowledge and compassion, and it has to feature somewhere on existing human scales of valuation. It has to "weigh" something, and fetch a token amount of money—just as the precept has to take a certain amount of time and effort to perform, and the text has to be read as part of scripture, for them to be the basis for claims about the whole of the law or the whole of scripture.

The text from Matthew 10 suggests that there is no point on the scale of inner-worldly valuation (the selling and buying of lives, for however many pennies) where that which is bought and sold is "unperceived" by God. It calls forth a primary response of respect, drawing attention at once to the bird's inability to *command* that respect (its vulnerability, its "lightness") and to the possible consequences of refusing the respect—inability to acknowledge that the value of a *human* life is secured in its relation to God and ultimately in no other way. At the same time, and to the chagrin of certain twenty-first-century readers, Matthew 10:29 acknowledges the buying and selling of sparrows—for almost nothing—and the much greater economic significance of human lives.

Matthew 10:29–31 affirms, then, we might say, a set of important penultimate relationships and judgements. Perhaps it is all right, and even unavoidable, to set a price on sparrows and to render them exchangeable—or even, within certain significant public-spending debates, to set a price on human lives (considerably higher than the price of sparrows). The discussion above of the parable in *Deuteronomy Rabbah* suggests a further move: perhaps it is all right, and even unavoidable, to make judgements about the relative "weight" of *precepts*, in a certain sense setting prices on them—for example, to regard the setting free of a mother bird as of less moment than the honoring of one's parents. The various interpretations I have discussed, in their evaluation of the bird's-nest precept in its textual form, suggest a further move beyond this. Perhaps it is all right, and even unavoidable, to engage in the extraction of value from *texts*—to read them "for" particular purposes, to exchange them for concepts more usable in contemporary discussions, and to make decisions about which, at any particular point, are worth most.

At the same time, the Matthean text sets up a way of rereading these penultimate relationships and judgements that will tend to transform them in the light of the ultimate. Perhaps it is *not* all right, for those called to respond to the world as God knows it, to reduce sparrows to their selling price, people to their value to the economy, precepts (as in the Talmudic discussion mentioned above) to generalized claims about "mercy," and texts to what they mean now for us. Perhaps it is not all right because the sparrow and the text, as well as the person (in an analogous but not identical sense), are in relation to God such that nobody can claim complete power over them without falsifying them; more than this, they are in relation to God such that they mediate the claim and call of God to the one who encounters them.

Following my discussion above of the bird's-nest precept "in the context of war," it should be noted that this latter move, in turn, protects the context of human action from destruction through exploitation. If sparrows are respected so that not all of them are bought and sold (or omitted from consideration in decisions about housing and farming), the species will continue; if people are not reduced to their economic value or other value-for-us, peaceful relationships can be built; and if the texts are not interpreted *away*, they retain their capacity to generate new and fruitful readings. As I suggested above in the discussion of the warfare context of the bird's-nest precept, the projection of a given system of inner-worldly valuation as *ultimate*—the claim (or the action that claims) that the sparrows or the people or the texts *are* their use-for-me—ends up destroying both the world and the agent.[45]

But is this in its turn an unacceptable explaining away of the bird's-nest precept, when I have already said that the latter should not be the

45. I am grateful to members of the Scriptural Reasoning Theory Group for discussions of the dynamics of remembering and forgetting (or movements between the complex–particular and the simplified–abstract) in economic life.

basis for general claims about law? Am I just finding a more subtle way to dispense with the specificities of the precept?

Here I want to return, after a long diversion, to Rupert of Deutz and the medieval interpreters, and to revisit the insight gained there that a Christian rereading of the bird's-nest precept has to be a christological reading. Taking Matthew 10:29 out of its context in fact misses much that could point to a christological reading of the bird's-nest precept. For this text occurs in the center of a dense passage—the commissioning of the Twelve—in which the risks incurred by the disciples of Jesus are enumerated in the context of recalling in advance Jesus' own death. It is a summons to action that has the identity and destiny of Jesus as its basis. Repeatedly the success, the security, and even the survival of the missionaries is relativized as an aim—relativized by the overriding importance of acknowledging Jesus[46] as the response to, and the prelude to, being acknowledged before God.[47] Set alongside the passion references and the verses on acknowledging and denying Jesus, the sparrow text acquires deeper connotations. Jesus will be sold by one of the Twelve for thirty pieces of silver, and he will be denied by another in exchange for that other's security. One way and another, he will be exchanged for "what he is worth" by people who fail to acknowledge him—and who take advantage of his vulnerability to this kind of reduction.

The text about the triviality and the vulnerability of sparrows, then, contributes to an understanding of what it means to "acknowledge" Jesus, and of the inseparability of Christology from ethical action. In a sense, this is to take up Rupert of Deutz's naming of Christ as the one in and by whom the law is fulfilled—but it is to do this without assuming that the law is thereby dispensed with. Christ not only does the law; he does what the law does.[48] In my reading, then, he does what the bird's-nest precept does. So,

46. Matt 10:32, 33: "Everyone therefore who acknowledges me before others, I also will acknowledge before my Father in heaven; but whoever denies me before others, I also will deny before my Father in heaven." 10:40: "Whoever welcomes you welcomes me, and whoever welcomes me welcomes the one who sent me."

47. And the "summary" of this is v. 39: "whoever finds her life will lose it, and whoever loses her life for my sake will find it."

48. Matt 23:37 (and its parallel, Luke 13:34), in which Jesus represents himself as a "mother bird" in the context of violence against the messengers of God, gains a further resonance in the light of this claim: "Jerusalem, Jerusalem, the city that kills the prophets and stones those who are sent to it! How often have I desired to gather your children together as a hen gathers her brood under her wings . . ." For a medieval commentary on Deut 22:6–7—the only one I have found—that makes use of this connection, albeit in a different way, see Bruno of Segni, *Expositio in Pentateuchum*, in PL 164:522B.

he interrupts the pattern of violence and exploitation, marks the breadth of divine compassion and the point from which human compassion can be learned, generates possibilities of life that transcend the competing concerns of any given moment, and does this affirming rather than denying ongoing and particular material relations of dependence. The Christ-centered rereading for which this text calls, I suggest, is a summons to Christian readers, firstly, to *acknowledge the claim and call of God in the vulnerable other they encounter*, and secondly, to *acknowledge that vulnerable other as the source of their life*—and to learn to do this in learning to acknowledge Christ. The response to this summons has to be enacted in relation to whatever is "come upon"—but the habits of mind that will make its enactment possible can be developed, as it were, in advance.

CONCLUSIONS: FINDING TWENTY-FIRST-CENTURY BIRD'S NESTS

We seem to have come a long way from the concerns with environmental ethics with which this article began, and perhaps even further from any real mother bird currently sitting on a nest and likely to be disturbed (or not) by someone in search of food. Have I taken the reading too far away from the very material concerns with which, after all, contemporary interest in this passage began—concerns about nonhuman animals and the nonhuman creation—and further away still from the literal sense of the biblical text? It is right, in the terms I have set out, to worry that this article might have managed, as it were, to kill the mother bird without letting her go. My readings, and my readings of the readings of others, point to a certain priority of respect or compassion in the response to the mother bird: if she is encountered *first* in herself, in her strangeness, in her unassimilability to human categories (the category of the enemy, the category of the food source), she can *then* be read as part of the context that sustains human life.

The same principle lies, I would argue, at the base of any adequate Christian environmental ethics; there is a proper concern for the sustainability of human existence and for the environmental conditions that make this possible, but one's own survival or the survival of one's own species is not the overarching framework—and if it becomes such, the result is likely to be a systematic inability to interpret the demands placed on one by whatever is "found." After all, it should be recalled that the *precept* in this text is the setting free of the mother bird (strictly speaking, there are two precepts here: one negative, "you shall not take . . ."; and one positive, "you shall let the mother bird go"); the taking of the eggs and the young is only *permitted*.

Likewise, I have argued following the discussion of medieval interpretations, it is particularly important for the Christian interpreter, in encountering a text such as this, to be warned against readings that do not allow the text to remain strange, or that make its strangeness primarily something to be fought against and defeated. The concern in the Talmud, taken up by Maimonides, that the command of God should not be "reduced to mercy"—that the strangeness of the bird's-nest precept should not be explained away within a larger framework of more rational theology—can be interpreted as a response to the vulnerability of this text, which is comparable to the vulnerability of the bird herself; and as the bird's-nest precept acts as a representative of *all* the commands, it points to the vulnerability of all of them to interpretive violence.

To counterbalance this, we should of course say that the taking of the eggs and the young is *really* permitted; and it can be assumed that it is necessary to sustain life. There is no escape from the relationships of material dependence in which we exist—just for that reason, the possibility of excessive or destructive exploitation is always present. I would suggest that the bird's-nest precept, both in the context of environmental ethics and in the context of biblical interpretation, puts to Christian readers the question of what it means to recall and acknowledge Christ not only in the face of the human other but also in the innumerable given sources of our material and social existence.

I conclude with one further reflection on the contemporary resonances of the bird's-nest precept in relation to human lives. I have said or suggested that twenty-first-century readings of this text have mainly been inspired by environmental concerns. As it happens, my work on this chapter coincided with teaching a course on Jewish and Christian post-Holocaust thought. Gisella Perl's memoir of her time as a doctor in Auschwitz—secretly killing babies born in the death camp in order to save their mothers from certain selection for the gas chambers—makes terrifying reading alongside Deuteronomy 22:6–7.[49] It makes even more terrifying reading alongside the various appeals in contemporary politics to the need to sacrifice some lives for the sake of a greater good—most of all where in Christian theology the death of Christ for the sake of

49. Perl, *I Was a Doctor in Auschwitz*, extract reprinted in Rittner and Roth, eds., *Different Voices*, 106–18.

all is used to justify such reasonings. The first lesson to be learned for a post-Holocaust and post-September-11 reading of the bird's-nest precept should, I suggest, be to attend to the responses of compassion that constitute a protest against the situation that makes the "sacrifices" necessary—the protest heard in Perl's mourning for the deaths of the children she killed. The twenty-first-century reader of the bird's-nest precept can learn (with Maimonides and Nachmanides, among others) to expand circles of compassion and to remember the acts of violence that have been concealed.

19 Literal Reading and Other Animals II

The Animals We Write On

ANIMALS IN THE MARGINS?

CAROL ADAMS, IN *NEITHER Man nor Beast*, suggests that nonhuman animals in Christian history do not even get as far as being "marginalized." They are, literally and figuratively, what we write both our central texts and our marginalia onto.[1] When we look at the Dead Sea Scrolls, to use Adams's example, we focus on the text and not on the animal skin. We do not see a dead animal; we see a writing surface. The very act of writing the text reduces the animal not only to voicelessness, but to invisibility as anything other than a resource for human use. Writing on animals is, for Adams, metonymic for a set of cultural practices that render animals invisible as agents and sufferers, and that thus prepare the way for ontologies of the animal that deny the significance of animal action and suffering. In Adams's accounts, practices (here, writing on animal skins) ground an epistemology (animals cannot be seen or known as agents or patients) that gives rise to an ontology (animals are "completely other than us" or "made for our use") which in turn provides the basis for the practices. I have written elsewhere about the usefulness for Christian theology and ethics of this basic account of how attitudes to animals are formed.[2] In this chapter I wish to focus more on the arresting

1. *Neither Man nor Beast*, 203.

2. Muers, "Seeing, Choosing and Eating."

image of "writing on animals," and to explore whether and how this is how Christian texts work. Following on from the previous chapter, I shall suggest that the question of how to read nonhuman animals in texts has much to do with the question of how to treat the "literal sense."

When I saw a fragment of a Dead Sea Scroll at a recent exhibition of Jewish, Christian, and Muslim sacred texts I did not—as Adams predicted I would not—think much about the animal on whom it was written. There were, however, at the same exhibition, innumerable animals on whom one could not but focus—the animals that did make it into the margins, and often beyond the margins, of the sacred texts, chiefly of Christianity but also to some extent of Judaism. Initial capitals were illuminated with or as animals; marginal notes were written in micrographia in the forms of real or imaginary animals; animals crept around the pages and worked their way into the texts. They arrested the eye immediately, whether or not the text was in a language or a script one could decipher—they held up the reading. I wondered what these animals, taken together, meant, and why it seemed to make no sense to ask what any one, taken individually, "meant"—and whether the answers to either of these questions would help to clarify my doubts about Adams's presentation of the animals we write on.

The marginal animals in the illustrated manuscripts are not, it seems to me, being instrumentalized in the service of a larger project of meaning making. If the *text* stands at this point for the larger project of meaning making, the marginal animals if anything detract from it. Quite often, they make the text considerably harder to read. (I could not imagine actually trying to follow the micrographia around the twists and turns of a serpent in order to make out the marginal note). In their very gratuity, their oddness, their apparent irrelevance, they seem to invite a pause before reading.[3] They make the text more opaque; they invite attention to the materiality of the book, the inks, even the writing surfaces. Viewed in an exhibition behind a glass case, by people who are not trained in the interpretation of the scripts they surround, they reinforce the sense of the text itself, before any reading, interpretation or application, as sheer given, as object over against its readers. One thinks, it is remarkable *that this is*. One is invited to wonder. The marginal animals reinforce a sense of the text's resistance to, and capacity to exceed, any particular use to which it is put by its interpreters.

3. I am indebted to Ben Quash and others for comments in, and on, a conversation in the Scriptural Reasoning Theory Group that suggested this idea to me.

Of course, these marginal animals are not flesh and blood, and they are fashioned according to a particular scribe's or artist's intention. They are being used to say something—even if what they are there to say is, "Pause, look, do not read too quickly, do not consume too quickly." So it is important not to jump from the marginal animals to an assertion that the deepest instinct of the Christian tradition is not to write on animals but to wonder at them. Nonetheless, it is worth asking: is it coincidental that it is so often animals—rather than anything else—that appear to interrupt reading? We know that people enjoy drawing animals; there is a playful exuberance about these marginal beasts that would be hard to attain with inanimate objects. There may also, however, be an aspect of the texts themselves that invites us to let the animals appear, not only in the margins but on the capitals (before the beginning)—and that might make us think twice about writing on them in such a way as to write them out.

In beginning to explore this idea, I want first to consider an earlier and influential account of "writing on animals," and an intriguing absence within it.

BEAST AND "MAN" IN THE BIBLE

Mary Midgley presents, in *Beast and Man* (and elsewhere), an extensive, lucid, and damning indictment of various ways in which Western culture, and in particular its anthropology, has been written on animals.[4] The "beast," generally and by species, has been used for centuries, Midgley demonstrates, as the negative or positive foil for humanity. From the commonest proverbs (the "greedy pig," the "sly dog") to the seminal texts of modern ethics (Midgley has much to say about the "Kantian beast"), animals have been used as building blocks for models of humanity as it should or should not be. Animals have not—this is Midgley's key point—been permitted to appear as themselves; so the more complex lessons that might thereby have been learned about humanity and the world we inhabit have been lost. The actual behavior of wolves in the wild, with its numerous intriguing analogies to aspects of human social behavior, is of no concern in the claim that "man is a wolf." Animals are made to carry moral weight, positive or negative, as it suits our larger projects of self-interpretation. The use of animals to symbolize negative moral characteristics (as is most common) does not, Midgley recognizes, *inevitably* result

4. Midgley, *Beast and Man*, esp. ch. 2.

in the ill treatment of the animals themselves. Nonetheless, she is clear that both we and the other animals lose something by our propensity to write ourselves on animals; we lose *inter alia* the ability to recognize ourselves as animals, and they do often suffer ill treatment as a result of our failure to recognize them as kin.

The evidence Midgley marshals for the historical aspect of her argument is extensive and persuasive. For the theologically minded reader there is, however, one very noticeable gap: she adduces no examples from the Bible. The story she tells begins in classical philosophy; the "Christianity" that appears in her pages is a Christianity that traces its intellectual lines of descent through Platonism and Stoicism.[5] Her only biblical example, as I shall discuss below, is used to support her own position over against the myth of the beast.

Why is this? My hypothesis is that Midgley adduces no examples from the Bible of animals being used as negative or even positive images of human traits because there are rather few such examples to use. The biblical writers do not often or consistently use animals in this way. This is a surprising hypothesis to be able to advance. The picture Midgley paints is readily recognizable, and the temptation, especially having read her discussion, is to assume that this happens everywhere. Indeed, in investigating my hypothesis I found several initially promising pieces of counterevidence, which on investigation proved not to be so (or not *obviously* to be so). For example, Ecclesiastes 3:21—"Who knows whether the human spirit goes upwards and the spirit of animals goes downwards to the earth?"—has been read as emphasizing the difference between humanity and the "beasts that perish."[6] In context, however, it makes more sense as a reminder that we are *like* the beasts, i.e., that we perish. Is there an anxiety about becoming too closely identified with the animal, evident in some (Christian) commentaries but rather less evident—or at least, subjected to critique—in Ecclesiastes?

There are, of course, several examples in the Hebrew Bible of the comparison of people with specific animals, often to the implied

5. Ibid., 47.

6. Thus Matthew Henry: "The soul of a beast is, at death, like a candle blown out—there is an end of it; whereas the soul of a man is then like a candle taken out of a dark lantern, which leaves the lantern useless indeed, but does itself shine brighter. This great difference there is between the spirits of men and beasts." *Exposition of the Old and New Testament*, loc cit.

detriment of the animals and of any people who are "like" them.[7] It is perhaps noteworthy that many of these occur within dialogue, and are often in the mouths of characters whose perspective the reader is not expected to share. Besides the example discussed below, we might recall the negative uses of "dog" in 1 Samuel 17:43 (Goliath) and 24:14 (David describing himself); and 2 Samuel 9:8 (Mephibosheth) and 16:9 (Abishai, in a comment immediately contradicted by David). Wild dogs and lions also appear in more threatening guise as images of human enemies—notably in Psalm 22, where the point appears to be less to denigrate the enemies than to emphasize the danger faced by the psalmist. (Note also the comparisons with snakes in Ps 58:4; 140:3). The blessing of Jacob (Gen 49:1–27) has perhaps the densest concentration of animal comparisons—used of tribes rather than individuals. The condemnation of Israel's rulers in Zephaniah 3:3f. and the parallel in Ezekiel 22:25–27 probably comes closest to the sort of negative comparison that Midgley finds pervasive in Western thought. Commentaries on these texts tend to take for granted the appropriateness of comparing rulers to "lions" and "wolves"—pausing only to note that the lion, as the more "noble" animal, is a suitable image for the princes.[8]

The book of Proverbs is perhaps the main place where those seeking to undermine the hypothesis advanced here might look for evidence. Here, certainly, there are repeated appeals to nonhuman animals as sources of wisdom for human life. Animals are frequently teachers of wisdom and of virtue by positive example (as, famously, Prov 6:6–8—"Go to the ant, you lazybones; consider its ways, and be wise . . ."; see also 28:1; 30:24–31), but they also function as exemplars of folly (7:22–23; 26:3; 26:11). Particularly in this second group of examples, there does seem to be an attempt to associate folly—being less than a human being should be—with being animal-like. It is particularly noteworthy that the first two—with the ox led to the slaughter and the wild animals trapped (7:22–23); the horse whipped and the donkey bridled (26:3)—refer explicitly to human domination of nonhuman animals. The fool by his folly relegates himself to the status of "animal" and receives similar treatment. It would be foolish in me to deny that there are some signs here of the tendency of which Midgley speaks—to use the animals as the negative

7. The major exception seems to be the lion, which is often the object of positive comparison—though not, as others have noted, nearly as frequently or consistently as in other bodies of ancient literature that helped to shape Western Christianity.

8. See for example Zimmerli, *Ezekiel*.

foil for good human behavior—and some material here that could be taken up by those who developed the full-scale "moralization" of animals in (for example) the bestiary tradition. Even here, however—and perhaps also in some of the texts Midgley does discuss—there seems to be rather more demand for attention to the animals themselves than would be compatible with obscuring their real characteristics in the way Midgley describes. The "lazybones" is invited to *go to* and *consider* the ant. As I shall suggest in the discussion that follows, this can be linked to calls elsewhere in the Hebrew Bible to "consider" nonhuman animals, which are *not* obviously linked to any particular lesson about human moral behavior.

The counter-examples notwithstanding, several commentators have noticed that the Hebrew Bible (at least) is not very interested in animals as tools for human self-definition. Boria Sax, for example, locates the Nazi symbology of animals in Germany's pre-Christian and classical (particularly Greek) inheritances, and contrasts this with the attitude evinced in the Hebrew Bible.[9] Stephen Webb, while very anxious to assert that the Hebrew Bible teaches human *superiority* over animals (something I would dispute), nonetheless emphasizes the extent to which animals in this text are permitted to "be themselves," rather than representing aspects of human behavior or acting as negative foils for humanity.[10]

So, are the marginal animals surrounding biblical texts in keeping with at least some of the appearances of nonhuman animals within the texts? I shall turn to the source of Midgley's biblical quotation—the book of Job—in order to explore this more closely.

BEHEMOTH AND THE BEASTS

Two passages in the book of Job illustrate neatly the potential critique of "writing on animals" that emerges from the Hebrew Bible. One of the few biblical examples outside Proverbs of the use of a negative characterization

9. Sax, *Animals in the Third Reich*, 19.

10. Webb, *Good Eating*, 36–39. Obviously there are many interesting animals in the Hebrew Bible, and many of them acquire symbolic weight that goes beyond simply allowing them to "be themselves"—consider Balaam's ass or Leviathan. The key point Webb is making, however, with which I would largely want to concur, is that these animals do not acquire their importance by being ordered towards human ends or used as the basis for a picture of humanity. (In fact, in both those cases, rather the reverse is true!)

of animals to (implicitly) exalt human beings is in Job—and, significantly, it is put in the mouth of one of the unreliable witnesses, the friends who are declared at the end not to have spoken what is right. "Why are we counted as beasts [*behemah*] and stupid [*tamah*, vile] in your sight?" asks Bildad (18:3). The last thing the friends want to be is *behemah*. Job insults them by treating them as *behemah*. *Behemah* are not human and not us. Perhaps there is a direct reference here to Job's call to the friends to learn from the beasts (12:7); something in the situation has apparently triggered an anxiety about getting too close to beastliness.

In the whirlwind speeches—the section of the book quoted by Midgley—the voice of God, at the climax of a series of instructions to Job to contemplate the nonhuman creation, calls on Job to look at Behemoth (40:15).[11] As several commentators note, Behemoth, grammatically the plural of *behemah*, can be plausibly translated "the Beast." Even if Behemoth is (as has often been argued) a hippopotamus, he looms larger than do the various other named animals that precede him; and this effect he has within the text cannot altogether be accounted for through the suggestion that he is the mythical cosmic ox. Behemoth is all the beasts summed up (or whatever the animal equivalent of "personified" would be) in a single, larger-than-life Beast.

What happens when Job's attention, and the reader's attention, is directed to Behemoth? Behemoth is viewed first as something *close* to Job. Thus Norman Habel: "Behemoth and Job have a common origin, and their destinies are bound up together in some way." Behemoth is not, Habel notes, introduced with a rhetorical challenge to Job, as something over which he is called to display his (in fact non-existent) power; "Job is not called on to do anything except look, listen and learn."[12] Behemoth is not something wholly other than Job, or by implication than anyone else. Perhaps there is in fact not so much difference between Job's friends and the *behemah*. Perhaps part of their problem is that they are not prepared either to look at *behemah* or to see themselves as *behemah*.

But then the description of Behemoth (as, even more so, the description of Leviathan that follows it) invites contemplation of its otherness, its givenness, its non-negotiability, its persistence over against any attempts to assimilate it for human use. *Behemah*, or at least some

11. For what follows I am much indebted to Susannah Ticciati, whose *Job and the Disruption of Identity* has shaped the reading of Job presented here—although it includes little explicit discussion of Behemoth.

12. Habel, *Book of Job*, 558.

of them, may be there for the taking; but Behemoth is not. Like all the other animals in this second whirlwind speech, Behemoth first appears in all its fascinating detail at the margins of Job's complaint and then, by divine invitation, starts to take over.[13] It holds up the search for meaning in the reading of the book. By this stage, after all, we have "got the point," have the feeling Job has got the point, and want to skip to the end; but we are being told to take a look at Behemoth, apparently for no particular reason. Rather few potted summaries of the "meaning of Job" have much to say about Behemoth, save as a rather elaborate illustration.

I have suggested, however, that Job is invited to look at Behemoth because he has something in common with it—namely, they are both creatures (or, if the Greek text is to be followed, that Behemoth is "with" Job). This has two functions. First, once Job or the reader has been freed from any need to define himself by his non-beastliness, Job or the reader might be able to acknowledge various other characteristics he has in common with Behemoth. Second, *both* Job *and* Behemoth (and all the other "beasts") have a relation to God that renders them properly ungraspable. They are not there simply to be ciphers in, or parchments for, other people's texts. In wondering at Behemoth, Job can wonder at himself—but he does not have to ground that wonder in any particular mark of his superiority over the beasts.[14] He is freed to be "man" without being "not-beast"—and thereby freed to look at Behemoth as something other than a threat requiring material or symbolic subjugation.[15]

This invites a further reflection about the place of Behemoth within the text as a whole, and on what happens when people read about Behemoth. Behemoth does not, I have suggested, add to the "point" of the text and does not help anyone draw a better or clearer moral from Job. Behemoth seems, like the marginal animals, to hold up the search for meaning. As such, Behemoth recalls for the reader the text's own ungraspability—its resistance to, and persistence over against, attempts to

13. Ticciati discusses the extent to which the whirlwind speeches repeat the vocabulary of Job's own initial complaint, but make nonhuman nature the central focus rather the marginal illustration of Job's story. Ticciati, *Job*, 102–9.

14. See, for a further discussion of this point in terms of the centrality of election for Job's identity, Ticciati, *Job*, 109–15. I owe to David Clough the idea of using the doctrine of election to reconstrue the relationship between humanity and the other animals.

15. As several commentators note, Behemoth, as described, is a non-threatening creature (to humans or other animals—his vegetarian diet is the first detail mentioned; Job 40:15).

reduce it to its interpretations. The elaborate description with no apparent point forces the reader to focus, to use more standard terminology, on the text in its literal sense. Both Behemoth in the world and Behemoth in the text resist being turned, through interpretation, into something other than their particular and puzzling selves.

CONSUMING THE PIG

This, the suspicious reader might say, is all very well, but Christian tradition clearly does go in for the symbolic consumption of animals. Indeed, Ingvild Gilhus has recently argued that the symbolic consumption of animals is *characteristic* of Christianity in late antiquity, marking it off from the Graeco-Roman context within which "real" animals were accorded more religious significance. Christianity from the New Testament onwards, Gilhus claims, allegorizes animals[16] and thereby "points away from their inherent value as animals and locks them forever into human hermeneutical processes." Like Midgley, whom she quotes with approval, Gilhus traces Christianity's lineage (as regards attitudes to animals) primarily through Stoicism and Platonism, although she assumes that the "Judaeo-Christian" tradition has an inherent tendency towards the symbolic consumption of animals. Christianity, in Gilhus's account, is responsible for significant innovations and developments in the late antique symbolization of animals and in the binary polarization of the human and the animal—for example, the "systematic use of animals to describe religious dissenters."[17]

The Christian propensity to turn animals into symbols is perhaps most obvious of all where there is a desire to render insignificant the literal consumption of animals, that is, in reading the Hebrew Bible's food laws in the context of (imagined or real) disputes with Judaism. Many of the more shameful aspects of this history are well known, such as the symbolic association of Jews with "carnal" interpretations of animal texts, and hence with carnality and "bestiality" (in multiple senses, all of them negative). Animals and Jews—the animals Jews do not eat and the animals

16. Ingvild Gilhus, *Animals, Gods and Humans*, 167–72, esp. 172. Many aspects of Gilhus's reading of the New Testament texts could be queried, not least her labeling of many of them as "allegorical."

17. Gilhus, *Animals, Gods and Humans*, 264; and see her discussion of Epiphanius on 238–42. She does admit that this was picking up and developing an older Graeco-Roman tradition of comparing one's enemies with beasts.

they symbolically become (to name names, the pigs[18])—have frequently been the unthematized basis of definitions of Christian identity. Biblical interpretation, with the food laws relating to animals as a key set of texts, has of course been crucial in the various historical shifts in Christian attitudes towards Jews and Judaism.[19] Are animals (and especially pigs) in this context simply something on which Christians write their arguments, their polemics, or their caricatures? It would certainly seem that, in their disputes with Jews over the food laws and their interpretation, Christians have had a particular interest in not allowing pigs to appear *as pigs*. Nonetheless, I would suggest that there is scope even within the tradition of Christian reinterpretation of the food laws for the animals themselves to reappear, to attract attention, and perhaps to claim their kinship with us.

Augustine's *Reply to Faustus the Manichaean* provides an intriguing example of, and source for, the tradition of reinterpreting animals in the food laws.[20] Recall that in this text Augustine is fighting, as it were, on two fronts: directly against the Manichaean who rejects the Old Testament and its God altogether, and indirectly against Judaism, or against the charge that the acceptance of the Old Testament necessarily implies the acceptance of Jewish interpretations. A theology of creation, and a theory of signs and their interpretation, are implicitly brought to work in the reading of, or writing on, the pig.

One of Augustine's striking moves is to compare the pig—and its positive/permitted counterpart, the lamb—to a word. "For instance, a pig and a lamb are both clean in their nature, for every creature of God is good; but, symbolically, a lamb is clean and a pig unclean. So the words 'wise' and 'fool' are both clean in their nature, as words composed of letters, but fool may be called symbolically unclean, because it means an

18. See Fabre-Vassas, *Singular Beast* for a fascinating analysis of the history of the pig as focal symbol of Christian identity over against Judaism in medieval Europe.

19. David Grumett's work (in Grumett and Muers, *Theology on the Menu*) draws attention to the numerous contexts in which Hebrew Bible food laws had continuing "literal" force for Christians, for many centuries. It has been proposed by Abigail Firey (see "Letter of the Law") that the Carolingian interpreters effected a major shift both in attitudes to Judaism and in attitudes to the food laws by developing extended "spiritual" interpretations of these texts. Grumett's research suggests that the picture is somewhat more complicated. The relationship between readings of the Old Testament and Christian dietary restrictions was never a straightforward reading off of laws taken to be directly binding on all Christians, although the Old Testament (and not merely Acts 15) did exert significant influence on decisions on dietary questions during the conversion of northern Europe.

20. Augustine, *Reply to Faustus* 6.7.

unclean thing." We might assume that, at this point, by being turned into something "symbolically unclean" the pig has thus been written, as it were, all over, such that it cannot appear as anything other than a determinate unit of meaning; its pigness has been consumed by what it signifies. This is not, however, the full force of Augustine's comparison. Rather, confronted with the Manichaean who wants to deny the goodness of creation, he goes to some length to emphasize the goodness of words *as things*, and the goodness of "wordness" itself, of the capacity to signify. He encourages people to pause where they usually do not pause—in contemplating the words themselves. "Fool" is, he says, as good a word as "wise"; the things signified are vastly different, but the words are equally good as sounds, and equally good *at being words*. Likewise, the pig and the lamb are both included within the creation that God sees to be good. They are (in a derived but real way) good "in themselves," good at being the particular creatures they are, and they are also good at being signifiers of divine meaning.

Augustine notes that the pig, in the context of biblical revelation, comes to signify folly rather than wisdom; but that casts no aspersions on the pig itself. It turns out that Jewish avoidance of pork in obedience to the law is, for Augustine, an absolutely indispensable stage in the "reading" of the pig; without it, the pig means nothing in particular.[21] Even once the pig has been given its symbolic meaning, however, the unconsumed pigs (and for that matter the consumed lambs) remain visible as things, as good parts of the good creation, whose significance exceeds human attempts to exhaust or control it. God gives the pig its meanings through the history of revelation, and it retains its surplus of potential and future meaning—a surplus that can be glimpsed as people contemplate its created pigness.

It seems to me that Augustine in this text makes the pig less into a blank writing surface than into a decorated letter. He does, of course, proceed fairly swiftly to describe his opponents as pigs, which is precisely the sort of move identified by Gilhus as characteristic of Christians' symbolic consumption of animals.[22] What Augustine (unlike Epiphanius) does not do, however, is to make his opponents "bestial" and only himself human.

21. Jeremy Cohen is among the scholars to draw attention to the relatively positive interpretation of Judaism—at least when compared to that of late medieval writers—implied by Augustine's biblical hermeneutics. See his *Living Letters of the Law*, esp. ch. 1.

22. Gilhus also describes the Manichaean avoidance of animal flesh as evidence of "a more compassionate ethic towards the animal world than [that of] Christians" (*Animals, Gods and Humans*, 260), while noting that this abstinence had "little to do with concern for the well-being of animals" (261)!

The texts from which he is working simply do not allow him to make so much of the dividing line between human and nonhuman animals. He has to assign animal characters to *everyone*—the pigs to the Manichaeans, the lambs to the orthodox. Animalness *as such* is not used to define the bad, the other-than-human, or the other-than-us. Even the use of animal-based insults has a range of different possible implications and underlying logics. The bestialization of the Jew in the later Middle Ages, for example, was linked to a binary construction of humanity and the "beasts" that does not appear in the text I have been considering.

That is all very well, Adams (or somebody arguing her line) might say, again, but would it not have been better for the pigs—or especially for the lambs—if they had not been written on at all? They are, after all, still being treated as "words" and as "meat";[23] they are symbolically consumed to form the social bodies of religious communities, and they are literally consumed by the people who make this symbolic use of them. Could the texts not simply leave them alone? Once the nonhuman animals have appeared and have been allotted meanings within a theological system, there is always the possibility that they will be reduced to *just these* meanings, that it will come to be thought that they matter only insofar as they serve to hold up these systems—to feed us meat or to teach us a lesson.

This is a fair point, and one against which there is no easy defense. We have already seen that even within the Hebrew Bible—which I have held up in the first instance as the key source for Christian resistance to the symbolic consumption of animals—examples can be found that look to the suspicious reader like "writing on animals." Christians are bound not only to read and reread these scriptural texts but to read and reread a tradition of interpretation that *does* frequently mandate the symbolic consumption of animals. It is no doubt true, as Midgley, Adams, and many others argue, that Christian thought has tended to work—in the West at least—for the instrumentalization of nonhuman animals and for the drawing of sharp dividing lines between "man" and "beast." My discussion should not be taken as a defense of "Christianity" in general (still less of the questionable "Judaeo-Christian tradition") against this accusation.

Nonetheless, I do want to highlight the fact that the Christian inheritance of "the West" includes not only the animals we write on but also the animals we *draw in*. We live with the other animals; ignoring them

23. Adams, with other animal ethicists, has discussed extensively the processes (material and cultural) by which many individual "animals" become the mass noun "meat"; see for example *Neither Man nor Beast*, ch. 6. See also Vialles, *Animal to Edible*.

altogether in our texts is not an option (and even if it were, it would not necessarily mean that we related to them better). We also, in one way or another, live off the other animals, materially and symbolically; we interpret them and learn from them, and even if we do not eat or wear them we need them to maintain liveable environments for us. They are drawn into our lives and our texts, and once they have been drawn in they are in some way at risk. The question is whether we can draw them in to our spheres of interest and concern without consuming them completely.

This is, as I have attempted to indicate in this article, linked to further questions about how Christians negotiate the relationships between literal and non-literal or more-than-literal interpretations of the biblical texts themselves—and about how they negotiate their relationships to Judaism and to Jewish readings. Negative assessments of "the animal," "the literal," and "the Jew" have often gone together in Christian history, with results ranging from the faintly problematic to the disastrous. For multiple reasons, therefore, it may be time to look again at the animals in the margins.

Bibliography

Adams, Carol J. *Neither Man nor Beast: Feminism and the Defense of Animals*. New York: Continuum, 1994.

Adams, Nicholas. *Habermas and Theology*. Cambridge: Cambridge University Press, 2006.

Anderson, G.W. "A Note on Psalm 1:1." *Vetus Testamentum* 24/2 (April 1974) 231–33.

Arberry, Arthur J. *The Koran Interpreted*. 2 vols. London: George Allen & Unwin, 1955.

Augustine of Hippo. *Confessions*. Translated by R.S. Pine-Coffin. Harmondsworth: Penguin, 1961.

———. *De doctrina christiana*. Translated by J. F. Shaw. In *Nicene and Post-Nicene Fathers*, ser. 1, vol. 2, *St. Augustin's City of God and Christian Doctrine*, 513–97. Edited by Philip Schaff. New York: Christian Literature Company, 1886. Online at the Christian Classics Ethereal Library: http://www.ccel.org/ccel/schaff/npnf102.v.html.

———. *Enarrationes in Psalmos*. Patrologia latina 36. Edited by J.-P. Migne. Paris, 1844–64. Online: http://www.sant-agostino.it/latino/esposizioni_salmi/index2.htm. ET: *Nicene and Post-Nicene Fathers*, ser. 1, vol. 8, *Expositions on the Book of Psalms*. Edited by A. Cleveland Coxe and Philip Schaff. New York: Christian Literature, 1888. Online at the Christian Classics Ethereal Library: http://www.ccel.org/ccel/schaff/npnf108.

———. *Reply to Faustus the Manichean*. Translated by Richard Stothert. In *Nicene and Post-Nicene Fathers*, ser. 1, vol. 4, *St. Augustin: The Writings Against the Manichæans and Against the Donatists*, 151–345. Edited by Philip Schaff. New York: Christian Literature, 1887. Online at the Christian Classics Ethereal Library: http://www.ccel.org/ccel/schaff/npnf104.iv.ix.viii.html.

———. *Sermons on Selected Lessons of the New Testament*. Translated by R. G. Macmullen, edited by E. B. Pusey. Oxford: John Henry Parker, 1844.

Balthasar, Hans Urs von. *The Dramatis Personae: The Person in Christ*. Vol. 3 of *Theo-Drama: Theological Dramatic Theory*. Translated by Graham Harrison. San Francisco: Ignatius, 1992.

Barker, Kenneth, editor. *The NIV Study Bible*. Grand Rapids: Zondervan, 1985.

Barth, Karl. *Church Dogmatics* III/1: *The Doctrine of Creation*. Edited by G. W. Bromiley and T. F. Torrance. Edinburgh: T. & T. Clark, 1958.

———. *Protestant Theology in the Nineteenth Century: Its Background and History*. London: SCM, 1972.

Bauer, Uwe F. W. "Anti-Jewish Interpretations of Psalm 1 in Luther and in Modern German Protestantism." *Journal of Hebrew Scriptures* 2 (1998). Online: http://www.arts.ualberta.ca/JHS/Articles/article8.pdf.

Bede. *In Pentateuchum commentarii: Explanatio in quintum librum Mosis*. In Patrologia latina, edited by J.-P. Migne, 91:189–393. Paris, 1844–64. Online: http://www.archive.org/details/patrologiaecurs73unkngoog.

Benstein, Jeremy. "The Earth's Reward." *The Jerusalem Report*, September 11, 2000. Online: http://www.heschelcenter.org/text_files/earth_reward.html.

Berger, Teresa, editor. *Dissident Daughters: Feminist Liturgies in Global Context*. Louisville: Westminster John Knox, 2001.

Berry, Wendell. *The Gift of Good Land: Further Essays Cultural and Agricultural.* San Francisco: North Point, 1981.

Bonhoeffer, Dietrich. *Ethics*. Translated from the German ed. by Ilse Tödt et al.; English ed. by Clifford J. Green, translated by Reinhard Krauss et al. Dietrich Bonhoeffer Works 6. Minneapolis: Fortress, 2005.

Bouma-Prediger, Steven. *For the Beauty of the Earth: A Christian Vision for Creation Care*. Grand Rapids: Baker, 2001.

Braude, William G., translator. *The Midrash on the Psalms*. Yale Judaica Series 13. New Haven, CT: Yale University Press, 1959.

Brownlee, William H. "Psalms 1–2 as a Coronation Liturgy." *Biblica* 1971 (52) 321–36.

Bruce, F. F. *The Hard Sayings of Jesus*. Downers Grove, IL: InterVarsity, 1983.

Brueggemann, Walter. "The Trusted Creature." *Catholic Biblical Quarterly* 31 (1969) 484–98.

Bruno di Segni. *Expositio in Pentateuchum: Expositio in Deuteronomium*. In Patrologia latina, edited by J.-P. Migne, 164: 505–50. Paris, 1844–64. Online: http://www.archive.org/details/patrologiaecurs22unkngoog.

Buell, Denise Kimber. *Making Christians: Clement of Alexandria and the Rhetoric of Legitimacy*. Princeton, NJ: Princeton University Press, 1999.

Bullough, Sebastian. "The Question of Metre in Psalm 1." *Vetus Testamentum* 17/1 (Jan 1967) 42–49.

Byassee, Jason. *Praise Seeking Understanding: Reading the Psalms with Augustine*. Grand Rapids: Eerdmans, 2007.

Carmichael, Calum M. *The Laws of Deuteronomy*. Ithaca, NY: Cornell University Press, 1974.

Carter, Pam. *Feminism, Breasts, and Breast-Feeding.* Basingstoke: Macmillan, 1995.

Christensen, Duane L. *Deuteronomy 21:10—34:12*. Word Biblical Commentary 6b. Nashville: T. Nelson, 2002.

Churchill, Winston S. *Onwards to Victory: War Speeches, 1943*. Compiled by Charles Eade. Winston Churchill's War Speeches 4. London: Cassell, 1944.

Clifford, Richard J. "The Bishops, the Bible and Liturgical Language." *America*, May 27, 1995, 12–16. Online: http://cba.cua.edu/clif.cfm.

———. *Deuteronomy: With an Excursus on Covenant and Law.* Old Testament Message 5. Wilmington, DE: M. Glazier, 1989.

Clifford, Richard J., and Chrysogonus Waddell. "'A Christological Interpretation of Psalm 1?': An Exchange between Fr. Richard Clifford and Fr. Chrysogonus Waddell." *Communio* 22/4 (1995) 749–52.

Clines, David J. A. "Psalm 2 and the MLF (Moabite Liberation Front)." In *Interested Parties: The Ideology of Writers and Readers of the Hebrew Bible*, 158–85. Journal for the Study of the Old Testament Supplement Series 205; Gender, Culture, Theory 1. Sheffield: Sheffield Academic, 1995.

Cohen, Jeremy. *Living Letters of the Law: Ideas of the Jew in Medieval Christianity*. Berkeley: University of California Press, 1999.

Cook, Samuel. *Ta Diapheronta, or, Divine Characters*. Edited by Christopher Barker and William Garrett. London: Adoniram Byfeild, 1658. Online: http://books.google.co.uk/books?id=MtPNAAAAMAAJ.

Craigie, Peter C. *The Book of Deuteronomy*. New International Commentary on the Old Testament. London: Hodder and Stoughton, 1976.

———. *Psalms 1–50*. Word Biblical Commentary 19. Waco, TX: Word, 1983.

Creach, Jerome. "Like a Tree Planted by the Temple Stream: The Portrait of the Righteous in Psalm 1:3." *Catholic Biblical Quarterly* 61/1 (1999) 34–46.

Croy, N. Clayton. *The Mutilation of Mark's Gospel*. Nashville: Abingdon, 2003.

Dandelion, Pink. *The Liturgies of Quakerism*. Aldershot: Ashgate, 2005.

Davies, Andrew. "Hand to the Plough (Luke 9:57–63)." Sermon delivered at the Aberystwyth Conference of the Evangelical Movement of Wales, August 16, 1984. Audio recording. Online: http://www.emw.org.uk/sermons/?sermon_id=81.

Dawood, N. J., translator. *The Koran: With a Parallel Arabic Text*. London: Penguin, 1999.

Delaney, Carol. "The Meaning of Paternity and the Virgin Birth Debate." *Man* 21 (1986) 494–513.

Deleuze, Gilles. *Difference and Repetition*. Translated by Paul Patton. London: Athlone, 1994.

Dodd, C. H. *Parables of the Kingdom*. London: Religious Book Club, 1942.

Dutcher-Walls, Patricia. "The Circumscription of the King: Deuteronomy 17:16–17 in Its Ancient Social Context." *Journal of Biblical Literature* 121/4 (2002) 601–16.

Einwechter, William O. "Christ's Political Authority and the Church's Witness and Service." *Christian Statesman*, September–October 2001. Audio recording. Online: http://www.sermonaudio.com/sermoninfo.asp?SID=91006165711.

Epstein, Isidore, editor. *Babylonian Talmud: New Hebrew-English Edition, Tractate Ḥullin*. Translated by Eli Cashdan. London: Soncino, 1980.

Fabre-Vassas, Claudine. *The Singular Beast: Jews, Christians and the Pig*. Translated by Carol Volk. New York: Columbia University Press, 1997.

Fessio, Joseph. "'Blessed is the Man . . .'" In *The Catholic World Report*, February 1994, 64.

Firey, Abigail. "The Letter of the Law: Carolingian Exegetes and the Old Testament." In *With Reverence for the Word: Medieval Scriptural Exegesis in Judaism, Christianity, and Islam*, edited by Jane Dammen McAuliffe et al., 204–23. New York: Oxford University Press, 2003.

Ford, David F. *Christian Wisdom: Desiring God and Learning in Love*. Cambridge Studies in Christian Doctrine 16. Cambridge: Cambridge University Press, 2007.

Ford, Gina. *The Contented Little Baby Book*. London: Vermilion, 1999.

Frei, Hans W. *Types of Christian Theology*. Edited by George Hunsinger and William C. Placher. New Haven, CT: Yale University Press, 1992.

Friedriksen, Paula. "Augustine and Israel: *Interpretatio ad litteram*, Jews and Judaism in Augustine's Theology of History." *Studia Patristica* 38 (2001) 119–35.

———. *Augustine and the Jews: A Christian Defence of Jews and Judaism*. New York: Doubleday, 2008.

Gilhus, Ingvild. *Animals, Gods and Humans: Changing Attitudes to Animals in Greek, Roman and Early Christian Thought.* London: Routledge, 2006.

Glossa ordinaria. In Patrologia latina 113, edited by J.-P. Migne. Paris, 1844–64. Online: http://www.archive.org/details/patrologiaecurs04migngoog.

Green, Melody, and David Hazard. *No Compromise: The Life Story of Keith Green.* Nashville: T. Nelson, 2008.

Greer, Rowan A. *Theodore of Mopsuestia; Exegete and Theologian.* Westminster: Tufton, 1961.

Greidanus, Sidney. *Preaching Christ from the Old Testament: A Contemporary Hermeneutical Method.* Grand Rapids: Eerdmans, 1999.

Grosz, Elisabeth. "Feminist Futures: The Time of Thought." *Tulsa Studies in Women's Literature* 21/1 (Spring 2002) 13–20.

Guibert of Nogent. *De Incarnatione contra Iudaeos.* In Patrologia latina, edited by J.-P. Migne, 156:489–526. Paris, 1844–64. Online: http://www.archive.org/details/patrologiaecurs05unkngoog.

Habel, Norman C. *The Book of Job.* Old Testament Library. London: SCM Press, 1985.

Hardy, Daniel W. "Societal Economics and the Kingdom of God: A Consideration of Two Parables of the Kingdom (Matthew 18:21–35 and 20:1–16)." *Journal of Scriptural Reasoning* 5.2 (July 2005). Online: http://etext.lib.virginia.edu/journals/ssr/issues/volume5/number2/ssr05_02_e03.html.

Henry, Matthew. *An Exposition of the Old and New Testament*, vol. 3, *Job to Song of Solomon.* Edited by G. Burder and John Hughes. London: Samuel Bagster, 1811. Online at the Christian Classics Ethereal Library: http://www.ccel.org/ccel/henry/mhc3.Ec.iv.html.

Higton, Mike. *Deciding Differently: Rowan Williams' Theology of Moral Decision Making.* Grove Ethics Series 162. Cambridge: Grove, 2011.

———. *Difficult Gospel: The Theology of Rowan Williams.* London: SCM, 2004.

Hilary of Poitiers. *Homilies on the Psalms.* In *Nicene and Post-Nicene Fathers*, ser. 2, vol. 9, *Hilary of Poitiers, John of Damascus*, 235–48. Edited by Philip Schaff. New York: Christian Literature, 1898. Online: http://www.ccel.org/ccel/schaff/npnf209.ii.vi.ii.i.html.

Hill, Robert C. "His Master's Voice: Theodore of Mopsuestia on the Psalms." *Heythrop Journal* 45 (2004) 40–53.

———, editor. *Theodore of Mopsuestia: Commentary on Psalms 1–81.* Writings from the Greco-Roman World 5. Atlanta: SBL, 2006.

Høgenhaven, Jesper. "The Opening of the Psalter: A Study in Jewish Theology." *Scandinavian Journal of the Old Testament* 15/2 (2001) 169–80.

Horrell, David G., et al., editors. *Ecological Hermeneutics: Biblical, Historical and Theological Perspectives.* London: T. & T. Clark, 2010.

Howgill, Francis. "Testimony Concerning the Life, Death, Tryals, Travels and Labours of Edward Burrough." In *The Memorable Works of a Son of Thunder and Consolation.* London, 1672.

Jenkins, Allan K. "Erasmus' Commentary on Psalm 2." *Journal of Hebrew Scriptures* 3 (2000–2001). Online: http://www.arts.ualberta.ca/cocoon/JHS/a015.html.

Jenkins, Timothy. *Religion in English Everyday Life.* Methodology and History in Anthropology 5. New York: Berghahn, 1999.

Jensen, Joseph. "Inclusive Language and the Bible." *America*, November 5, 1994, 14–18. Online: http://cba.cua.edu/jen.cfm.

———. "Watch Your Language: Of Princes and Music Directors." *America*, June 8, 1996, 7–11. Online: http://cba.cua.edu/princes.cfm.

Jobes, Karen H. "Got Milk? Septuagint Psalm 33 and the Interpretation of 1 Peter 2:1–3." *Westminster Theological Journal* 64/1 (2002) 1–14.

Johnston, Robert M. "'The Least of the Commandments': Deuteronomy 22:6–7 in Rabbinic Judaism and Early Christianity." *Andrews University Seminary Studies* 20/3 (1982) 205–15.

Katz, Claire Elise. *Levinas, Judaism, and the Feminine: The Silent Footsteps of Rebecca*. Bloomington: Indiana University Press, 2003.

Kepnes, Steven. "A Handbook for Scriptural Reasoning." In *The Promise of Scriptural Reasoning*, edited by C. C. Pecknold and David F. Ford, 23–39. Malden, MA: Blackwell, 2006.

———. "Adam/Eve: From Rabbinic to Scriptural Anthropology." *Journal of Scriptural Reasoning* 4/2 (October 2004). Online: http://etext.lib.virginia.edu/journals/ssr/issues/volume4/number2/ssr04_02_e01.html.

Khan, Muhammad Muhsin, and Muhammad Taqi-ud-Din al-Hilali. *The Noble Quran in the English Language*. Riyadh, Saudi Arabia: Dar-us-Salaam, 1997.

Kraus, Hans-Joachim. *Psalms 1–59: A Commentary*. Translated by Hilton C. Oswald. Minneapolis: Augsburg, 1988.

Lawler, Steph. *Mothering the Self: Mothers, Daughters, Subjects*. London: Routledge, 2000.

Levinas, Emmanuel. *Totality and Infinity: An Essay on Exteriority*. Translated by Alphonso Lingis. Pittsburgh: Duquesne, 1969.

Lings, Martin. *Muhammad: His Life Based on the Earliest Sources*. Vermont: Inner Traditions, 1983.

Linzey, Andrew, and Dan Cohn-Sherbok. *After Noah: Animals and the Liberation of Theology*. London: Mowbray, 1997.

Lowth, Robert. *Lectures on the Sacred Poetry of the Hebrews*. Translated by G. Gregory. Rev. ed. Boston: Joseph T. Buckingham, 1815.

Luther, Martin. "Preface of Jesus Christ" and "Preface to the Scholia." In *First Lectures on the Psalms [Dictata super Psalterium] I: Psalms 1–75*, edited by Hilton C. Oswald, 6–10. Luther's Works 10. St. Louis: Concordia, 1974.

———. *Selected Psalms [Operationes in Psalmos] III*. Edited by Jaroslav Pelikan. Luther's Works 14. St. Louis: Concordia, 1958.

McConville, Gordon. *Deuteronomy*. Apollos Old Testament Commentary. Leicester: InterVarsity, 2002.

Michaels, J. Ramsey. *1 Peter*. Word Biblical Commentary 49. Waco, TX: Word, 1988.

Midgley, Mary. *Beast and Man: The Roots of Human Nature*. Ithaca, NY: Cornell UP, 1978.

Freedman, H., and Maurice Simon, editors. *Midrash Rabbah*, vol. 7, *Deuteronomy and Lamentations*. Translated by J. Rabbinowitz and A. Cohen. London: Soncino, 1939.

Milbank, John, et al. "Suspending the Material: The Turn of Radical Orthodoxy." In *Radical Orthodoxy: A New Theology*, 1–20. London: Routledge, 1998.

Miller, Patrick D. *Deuteronomy*. Interpretation. Louisville: John Knox, 1990.

Muers, Rachel. *Keeping God's Silence: Towards a Theological Ethics of Communication*. Oxford: Blackwell, 2004.

———. "Seeing, Choosing and Eating: Theology and the Feminist–Vegetarian Debate." In *Eating and Believing: Historical and Contemporary Perspectives on*

Vegetarianism and Theology, edited by David Grumett and Rachel Muers, 184–97. London: Continuum, 2008.

———. "Sign of Jonah: Aide Memoire of Cambridge Society for Biblical Reasoning (CSBR)." *Journal for Scriptural Reasoning* 3/1 (June 2003). Online: http://etext.lib.virginia.edu/journals/ssr/issues/volume3/number1/ssr03-01-e03.html.

Muers, Rachel, and David Grumett. *Theology on the Menu: Asceticism, Meat and Christian Diet*. London: Routledge, 2010.

Nachmanides. *Commentary on the Torah*. Translated by Charles B. Chavel. New York: Shilo, 1971.

Neher, Andre. *The Exile of the Word: From the Silence of the Bible to the Silence of Auschwitz*. Translated by David Maisel. Philadelphia: Jewish Publication Society of America, 1980.

Odes of Solomon. Edited and translated by Rendel Harris and Alphonse Mingana, 2 vols. Manchester: Manchester University Press, 1916–20. Online: http://www.archive.org/details/odespsalmsofsolo01harruoft (text); http://www.archive.org/details/odespsalmsofsolo02harruoft (translation).

O'Donovan, Oliver. "*Usus* and *Fruitio* in Augustine's De Doctrina Christiana I." *Journal of Theological Studies*, n.s., 33/2 (1982) 361–97.

O'Keefe, John J. "'A Letter That Killeth': Toward a Reassessment of Antiochene Exegesis, or Diodore, Theodore, and Theodoret on the Psalms." *Journal of Early Christian Studies* 8/1 (2000) 83–104.

Ochs, Peter. *Peirce, Pragmatism and the Logic of Scripture*. Cambridge: Cambridge University Press, 1998.

Ochs, Peter, and Nancy Levene, "Introduction." In *Textual Reasonings: Jewish Philosophy and Text Study at the End of the Twentieth Century*, edited by Peter Ochs and Nancy Levene, 2–27. Grand Rapids: Eerdmans, 2002.

Olley, John. "Mixed Blessings for Animals." In *The Earth Story in Genesis*, edited by Norman C. Habel and Shirley Wurst, 130–39. Earth Bible Series 2. London: Continuum, 2000.

Parsons, Michael. *Martin Luther's Interpretation of the Royal Psalms: The Spiritual Kingdom in a Pastoral Context*. Lewiston, NY: E. Mellen, 2009.

Perl, Gisella. *I Was a Doctor in Auschwitz*. Salem, NH: Ayer, 1984. Extracts reprinted in *Different Voices: Women and the Holocaust*, edited by Carol Rittner and John K. Roth, 106–18. St Paul: Paragon, 1993.

Piper, John. "The Other Dark Exchange: Homosexuality." Sermon delivered in Bethlehem Baptist Church, October 11, 1998. Online: http://www.soundofgrace.com/piper98/10-11-98.htm.

Quaker Faith and Practice: The Book of Christian Discipline of the Yearly Meeting of the Religious Society of Friends (Quakers) in Britain. London: Yearly Meeting of the Religious Society of Friends (Quakers) in Britain, 2008. Online: http://qfp.quakerweb.org.uk/qfp19-08.html.

Rabanus Maurus. *De Universo*. In Patrologia latina, edited by J.-P. Migne, 111:9–612. Paris, 1844–64. Online: http://www.archive.org/details/patrologiaecurs164unkngoog.

———. *Enarratio super Deuteronomium*. In Patrologia latina, edited by J.-P. Migne, 108:837–998. Paris, 1844–64. Online: http://www.archive.org/details/patrologiae00unknuoft.

Rad, Gerhard von. *Old Testament Theology*. Vol. 1. Translated by D. M. G. Stalker. Edinburgh: Oliver and Boyd, 1962.

Razi, Fakhr al-Din al-. *Mafatih al-Ghayb (al-Tafsir al-Kabir)*. Cairo: al-Matba'a al-Misriyya, 1933.

Richardson, Kurt Anders. "*Imago Dei*: Anthropological and Christological Modes of Divine Self-Imaging." *Journal of Scriptural Reasoning* 4/2 (October 2004). Online http://etext.lib.virginia.edu/journals/ssr/issues/volume4/number2/ssr04_02_e02.html.

Rupert of Deutz. *De sancta Trinitate et operibus eius: In Deuteronmium*. In Patrologia latina, edited by J.-P. Migne, 167:917–98. Paris, 1844–64. Online: http://books.google.co.uk/books?id=0IetgvZmQ7cC.

Saheeh International. *The Qur'an: Arabic Text with Corresponding English Meanings*. Jeddah, Saudi Arabia: Abul-Qasim, 1997.

Salmon, Marylynn. "The Cultural Significance of Breastfeeding and Infant Care in Early Modern England and America." *Journal of Social History* 28/2 (1994) 247–69.

Sax, Boria. *Animals in the Third Reich: Pets, Scapegoats, and the Holocaust*. London: Continuum, 2000.

Schweickart, Patrocinio P. "Reading Ourselves: Towards a Feminist Theory of Reading." In *Speaking of Gender*, edited by Elaine Showalter, 17–44. London: Routledge, 1989.

Second Council of Constantinople. "Anathemas against the Twelve Chapters." In *Decrees of the Ecumenical Councils*, edited by Norman P. Tanner, 114–22. Washington, DC: Georgetown University Press, 1990.

Segal, Eliezer. "Justice, Mercy and a Bird's Nest." *Journal of Jewish Studies* 42 (1991) 176–95.

Seiss, Joseph A. *The Apocalypse: A Series of Special Lectures on the Revelation of Jesus Christ, with Revised Text*. 8th ed. New York: Charles C. Cook, 1901.

Shildrick, Margrit. *Leaky Bodies and Boundaries: Feminism, Postmodernism and (Bio) Ethics*. London: Routledge, 1997.

Spurgeon, C. H. *The Treasury of David*. 7 vols. New York: Marshall Brothers, 1869. Online at *The Spurgeon Archive*: http://www.spurgeon.org/treasury/treasury.htm.

Steyn, Gert J. "Psalm 2 in Hebrews." *Neotestamentica* 37/2 (2003) 262–82.

Taylor, William. "How to Pitch a Tent: A Beginner's Guide to Scriptural Reasoning." London: St. Ethelburga's Centre for Reconciliation and Peace, 2008. Online: http://www.scripturalreasoning.org/resources.php.

Thomas Aquinas. *Commentary on the Psalms*. Translated by Stephen Loughlin et al. Online at the Aquinas Translation Project: http://www4.desales.edu/~philtheo/loughlin/ATP/.

———. *Summa Theologiae* 1a.1. In *Summa Theologiae* 1: *Christian Theology*, translated by Thomas Gilby. Cambridge: Cambridge University Press, 2006.

———. *Summa Theologiae* 1a.90–102. In *Summa Theologiae* 13: *Man Made to God's Image*, translated by Edmund Hill. Cambridge: Cambridge University Press, 2006.

Ticciati, Susannah. *Job and the Disruption of Identity: Reading beyond Barth*. London: Continuum, 2005.

Timmer, David. "Biblical Exegesis and the Jewish-Christian Controversy in the Early 12th Century." *Church History* 58 (1989) 309–21.

Truth, Sojourner. "Ain't I a Woman?" Speech to 1851 Women's Convention, Akron Ohio, as recalled by Frances Dana Gage in the *National Anti-Slavery Standard*, May 2 1863. Online at the *Modern History Sourcebook*: http://www.fordham.edu/halsall/mod/sojtruth-woman.html.

Tyng, Dudley. "Theodore of Mopsuestia as an Interpreter of the Old Testament." *Journal of Biblical Literature* 50 (1931) 298–303.

Usmani, Muhammad Taqi. *The Meanings of the Noble Qur'an*. Karachi: Maktaba Ma'ariful Quran, 2007.

Van Engen, John H. *Rupert of Deutz*. Berkeley: University of California Press, 1983.

Vialles, Noélie. *Animal to Edible*. Cambridge: Cambridge University Press, 1994.

Waddell, Chrysogonus. "A Christological Interpretation of Psalm 1?: The Psalter and Christian Prayer." *Communio* 22 (Fall 1995) 502–21.

Webb, Stephen H. *Good Eating: The Bible, Diet, and the Proper Love of Animals*. Grand Rapids: Brazos, 2001.

Weiss, Roslyn. "Maimonides on *shilluah ha-qen*." *Jewish Quarterly Review* 79 (1989) 345–66.

Weren, Wim. "Psalm 2 in Luke-Acts: An Intertextual Study." In *Intertextuality in Biblical Writings: Essays in Honour of Bas van Iersel*, edited by Sipke Draisma, 189–203. Kampen: Uitgeversmaatschappij J. H. Kok, 1989.

Williams, Rowan. "Knowing Myself in Christ." In *The Way Forward?: Christian Voices on Homosexuality and the Church*, edited by Timothy Bradshaw, 12–19. London: Hodder and Stoughton, 1997.

Williams, Thomas. "Biblical Interpretation." In *The Cambridge Companion to Augustine*, edited by Eleonore Stump and Norman Kretzmann, 59–70. Cambridge: Cambridge University Press, 2001.

Young, Peter. "The Book of Psalms." In *The Old Testament according to the Authorized Version*, vol. 3, *Poetical Books: Job to Song of Solomon*. London: SPCK, 1878.

Zimmerli, Walther. *Ezekiel: A Commentary on the Book of the Prophet Ezekiel*. Translated by Ronald E. Clements, edited by Frank Moore Cross and Klaus Baltzer. Philadelphia : Fortress, 1979–83.

Scripture Index

Subject/Person Index